THE OLD FARMER'S ALMANAC SAMPLER

THE OLD FARMER'S ALMANAC SAMPLER

Edited by

ROBB SAGENDORPH

IVES WASHBURN, INC.

NEW YORK

Library of Congress Catalog Card No.: 57-11045

MANUFACTURED IN THE UNITED STATES OF AMERICA

VAN REES PRESS • NEW YORK

PREFACE

TO such a book as this *Sampler, The Old Farmer's Almanac,* first published in the year 1792 for the year 1793, and now in its 165th continuous year, lends itself particularly well. Each edition, topical and timely by its very nature, has nevertheless contained gems of wit, wisdom, and entertainment which have withstood the danger of repetition year after year. Yet, like the Bard of Avon, the *Almanac* rarely repeats itself and, as a result, this mass of material, which some have called the "sinews of American thought," has remained available only to the few owners of complete sets, and only to those owners with eyes strong enough to read the old-fashioned small print and the patience to sort the wheat from the chaff.

As the title *The Old Farmer's Almanac Sampler* implies, a sampling from these past issues, rather than a collection, is intended. As you will note in the table of contents, the samples are placed with fellows of their own kind: poems of spring with other poems of spring, anecdote with anecdote, Farmer's Calendar with a focus on the orchard beside another like it, etc.

The opening chapters on history, weather, and astronomy—all of them strong colors in the pattern of this book—represent years of research, added to experience as *Almanac* editor and publisher, to learn the truths, if there were such, in many apocryphal stories about the *Almanac,* and to establish in my own mind a faithful summary of what this *Almanac* stands for, without fear of any factual contradiction. Such a summary, made up as it is from small bits garnered here, there, and clear around the world, is not easily come by and will not be found in one place anywhere but here.

You will also find short introductory essays preceding the sections of the Seasons in Rhyme and the Farmer's Calendars. These were written by Benjamin M. Rice, who has been author since 1940 of all the Farmer's Calendars used in the *Almanac* itself. Mr. Rice also helped decide which samples to use of the *Almanac*'s Anecdotes and Pleasantries and has cheerfully loaned his advice and help throughout.

Donald Day and Clara Pearce, in first suggesting which of the poems and Farmer's Calendars seemed most quotable, might also be considered co-editors of this book.

As with the *Almanac*, to Phyllis Worcester, loyal Secretary, and to my good wife, Beatrix, acknowledgment is gladly given here. "Indispensable" remains the only word which will describe their efforts, affection, and understanding.

ROBB SAGENDORPH

Dublin, New Hampshire
April 9, 1957

CONTENTS

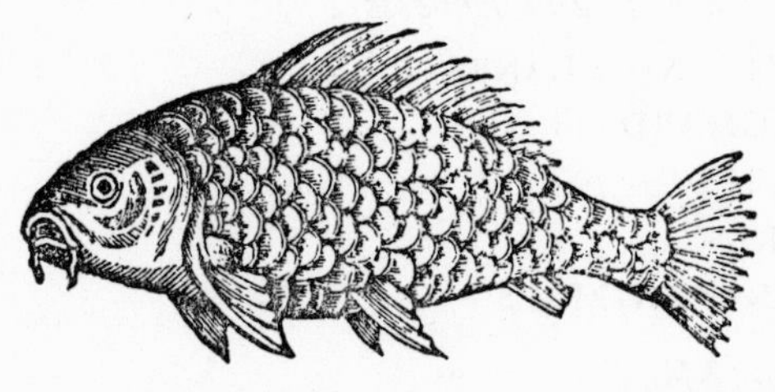

THE OLD FARMER'S ALMANAC SAMPLER

[No. I.]

THE

FARMER's ALMANAC,

CALCULATED ON A NEW AND IMPROVED PLAN,

FOR THE YEAR OF OUR LORD

1793:

Being the first after Leap Year, and seventeenth of the Independence *of* America.

Fitted to the town of BOSTON, but will serve for any of the adjoining States.

Containing, besides the large number of ASTRONOMICAL CALCULATIONS and FARMER'S CALENDAR for every month in the year, as great a variety as are to be found in any other Almanac, *Of* NEW, USEFUL, *and* ENTERTAINING MATTER.

BY ROBERT B. THOMAS.

"While the bright radient sun in centre glows,
The earth, in annual motion round it goes;
At the same time on its own axis reels,
And gives us change of seasons as it wheels."

Published according to Act of Congress.

PRINTED AT THE Apollo Press, IN BOSTON,
BY BELKNAP AND HALL.
Sold at their Office; State Street; also, by the *Author* and *M. Smith, Sterling*.
[*Sixpence single, 4s. per dozen, 40s. per groce.*]

Title page, volume I, number 1, of *The Old Farmer's Almanac.* The "Old" was inserted in the title about 1830 to distinguish this almanac from its imitators.

I.

THE FAMILY TREE

FEW PEOPLE realize that, since the beginning of mankind, almanacs have had a place in the lives of most of us. The record reveals that the oldest almanac we have on hand now is the thirteen-acre pyramid at Gizeh, the almanac used by King Khufu, or Cheops, in 1700 B.C. Somewhat less cumbersome is a Sumerian farmer's almanac tablet also dated about 1700 B.C. This was found in 1950 not far from modern Baghdad, is 108 text lines long, and to move it would test the strength of a fair-sized ox.

Scholars have not yet settled the argument as to just when Hesiod's famous *Works and Days* was published. Some say 700 B.C., others 300 A.D. But they agree that a stone now in the British Museum, contemporary with Ramses the Great (1292-1225 B.C.), with the unfortunate days of the year marked on it in red, the fortunate ones in black, is certainly one of the oldest almanacs in existence. And there is little difficulty in tracing the popularity of almanacs down through Babylonian, Egyptian, Grecian, Roman, and Arabic civilizations.

When man tired of building pyramids the portals of which he had to use to observe, let us say, the rising of the Pleiades in order to know when the season for planting had arrived, he took to more portable almanacs.

King Athelstan's "Psalter," for example, in 703 A.D. was but a four-sided stick. The king's subjects needed only to face the correct side to the sun to learn at once which day of the week was at hand—particularly Sunday. There were lunar tables on it, too—the first on record.

But it was not until well into the tenth century that almanacs became repositories of astrology, quack medicine, proverbial wisdom, and popular superstition. Friday became a Black Day, for instance, because this was the day of the killing of Abel, the slaughter of the Innocents, the beheading of John the Baptist.... Can you name the other ten reasons? Each month came to have at least two really bad days, except April which had but one—that on which the terrible Walpurgis appeared to make a night of demons, witches, and terror.

And in the Savilian Library in London you may see Peter Docia's 1300 A.D. almanac, the first to introduce that awful "Man

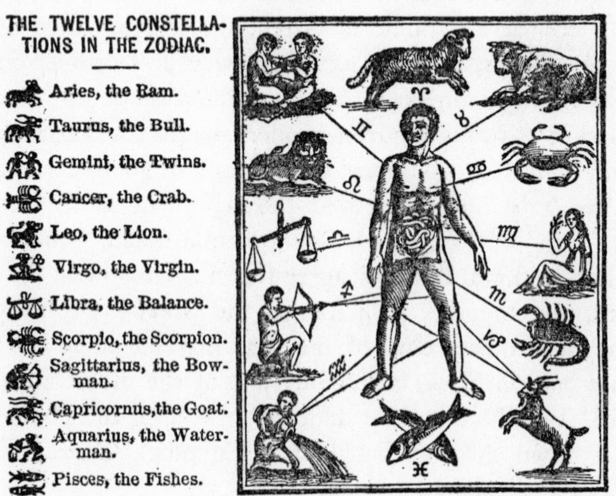

of the Signs" with his bowels on view which has appeared in nearly every almanac since that day. Through the signs attributed to such a man astrologists have falsely interpreted the supposed influence on each of us of the part of the heavens under which we are born. If a person is born under the sign of Aries, for example, he is likely to be headstrong or brilliant, according to astrology.

Some compensation for this dreadful trend toward the macabre is, however, to be found in the beautiful illuminated manuscripts which were being made at about this same time. The *Book of Hours* (1409) is one example. Here, just before the invention of printing, is man's skill with pen and quill at its most beautiful. Printed matter since then may rival but never equal or better the almanac manuscript of this kind. Some, like the Austrian almanac —the *Ulter Bauernkalender*, illuminated in 1370—continue today in printed form.

Symbols from the *Ulter Bauernkalendar:* The hand means "cold"; half-circle with cross means Sunday; 19 is the day of the month; and the animal on the left is Taurus the Bull, to indicate that was the moon's place on the eighteenth and nineteenth.

With the invention of printing one of the first almanacs to appear was Regiomontanus's *Astronomica of Manilius.* This appeared in Nuremberg in 1472 and is said to have been useful to Columbus in his discovery of the New World. The printing press was soon to test the mettle even of kings. Henry III in France in 1579, for example, had to forbid all political prophecy of any kind. Rabelais, in 1533, through his satirical almanacs, came to the attention of Francis I, and thus achieved fame. In Prussia, legislation was passed which made it lawful—in 1570—for "almanacs to tell more lies than truths." The story is also told that Frederick the Great became so annoyed with the poor quality of Prussian almanacs he requested his Royal Academy of Sciences to prepare a new version in 1750, and banned all the others. This it did, but when a certain husband brought one of these improved versions home to his *hausfrau,* she became so angered with its prosaic content she murdered him. The courts upheld her side and Frederick the Great was overruled... the old almanacs would continue as they had.

James I of England, however, was smarter than his royal contemporaries on the Continent. He welcomed the persecuted almanac makers from European shores with a royal monopoly on all almanac copyrights. These he granted to the Stationers Company, and the universities at Oxford and Cambridge. It mattered not to him what these almanacs said or did—the more copies sold, the more revenue for education.

But for the almanac makers themselves competition was not easy. Two were hanged on the suspicion they had started the Great London Fire of 1666 just to make sure their predictions did come true. Another predicted the death of his rival with less fortunate results than Benjamin Franklin later had in a similar experience in his *Poor Richard's.* Foulsham's *Old Moore's,* begun in 1697 and still published under the original copyright, made no sale at all one year because it failed to include the famous Man of the Signs. And John Partridge, as well known as any almanac editor of that day, had to quit because Jonathan Swift began circulating stories to the effect that people considered Partridge's prophecies remarkable because what happened—particularly in the matter of the weather—was always the opposite of what his almanac had predicted.

The oldest extant almanac printed in English is dated 1495. It was found in a chest in Edinburgh and then placed in the Bodleian Library. On its title page it says: "Flete Street by Wynkin de Woode." Exactly 144 years later, the second document to be struck off the New World's only printing press in Cambridge, Massachusetts, was the first American almanac, "Calculated by Mr. Peirce, Mariner." This was in 1639. There is no copy of this almanac now. But it is interesting to note that Captain Peirce at one time commanded such ships as the *Charity*, the *Ann*, the *Lion*, and the *Desire*. Out of Peirce's almanac grew the so-called Danforth almanacs, the one for 1649, America's oldest existing almanac, being in the Lenox Library in New York.

In the collection (America's largest) of the American Antiquarian Society at Worcester, Massachusetts, are the John Tulley almanacs from 1687 to 1702. Here may be found the first attempts to forecast American weather day by day, and prognostications like, "When the small stars are obscured at night, beware of tempests in the offing."

In passing, it is also interesting to note that Cotton Mather, famous New England Puritan clergyman, was editor of the *Boston Almanac* in 1683. But whatever may have been the religious influence of this grim Puritan on almanacs, it was not to last as anything more than the listing of Fast and Feast and Holy Days, a practice well known to almanac makers before and after him.

In the early part of the eighteenth century, two famous American almanacs appeared: *Poor Richard's Almanac*, by Richard Saunders (Benjamin Franklin's pen name), and that of Nathaniel Ames, Jr. Although the latter's outsold Franklin's many times over in their day, Franklin's is now much more sought after and prized. Up to 1905, for example, the highest price paid for an old almanac was $555. This was for the 1686 *Pennsylvania Almanac* by Samuel Atkins. One of the *Poor Richard's Almanacs* (1733-57), that for the year 1750, was being offered by Goodspeed's of Boston recently at $500. The *Ames' Almanacs* would probably do well to bring one-fiftieth of that.

Franklin was of course famous for his proverbs, and these may explain his latter-day popularity. For instance, a piece from one of his almanacs written as the harangue of a wise old man to people at an auction had a tremendous sale. It was translated into French and Greek as well.

There have been other almanacs started in this country before and after the one with which we are chiefly concerned. Of these, the *Daboll Almanac*, published in New London, Connecticut, is said to have a continuous publishing record from 1772 to the present day. It was used on board many of our whalers before the *Nautical Almanac* came along. A recent request to the publisher of the *Daboll Almanac* for confirmation of this unbroken record, however, brought no reply. Outside sources suggest a change of title or a missing year.

Leavitt's in New Hampshire lasted over a hundred years and Robinson's *Maine Farmer's Almanac*, begun after the turn of the nineteenth century, is still going strong. Josh Billings came into the picture for a few years in the 1870's with his *Farmer's Allminax*, the front cover of which included the words: "In Adams sin, we all jined in," and, "Being the 98th year of North American liberty and over 5000 years (if I don't disremember rong) since Adam did the bizness for us in the garden of Eden."

One almanac calling itself *The Farmer's Almanac*, formerly published in New Jersey and now published in Maine, occasionally bears the name of a compiler, David Young. Young, long since deceased, was unique in that he did the calculations for many more almanacs than his own, and thereby gained what few of these behind-the-scene calculators of astronomical and other matters have, a reputation of his own.

Few today, for example, have heard of Osgood Carleton. True enough, a statue of him which long stood in the State House is even now in the Boston Custom House. And there are records which tell of his eighteenth-century social and educational standing in Boston. Yet it was this New Hampshire-born citizen who did the calculations for the first *Farmer's Almanac* by Robert B. Thomas.

This Thomas almanac is an excellent example of its kind not only because it enjoys the longest unbroken (1793-) publishing record of any American periodical but also because its format and contents summarize pretty much all the almanac features known to man. It has the astronomy of the Babylonians, the farm calendars of the Sumerians, the prognostications of Virgil and Hesiod, the proverbs of Franklin, the wit of Swift.

Which is not to say that Robert B. Thomas, its founder, set out to include all these things in it. Provoked because Isaiah Thomas, father of American printing and an almanac maker too, would not sell him almanac sheets, this schoolteacher and bookseller of western Massachusetts decided he must have an almanac of his own.

"His own" is right. No almanac maker of any day or age ever left an impression of such depth or magnitude on any publication as did Robert B. Thomas on this one. Editor for some fifty-six years, his name is still carried on the front cover and, though he died in 1846, none of the nine or ten editors who have carried on for him since have seen fit to sign the annual Note to Correspondents with any name but his.

Robert B. Thomas lived the greater part of his life in the old Thomas Homestead in West Boylston, Massachusetts. His grandfather had attended Cambridge University in England and was a great lover of books. There in his grandfather's library Thomas found, for example, Ferguson's *Astronomy* from which he "imbibed the idea of calculating an almanac." He studied Ferguson during the few winters he taught school. Then, becoming interested in bookbinding and bookselling, he went to Boston. It was here in 1792, while attending the school kept by Osgood Carleton on Beacon Hill, that this *Almanac* was born.

His portrait and that of his wife, Hannah Beaman, may still be seen at the residence of Paul W. Parker in Rowley, Massachusetts, as well as at the American Antiquarian Society. You may also see his snuffbox and kerchief and his engineer's silver drawing set at the Parker home, as well as several household paper hatboxes. A man in Worcester seems to have the original transcripts in Thomas's own handwriting of the first issues and his one-horse shay (without wheels) may be purchased in Sterling, Massachusetts, for the modest sum of thirty-five dollars. In his home town, the Meeting House is said to bear his name.

APRIL 24, 1766 — MAY 19, 1846
at West Boylston, Mass.

He may be visualized as tall, straight, kindly, energetic, and observant. He makes known his presence and directs the affairs of the *Almanac* still because, as his successors know, that which he would not approve just doesn't belong.

Robert B. Thomas, it seems, was not too fond of personal publicity or personal identification with his *Almanac* except when it was necessary to ward off competitors and imitators. Though at one time he had over five hundred of these, none exist today. What he really did was to transfer the stamp of his own individuality to the *Almanac*—to make the *Almanac* the important thing. And so it is today.

The list of his successors as editors and publishers reads like this:

John H. Jenks	1847	through	1860
Charles L. Flint	1861	"	1869
John B. Tileston	1870	"	1871
Loomis J. Campbell	1872	"	1876
Horace E. Ware	1877	"	——
Robert Ware	——	"	1918
Frank B. Newton	1919	"	1932
Carroll J. Swan	1933	"	1935
Roger Scaife	1936	"	1940
Robb Sagendorph	1941	"	present

It is not clear who owned the copyright during the issues from 1793 through 1796. But beginning with that of 1797, one John West, a Boston bookseller, owned it and held on to it through the issue of 1808. After that, the names are as follows:

John West and Company	1809	through	1812
West and Richardson	1813	"	1818
West, Richardson & Lord	1819	"	1820
Richardson & Lord	1821	"	1829
Richardson, Lord & Holbrook	1830	"	1832
Carter, Hendee & Company	1833	"	1836
Charles J. Hendee & Co.	1837	"	1838
G. W. Palmer & Co.	1839	"	1839
Jenks & Palmer	1840	"	1847
Jenks, Palmer & Co.	1848	"	1851
Jenks, Hickling & Swan	1852	"	1855
Hickling, Swan & Brown	1856	"	1857
Hickling, Swan & Brewer	1858	"	1860
Swan, Brewer & Tileston	1861	"	1863
Brewer & Tileston	1864	"	1876
William Ware & Company	1877	"	1918
The Old Farmer's Almanack, Inc.	1919	"	1932
Carroll J. Swan	1933	"	1935
Mabel M. Swan	1936	"	1946
Swan, Swan, & Haynes	1946	"	——

Each in his or her or their own turn has carried on in the Thomas tradition. Under the Ware regime, for example, that marvelous book by Professor Kittredge of Harvard, called *The Old Farmer and His Almanac(k)* (Harvard University Press), first appeared. Carroll Swan rescued the old book from the ruins of bankruptcy, rebuilt it, and with his many friends, brought new blood and vitality to its veins. Little, Brown and Company, publishers, restored the ivy to its walls.

The present management team of Yankee, Incorporated, has its headquarters in Dublin, New Hampshire, in a farmhouse built in 1830. It, too, is doing well by the old *Almanac*. Circulation has grown to over a million from the less than 100,000 it had in 1940, when the present ownership took over; the advertising position is healthy; and reader interest is at a new high.

2.

OF THE WEATHER AND OTHER THINGS

TWO of the most strongly colored threads in this *Old Farmer's Almanac Sampler* are those of weather and astronomy. Long before there was any United States Weather Bureau or weather service of any kind, the American people, just as thousands do today, turned to the *Almanac* to find out what the weather would be—the next day, six months, and even a year ahead. Of course, Mr. Thomas must have made many a successful forecast to establish the reputation of his *Almanac* for accuracy. But in one instance at least, it is safe to say good fortune as much as any formula helped him out.

This must have happened as early as 1805, for one finds reference to it in a booklet printed in 1806. That year, Robert B. Thomas was stricken in the early spring with a bug or virus or whatever they called it then. Sick abed, he was unable to work on his *Almanac* manuscript for the forthcoming year. But deadlines—even if much earlier then—were deadlines. So when the printers, Munroe and Francis of Boston, were ready to set type for the thirteenth of July, they had no copy from Mr. Thomas for that day. They sent their "printer's devil" (office boy we would call him today) running from Boston to Sterling and the editor's bedside.

"Mr. Thomas," the boy exclaimed, "our firm must have your copy for July 13. What shall I tell them to put in?"

This is the inward month! Man shuts his door And turns his thought To what he holds, Of less and more,	In his most secret breast, That personal bin— What longer harvest, Of what worth, He has gathered in.

D. M.	D. W.	Aspects, Holidays, Heights of High Water, Weather, etc.	
1	Fr.	All Saints ♀ Gr. Hel. Lat. S. Hol. La. {8.4 8.4	*Clear,*
2	Sa.	All Souls ☾ in Apo. ☾ on Eq. {8.6 8.5	*blowy,*
3	F	20th S. a. T. "Wig" Season {8.9 8.6	*then*
4	M.	□♅☉ 1st Erie Canal bt. 1825 Will Rogers Day–Okla. {9.2 8.7	
5	Tu.	Fawkes Day Flood crest 1947 Gen. El. day {9.5 8.8	*clouds,*
6	W.	Billion dollar "drought relief" storm 1952—(6-17) {9.8 9.0	*snowy.*
7	Th.	The full "Beaver" Moon → In total eclipse {10.0 9.0	*Indian*
8	Fr.	☿ in Aph. A great "blazing starre" 1664 {10.2 9.1	*summer*
9	Sa.	The Pilgrims first sighted land 1620 Tides {— 10.3	*comes*
10	F	22nd S. a. P. ☾ runs high {9.1 10.3	*early*
11	M.	Veteran's Day Animals are hibernating Tides {9.1 10.3	*but*
12	Tu.	Confed. SS Alabama bt. U.S. Clipper Contest 1863 {9.1 10.2	*the*
13	W.	☌♂♆ Trad. Indian Summer {9.1 10.0	*rest of*
14	Th.	☌♅☾ Harvard Stadium dedicated 1903 {9.2 9.8	*Novem-*
15	Fr.	First wireless produced newspaper at sea 1899 {9.4 9.7	*ber with*
16	Sa.	☾ on Eq. "Where a whale can go I can follow." 1820 {9.7 9.7	*its*
17	F	22nd a. T. ♅ Stat. in R.A. {10.1 9.9	*gales*
18	M.	♀ Gr. El. E. ☌♃☾ ☾ in Peri. {10.6 10.0	*and*
19	Tu.	☌♆☾ ☌♂☾ Tides {11.1 10.2	*storms*
20	W.	17 ft. Army balloon burst at 140,000 ft. alt. 1949 Tides {11.4 10.3	
21	Th.	☌☿♄ Mayflower Compact Tides {11.6 10.2	*will*
22	Fr.	☌♄☾ ☌☿☾ ☾ rides low Tides {11.6 10.1	
23	Sa.	Most forgotten Am. anniversary 1618 Hol. Md. {— 11.3	*be*
24	F	24th a. P. Huron wreck 1877 {9.8 10.9	*some-*
25	M.	☌♀☾ 37 lb. Rainbow trout taken Idaho 1947 {9.5 10.4	
26	Tu.	Colossal Washington Statue erected Baltimore 1829 {9.2 9.8	*thing*
27	W.	Sea Cap'n Stetson k. by falling tree 1820 Tides {8.9 9.3	*to*
28	Th.	Thanksgiving Day Tides {8.6 8.8	*re-*
29	Fr.	☿ Gr. Hel. Lat. S. Str. Portland foundered 1898 {8.5 8.4	*mem-*
30	Sa.	St. Andrew ☾ in Apo. ☾ on Eq. {8.5 8.2	*ber.*

"If ice in November will bear a duck, nothing follows after but sleet and muck."

Farmer's Calendar.

"I am lately of the sluggish sort who likes nothing better than a nap on the sunny side of the house. But here is the contradiction, sir. I leap out of bed to take the morning with the eagerness of a young ram. The habit goes back to my youth when I had to be up betimes to perform the rugged chores that earned my breakfast. I hold no brief for the chores but in the doing of them I heard the voices of the morning, and those I have never forgotten.

"The world never speaks so sweetly as in those charmed hours. Man and nature do then commune in pious fellowship, though for me, I must confess, some part of those early hours belonged to our imbecile rooster. I needs must listen to his clarion, for he really could talk—at least in a way that seemed especially for me. I remember how many a morning he would crow, 'Martha Lee is not for thee,' a fact, alas, which I knew only too well. So he and I were part of the morning together.

"Not alone together, of course, for I delighted to hear the crows (late risers like all thieves) clear their pipes. Each spoke to me after his own fashion. There was my old philosopher. 'Slow, slow, slow,' he would say. There was Blackie, my watch-dog of crows, with his 'Be off, be off, be off, be off.' . . . And many other voices indeed. But now let us good-night—for we would not '**be off**' but **be up** betimes."

The late Squire Brown

Thomas, no doubt with a fever of 103, simply rolled over in bed and told him to go away.

"Put in anything, anything at all," he told the lad.

So the compositor set for that day:

July 13 ... "Rain, Hail, and Snow."

By the time Mr. Thomas was well again, he had, of course, forgotten all about the incident, and when he saw the proof sheets for July, it was too late. A number of the sheets had been printed; enough, anyway, so that when July 13 came around and it did "rain, hail, and snow," *The Farmer's Almanac* by Robert B. Thomas found "infallibility" added to its virtues.

But this wasn't all. There had been an almanac maker around for some years before Thomas started his whose name was Abraham Weatherwise. By his own confession one year in the preface of his almanac, he lived on the outskirts of the city of Boston in a shack on a dump. He claimed to have possession of a secret weather formula which he had learned through observing the stars between the cracks of the boards in the roof of his shack. And he maintained that, living practically in the open as he did, he had acquired a certain weather sensitivity enjoyed by very few.

Evidently, though the facts are long since lost to history, Abraham Weatherwise, forced to the wall by Thomas's July 13 coup, went to work with his secret formula for our man. Like Thomas himself, he has remained with this *Almanac* ever since as its weather forecaster. Naturally, in time, as did Mr. Thomas, he abandoned his earthly habitat. Yet his secret formula, as well as the Thomas format, with some variations and updating, is the one the present editors use today.

This secret formula has never been revealed to anyone other than the Thomas successors. By scientists it has been called nonsense, folderol, not as good as chance, ridiculous, and just plain luck. Yet last year when a Boston TV station invited the best weather brains in New England to join in a weather debate with the possessor of this formula, none of these scientists saw fit to risk their reputations or that of their profession. Actually, it was probably just as well, because the debate was to concern January, 1957, a month in which Abe Weatherwise once again saw his prophecies, made six months before, fulfilled with almost 100 per cent accuracy.

It must be pointed out here and now, however, that any comparison between Abe's methods, forecasts, or even his results and those of the United States Weather Bureau or other professional forecasters is not valid. Abe deals in weather trends over periods as short as a day or two at times, but in general his forecasts stretch over periods of three or four days, sometimes a week, or even two. And, in the long run, he prides himself mostly on how the seasons or even the years will turn out. The professional forecasters, on the other hand, limit themselves to accuracy over a one- or two-day period at the most—and even then make no real guarantees.

For a great many years *The Old Farmer's Almanac* was suitable only for Boston and places of similar latitude. The weather was calculated pretty much for the New England states and the astronomical correction tables took notice only of the slight differences in time between Boston and New England's larger cities. About fifteen years ago, however, astronomer Loring B. Andrews of the *Almanac* staff introduced correction tables for the entire United States, and Abe Weatherwise in his weather predictions naturally followed suit.

Scoff as one will at Old Abe and his "secret formula," it still remains true that:

... there now exists on Cape Cod a number of skating rinks for children provided by Grandma Dean of Hyannis, who over a period of years planned fund-raising outdoor square dances for which fair weather had been predicted by the *Almanac*.

... the skipper of an ocean-going yacht in the Bermuda Race in 1956 wrote that he found the *Almanac*'s warning, "Beware a strange event you may repent," invaluable when he was hundreds of miles offshore.

... a radio station in Chicago (WIND) ran a series of tests in

This cartoon, especially drawn for *The Old Farmer's Almanac* and Mr. Weatherwise by Francis W. Dahl, famous cartoonist of the *Boston Herald*, was published in the 1949 *Almanac*. It reveals for the first time a weather secret shared only by the Weather Bureau and ourselves. How Dahl discovered it, we wouldn't know. He may have been hiding in the barometer. We wouldn't put it past him.

1956 in which the *Almanac*'s forecasts were compared daily with those of the United States Weather Bureau and it found the *Almanac*'s were slightly better.

...the natives of Saskatchewan, Canada, as well as those of Penaguluru, Cuddapah, South India, have found the *Almanac*'s predictions accurate and helpful, and the latter have come to consider the editor of the *Almanac* as a befriending holy man.

...the United States Office of Censorship banned the *Almanac*'s weather forecasts during World War II as being of aid to the enemy and ruled that during this period they were to be called "Indications" and not "Forecasts."

...many a mother sets her daughter's wedding date, and many a hostess plans her garden parties, entirely by what the *Almanac* has to say.

...business conventions, golf tourney managers, soft-drink manufacturers, rainwear and anti-freeze makers, construction firms, summer theaters, traveling bands, even aviation pilots and bank presidents, go and plan by Old Abe's weather forecasts.

...even the experts, the highest-ranking meteorologists and scientists, will, at times, shamefacedly admit the *Almanac*'s formula has them stumped.

The forecasts, as they run in italics down through the *Almanac*'s right-hand Calendar pages, are in verse. Thus in 1951, when Mr. Eisenhower and Mr. Taft were having it out in the March New Hampshire primaries, the *Almanac* was saying for that time, "A Blizzard up to your Gizzard." As only chickens have gizzards, some might say such a forecast was equivocal. But heavy snow and ice did arrive, which cut down the audiences along Mr. Taft's slipping and sliding speaking tour to a disastrously low number.

Then there was the calamitous tornado in 1953 at Worcester, Massachusetts, which the *Almanac* within a day had predicted as "A bad squall and that's not all."

It has never been the policy of the *Almanac*'s editors to take seriously these and hosts of other successful forecasts. They realize, as did Mr. Thomas, that to know the weather the best rule is to wait and judge for one's self "after it has come what it may be." There is no scientific method known to man that will accurately forecast weather more than a day or so ahead. About as far as Old Abe and his secret formula can go is a determination of the trends it may indicate. These trends may be modified or magnified by what little scientific information available today seems pertinent. The process is somewhat similar to that which a Central Weather Intelligence Office would employ, with the full knowledge that though many times its findings will be worthless, now and again certain facts coming together will indicate an almost certain conclusion worth many times the cost of the entire operation.

In some years when the weather has been particularly capricious and gone pretty much against all forecasters, including Old Abe himself, many in the business (and today it is a large industry) lose heart and seek greener fields. This was the case with David Young in 1875, and also with the editor of *The Old Farmer's Almanac* in 1936. Young did not begin again until a quarter of a century had elapsed, but the omission of these forecasts from *The Old Farmer's Almanac* for one year created such protest (the press announced it was greater than the uproar when Teddy Roosevelt omitted the "In God We Trust" from the nickel) that the next year there was no alternative. Either the forecasts were resumed or, as 1936 sales showed, there would be no buyers for the next issue.

Whatever candid view Mr. Thomas and his successors may be said to hold of the *Almanac*'s weather predictions, the Astronomical Calculations and Data are and always have been inviolate. If one includes the necessary verifications, there are some 365,000 of these to be gone through each year. Except for an occasional letter broken on the press, these have remained remarkably free from error. Be it sunrise, sunset, length of day, sundial time, moonrise, moonset, moon southing, time and height of tides, hourly position of the planets and their relation to one another, moon's position in the heavens, eclipses, or whatever, any reader with this Almanac in hand may stand anywhere in the United States and tell almost to the minute exactly when and what is going to happen.

If anything, the *Almanac*'s readers follow this astronomy even more carefully than they do the weather. One year in the first decade of this century, the editor had the temerity to introduce a slight change in the order of the Astronomical Calculations columns. He shifted the Moon's Age column about one-quarter of an inch to the left.

Such a change, slight as it was, provoked the *Almanac*'s readers; for instance, a man from Nashua, New Hampshire, wrote in:

"I do not know who it was in your office who saw fit to make this change in the Moon's Age column but I wish to God he'd a died before he done it."

In more recent years, a little more space on the right-hand Calendar pages was provided for historical dates by omitting some of the repetitious daily heights of tides. This also brought a storm of protest. Fishermen up and down the Atlantic Coast, especially clam diggers, complained the omissions left their boats stranded high and dry on the beaches.

Many stories could be written of the anguish to editors the Astronomical Calculations have caused.

I remember, for instance, the last-minute rush, during World War II, caused by the United States Government change to War Time. The *Almanac* had been calculated by then, in fact was being set in type. The astronomer, Loring Andrews, was in North Africa, beaming, I believe, short-wave broadcasts over enemy territory. In government service, too, but nearer the plant, I found weekend leave available in which I could visit the printer and make the needed changes. This may sound simple enough, but try moving all those calculations an hour or two ahead some time and see what you run into.

I like the story, too, of the year when Isaiah Thomas, Jr., publisher of a competitive almanac for a few years, reached his astronomy deadline with no copy at hand. He learned his astronomer, a man named Graves, was far away in upper New York State. After

NOVEMBER, ELEVENTH MONTH.

ASTRONOMICAL CALCULATIONS.

☉'s Declination.	Days.	° ′	Days.	° ′	Days.	° ′	Days.	° ′	Days.	° ′
	1	14s. 30	7	16 20	13	18 01	19	19 31	25	20 47
	2	14 49	8	16 38	14	18 17	20	19 44	26	20 59
	3	15 08	9	16 55	15	18 32	21	19 58	27	21 10
	4	15 26	10	17 12	16	18 47	22	20 11	28	21 21
	5	15 45	11	17 29	17	19 02	23	20 23	29	21 31
	6	16 03	12	17 45	18	19 17	24	20 36	30	21 41

○ Full Moon, 7th day, 9 h. 32 m., morning, W.

☾ Last Quarter, 14th day, 4 h. 59 m., evening, W.

● New Moon, 21st day, 11 h. 19 m., morning, E.

☽ First Quarter, 29th day, 1 h. 57 m., morning, W.

KEY LETTERS REFER TO CORRECTIONS TABLE, PAGES 101-4, FOR ALL POINTS OUTSIDE NEW ENGLAND

Day of Year	Day of Month	Day of the Week	☉ Rises. h. m.	Key	☉ Sets. h. m.	Key	Length of Days. h. m.	Sun Fast. m.	Full Sea, Boston. Morn h.	Full Sea, Boston. Even h.	☽ Sets. h. m.	Key	☽ Souths. h. m.	☽'s Place	Moon's Age
305	1	Fr.	6 17	L	4 38	F	10 22	32	$6\frac{1}{2}$	$6\frac{3}{4}$	$12^{A}_{M}30$	G	$7^{P}_{M}30$	PSC	10
306	2	Sa.	6 18	L	4 37	F	10 19	32	$7\frac{1}{4}$	$7\frac{1}{2}$	1 27	H	8 12	PSC	11
307	3	F	6 19	L	4 36	E	10 17	32	8	$8\frac{1}{2}$	2 25	I	8 54	ARI	12
308	4	M.	6 21	M	4 35	E	10 14	32	$8\frac{3}{4}$	$9\frac{1}{4}$	3 23	J	9 37	ARI	13
309	5	Tu.	6 22	M	4 34	E	10 12	32	$9\frac{1}{2}$	$9\frac{3}{4}$	4 21	K	10 22	ARI	14
310	6	W.	6 23	M	4 32	E	10 09	32	10	$10\frac{1}{2}$	$5^{A}_{M}21$	L	11 09	TAU	15
311	7	Th.	6 24	M	4 31	E	10 07	32	$10\frac{3}{4}$	$11\frac{1}{4}$	rises	–	$11^{P}_{M}57$	TAU	16
312	8	Fr.	6 26	M	4 30	E	10 05	32	$11\frac{1}{4}$	$11\frac{3}{4}$	$5^{P}_{M}22$	E	—	—	—
313	9	Sa.	6 27	M	4 29	E	10 02	32	—	0	6 10	D	$12^{A}_{M}49$	G'M	17
314	10	F	6 28	M	4 28	E	10 00	32	$0\frac{1}{2}$	$0\frac{3}{4}$	7 04	D	1 42	G'M	18
315	11	M.	6 29	M	4 27	E	9 58	32	$1\frac{1}{4}$	$1\frac{1}{2}$	8 05	E	2 36	CNC	19
316	12	Tu.	6 31	M	4 26	E	9 55	32	2	$2\frac{1}{4}$	9 09	E	3 30	CNC	20
317	13	W.	6 32	M	4 25	E	9 53	31	$2\frac{3}{4}$	3	10 16	F	4 24	LEO	21
318	14	Th.	6 33	M	4 24	E	9 51	31	$3\frac{3}{4}$	4	$11^{P}_{M}25$	G	5 17	LEO	22
319	15	Fr.	6 34	M	4 23	E	9 49	31	$4\frac{3}{4}$	$5\frac{1}{4}$	—	–	6 09	VIR	23
320	16	Sa.	6 36	M	4 22	E	9 47	31	$5\frac{3}{4}$	$6\frac{1}{4}$	$12^{A}_{M}36$	H	7 00	VIR	24
321	17	F	6 37	M	4 21	D	9 45	31	$6\frac{3}{4}$	$7\frac{1}{4}$	1 47	I	7 52	VIR	25
322	18	M.	6 38	N	4 21	D	9 43	31	$7\frac{3}{4}$	$8\frac{1}{4}$	2 58	K	8 45	LIB	26
323	19	Tu.	6 39	N	4 20	D	9 41	30	$8\frac{3}{4}$	$9\frac{1}{4}$	4 10	L	9 40	LIB	27
324	20	W.	6 40	N	4 19	D	9 39	30	$9\frac{1}{2}$	10	$5^{A}_{M}22$	M	10 36	SCO	28
325	21	Th.	6 42	N	4 18	D	9 37	30	$10\frac{1}{4}$	11	sets	–	$11^{A}_{M}32$	SCO	29
326	22	Fr.	6 43	N	4 18	D	9 35	30	$11\frac{1}{4}$	$11\frac{3}{4}$	$5^{P}_{M}24$	D	$12^{P}_{M}29$	SGR	1
327	23	Sa.	6 44	N	4 17	D	9 33	29	—	0	6 21	D	1 25	SGR	2
328	24	F	6 45	N	4 16	D	9 31	29	$0\frac{1}{2}$	$0\frac{3}{4}$	7 19	E	2 18	CAP	3
329	25	M.	6 46	N	4 16	D	9 30	29	$1\frac{1}{2}$	$1\frac{1}{2}$	8 20	E	3 09	CAP	4
330	26	Tu.	6 48	N	4 15	D	9 28	28	$2\frac{1}{4}$	$2\frac{1}{2}$	9 20	F	3 57	AQR	5
331	27	W.	6 49	N	4 15	D	9 26	28	3	$3\frac{1}{4}$	10 18	G	4 42	AQR	6
332	28	Th.	6 50	N	4 15	D	9 25	28	$3\frac{3}{4}$	4	$11^{P}_{M}16$	H	5 25	PSC	7
333	29	Fr.	6 51	N	4 14	D	9 23	27	$4\frac{3}{4}$	5	—	–	6 07	PSC	8
334	30	Sa.	6 52	N	4 14	D	9 22	27	$5\frac{1}{2}$	6	$12^{A}_{M}14$	I	$6^{P}_{M}49$	PSC	9

dispatching a messenger on horseback to Graves for the copy, the anxious Thomas received only this reply:

"Sorry, Mr. Thomas, but I am on the shores of Lake Erie hiding behind a bush from which vantage point I intend to watch this great Battle of Lake Erie. The British have just now notified the Americans that one of their ships is not quite ready and so have asked that the battle be delayed not more than a day or so. After that I will get to your astronomy."

It is fortunate that all years have not been like this one of 1813 for almanac editors. Their lives, indeed, would have been much shorter than they have been.

Such astronomical pains, however, have paid off for this *Almanac.* Thomas was, if nothing else, adamant with regard to accuracy. Newspapers often used and still use his calculations on their front pages; public service companies turn their lights off and on by them; many Jewish synagogues light their candles *Almanac* in hand; on August 27, 1937, W. H. Desmond of Brockton, Massachusetts, won his freedom from a charge of "nighttime robbery" when his attorney was able to prove by the *Almanac* that the crime took place in daylight.

The most famous use of the *Almanac* in this regard, however, seems to have been during Abraham Lincoln's famous Armstrong murder trial, on May 7, 1858. The principal witness against Armstrong, Lincoln's client, was a man named Allen, who testified that at about eleven o'clock on the evening of August 29, 1857, he had seen the accused, from about 150 feet away, strike the murdered man. Mr. Lincoln inquired of the witness how he was able to see that far at that time of night. Allen replied he could see by the light of the moon. Lincoln then introduced the *Almanac* to show that on that night the moon had just completed its first quarter, that it set before midnight, and at the hour named by Mr. Allen was so dim, because it was near the western horizon, that it would have been impossible to see a blow struck by Armstrong with its light. The jury subsequently disagreed, and Armstrong was freed.

The North American Review for February, 1898, contains an article by James L. King, Librarian of the State of Kansas, which quotes an eyewitness to the *Almanac* episode, one Abram Bergen. A considerable controversy exists with regard to which of the many almanacs of the day Lincoln actually used. We have examined copies of most of those which might have been available. *The Old Farmer's Almanac* is the only one which, in addition to giving the time of the moonset as 11:39 P.M., also states that the moon was riding low on the evening of August 29.

Though astrology played a large part in almanac history, *The Old Farmer's Almanac* has never gone along with it. It is a popular "science" among many who should know better today, but Thomas and his successors have never included astrology in this *Almanac* except to scoff at it and warn their readers of its dangers. The informed do not need to be told how astrologers, using the configurations of the planets among other calculations, attempt to cast the horoscopes of men and nations.

We suppose people, looking at the strange little symbols which show the aspects of the planets on the Calendar pages, imagine this *Almanac* is up to the same tricks. It is not at all. The aspects are shown for what they are and no meaning is ever given them. As a matter of fact, astronomical time is on a different basis from that of astrology. The *Almanac*'s editors have often chuckled when letters come to the office asking for the moon's location on certain days in certain years. How much difference a variation in astronomical times can make in a horoscope! Perhaps such a half day could mean the difference between having a bewitching brunette in one's life instead of a vixen of a blonde.

Notwithstanding Thomas's firm stand against astrology, one does find him and his successors coming close at times to drinking at the pool of superstition. There are many references in past and present issues, for example, to the proper times of the moon in which to cut timber or plant one's garden, or for the best fishing and hunting. Scientists, like Arago, published long treatises in the nineteenth century purporting to prove there was nothing to it. Yet, even now, it is easy to find three believers (among farmers, that is) for two scoffers. And secretly at least, one must conclude that in all of us, superstition is not entirely dead. It is certainly not in the North Carolina sheriff who uses the *Almanac* for telling the full of the moon because he knows his jail will then become far more crowded than it usually is.

Another indication of at least toying with the occult was Thomas's introduction of the charming little zodiacal cuts which appeared first at the head of his Calendar pages in 1823, and have remained there ever since.

Certain of the woodcuts still appearing each year in *The Old Farmer's Almanac* can be traced back to one Abel Bowen, student, if not pupil, of Bewick, the famous English woodcut artist. Along with Alex Anderson, Bowen may be said to be America's first woodcut artist. In the days before the invention of mechanical engraving, Bowen's Boston and Massachusetts business in this line (1800 to about 1830) was a virtual monopoly. At times he and his associates numbered as many as sixty, and examples of their work and industry are to be found in many school as well as adult books of that day. *The Old Farmer's Almanac* title page now carries the same Abel Bowen woodcut which the latter prepared for Mr. Thomas about 1806.

The 166th Continuous Year of Publication 35¢

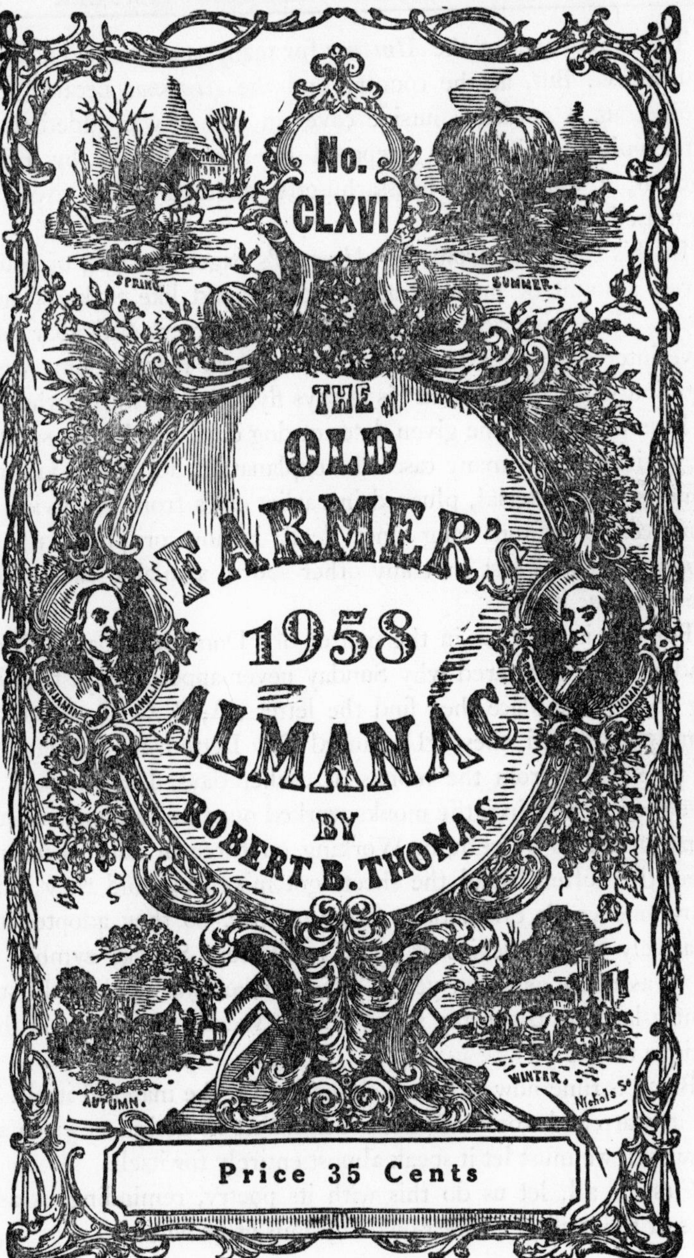

ANECDOTES, PLEASANTRIES, FARM CALENDAR EACH MONTH, PHOTOGRAPHS AND WOODCUTS.

☞ THIS IS THE ORIGINAL ROBT. B. THOMAS FARMER'S ALMANAC FIRST ISSUED IN 1792 FOR THE YEAR 1793.

Weather Forecast, Planting Tables.

PB

The front cover of the *Almanac* for many years carried a Bowen illustration. But, as the country and the *Almanac* became more prosperous, a so-called outside cover in yellow was added to the little volume. This was prepared for the *Almanac* by Henry Nichols, a Cambridge, Massachusetts, engraver. The cover has been used since 1851.

In this sampling from the *Almanac*'s pages there is, of course, a vast amount of material any reader would like to know more about. Many historical dates used on the Farmer's Calendar pages have interesting explanations for the modern reader. Some would question why "Old Colind" is always flying about during the Ides of March and how the given dates of dog days and Indian summer are arrived at. In many cases the explanation lies in the fact that some of this material, plucked in earlier days from the living experiences of editors long since dead, is now original with the *Almanac*. There just isn't any other source available earlier than the *Almanac* itself.

But this is not true in the matter of "Dominical Days." Many readers have wondered why Sunday never appears as just a plain big "S." In its place they find the letters, A, B, C, D, E, and F. Simply explained, these "Dominical Day Letters for Sunday" are an inheritance from the monks of earlier days. Long before the invention of printing, the monks worked out these almanac calculations on sheets of vellum. Working on three or four years at a time, they often found the sheets got mixed up, and they didn't know one year's calculations from another. So they adopted this relatively simple device of using a different Sunday symbol for up to as many as seven years. This number was apparently sufficiently large to cover any set of vellum sheets spread out on their antique tables.

But it is time now to take a closer look at the material itself. To see its warp and woof and that which makes its design so warm and beautiful, we must let it speak almost entirely for itself.

First of all, let us do this with its poetry, reminding us as it does of the cyclical and seasonal rhythms of its whole.

3.

THE SEASONS IN RHYME

SEASONS for *The Old Farmer's Almanac* have come and gone for a hundred and sixty-five years. But the seasons are not old. They are always new and different with a way of being what they will. They renew their youth and their loveliness, their cussedness and strangeness year after year, for all that we think we know all about them.

There has been a verse or poem atop each month of the *Almanac* since 1793. To quote all of them would have made a book containing over two thousand poems. We have had, therefore, to make a choice of what seemed most typical, and they are arranged according to the season of the year in which they first appeared.

SPRING

Though we mean no sacrilege to poetic endeavor, we have always thought most of the poems that may be gently called "of spring" were probably not written in springtime at all. For spring sings its own poetry about a world of love-making and birth and rebirth, a world of green, tender things, and soft winds, and the sound of streams that we have not heard for many a month—the wonder of a world coming to life around us. And the bluebird is its natural poet.

Our poet remembers spring and sings of it when the hot summers are on him or frosts and winter—and then he does so by true remembrance and in contrast to the world about him in other seasons. At that time he finds the true meaning of cloud and clod and bud and freshet and just what the bird had sung to him.

March is a boisterous fellow,
And undeterred by fear,
With many pranks proclaims himself
The tomboy of the year!

1931

'Tis April still, but April wrapt in cloud—
Month of sweet promise and of Nature's bliss,
When earth leaps up at heaven's reviving kiss,
And flouts at Winter lingering in her shroud.

John Dennis

What a charming month is May!
Hear each sighing lover say
Every maid the same replies,
In the echo of his sighs—
Hearts uniting—do not sever;
Be their month of May for ever.

1813

Apple blossoms, budding, blowing,
  In the soft May air:
Cups with sunshine overflowing—
Flakes of fragrance, drifting, snowing,
  Showering everywhere!

Lucy Larcom

Come haste to the muster, ye sweet little lasses,
  To dance on the green, like your grannam's of yore,
Where fiddles and sweethearts with charming caresses,
  Cake, candy, and custard are found in full store.

Enraptur'd Spring returns again,
The farmer plants the golden grain;
Hark, hark, the joy-inspiring grove,
Echoes to the voice of love.

1793

Now little Robin-Red-Breast,
  The Thrush, Tom-Tit, and Sparrow,
Awake the sluggard from his nest,
  And bid him plough and harrow.

1806

Now ere the snow forsakes the frozen soil,
The full-grown damsel quits her in-door toil;
And with her sweetheart, in the gliding sleigh,
Welcomes the moon, and steers the fiddler's way.

1802

RICH IN STONES

I farm a pasture where the boulders lie
As touching as a basket full of eggs,
And though they're nothing anybody begs,
I wonder if it wouldn't signify

For me to send you one where you live
In wind-soil to a depth of thirty feet,
And every acre good enough to eat,
As fine as flour put through a baker's sieve.

I'd ship a smooth one you could slap and chafe,
And set up like a statue in your yard,
An eolith palladium to guard
The West and keep the old tradition safe.

Carve nothing on it. You can simply say
In self-defense to quizzical inquiry:
"The portrait of the soul of my Gransir Ira.
It came from where he came from anyway."

Robert Frost

SUMMER

My uncle was an old man—or so he seemed to me—when I was very young. And yet, in the good hot summertimes, he shared my youth with me. He enjoyed with me things that seemed important then—as they do now. There were the owls at night and the whippoorwills, and the "creek, creek" of the night hawks about the housetop. The roll of the thunder, the sweet call of the bob-whites in those long-ago dusks, and all the things I shared with my uncle have always made for me the poetry of summer.

June's bridesman, poet o' the year,
Gladness on wings, the bobolink is here;
Half-hid in tiptop apple blooms he swings,
Or climbs against the breeze with quiverin' wings
Or, givin' way to 't in a mock despair,
Runs down, a brook o' laughter, thru the air.

James Russell Lowell

Lo! where the rosy-bosomed Hours,
  Fair Venus' train, appear,
Disclose the long-expecting flowers,
  And wake the purple year!

1904

White with its sun-bleached dust, the pathway winds
Before me; dust is on the shrunken grass,
And on the trees beneath whose boughs I pass;
Frail screen against the Hunter of the sky.

Whittier

The quiet August moon has come,
  A slumberous silence fills the sky,
The fields are still, the woods are dumb,
  In glassy sleep the waters lie.

W. C. Bryant

The brilliant poppy flaunts her head
  Amidst the ripening grain,
And adds her voice to swell the song
  That August's here again.

Helen Maria Winslow

Green in the valley and blue on the hill
And brown in the fields nearby,
A quiver of heat when the wind is still,
A bobwhite whistle, strong and shrill,
And a distant, sweet reply.

John L. Shroy

His sunburnt hands the scattering fork forsake,
And ruddy damsels ply the saving rake:
In rising hills the fragrant harvest grows,
And spreads along the hills in equal rows.

1801

The farmers grind and whet their scythes,
While haystacks in the meadows rise:
Green fields and shady groves appear,
And ripening harvest crowns the year.

1793

FALL

My good neighbor, Squire Brown, and I were spending an evening together—at his hearth, and with his Baldwin cider. The drink was sweet and light. I said I reckoned it gave every promise of getting better. That started him off and he crossed his boots as he began talking.

"You know, young feller, this here's a sad time of year. I've been reading poetry. Seems suitable now. But it ain't what it used to be. Look at these two books! *Newfangled stuff!*" sez he disgustedly.

The squire then slumped down with his boots straddled, taking his cider. So I let him be. But I poured me another glass and left him a copy of *The Old Farmer's Almanac.*

The husking's announced and the neighbors invited,
The boys in full glee and the girls all delighted;
When the labor is over they join in the cheer,
And a "smack" pays the labor for each ruddy ear.

1813

Now round goes the crackling wheel,
And foaming presses laughing syrup yield
For cider.

1799

Now the apples and pears and the peaches and plums,
'Tis said, are all ripe up at good Uncle Tom's
Oh, then, let us haste for the girls are all there;
And sweet is the fruit with the smiles of the fair.

1813

"Take the fruit I give you," says the bending tree,
"Nothing but a burden is it all to me.
Lighten ye my branches; let them toss in air!
Only leave me freedom next year's load to bear."

Lucy Larcom

More welcome than voluptuous gales,
  This keen, crisp air, as conscience clear:
November breathes no flattering tales;
  The plain truth-teller of the year,
Who wins her heart, and he alone,
Knows she has sweetness all her own.

Lucy Larcom

The woods stand close around,
  And the sound the leaves make
Is small and near, a green sound—
  This, for joy's sake,
Since joy is surely here.

High up there is a clear
  Way that the trees make
To show how blue and near
  Is heaven—for love's sake;
And love is surely here.

David Morton

Deep in the ashes one live ember
  Lingers two similes to show:
June in the arms of old December,
  A red rose in a drift of snow.

Frank Dempster Sherman

Harvest is gathered in
The grain, the grape, and all...
All that the labor meant

Is safely in the bin...
Safe for bin and stall—
Save the divine intent:

And that is safer still
In cells of mind and will,
That have their sleepy fill.

David Morton

WINTER

When it comes to winter the old farmer cannot help but be enclosed in his *own* winter. His little world is snug and secure, with chores done, the cattle fed, a warm stove or two going, and a crackling fireplace, and nothing frozen up—permanently, that is. He comes very close then, perhaps, to being a poet himself.

He remembers Whittier's "Snowbound"—the great northeast snowstorm with the "ghostly finger tips of sleet" brushing on the windowpanes all night, seeing next morning a gnome in white and the drifted shapes of the familiar walls and the bright-eyed country lads obeying the glad duty from their father:

"Boys, a path! What farmer boy
Counted such summons less than joy?"

What more shall we ask of poetry than that it carry the heart with it?

Oh, what a goodly and a glorious show;
The stately trees have decked themselves with white,
And stand transfigured in a robe of light;
Wearing for each lost leaf a flake of snow.

Richard Wilton

Now frowning *Winter* rears his head,
Array'd in all majestic dread;
Again his hostile standards rear,
To usher in the infant year.

1797

Bring from the winter woods
  What never the eye can see:
Flowers that the winter hoods,
  That stand, invisibly,
In frozen solitudes.
This is the winter daring:
  Of what we said would die,
Far on some winter faring
  From names we knew them by...
Give them the warmth of your caring,
  Prove that death is a lie.

David Morton

See bursting from the northern skies,
November's fierce successor rise;
Lo! devastation makes his way,
Oaks with a bow confess his sway.

1793

If Candlemas Day be fair and bright,
Winter will have another flight;
If on Candlemas Day it showers or rain,
Winter is gone, and will not come again.

1807

'Tis now the time from cribs to feed
The hardy ox and noble steed
The cattle fed—fuel within—
'Tis now the blissful hours begin.

1797

Now clouds the wintry skies deform;
In sullen vengeance roars the storm;
The snow which from yon mountain falls
Loads leafless trees and fills the vales.

1797

Behold, my fair, where'er we rove,
The naked hill, the leafless grove,
What dreary prospects round us rise,
The hoary ground, the frowning skies.

1795

4.

THE FARMER'S CALENDARS

ON THE right-hand side of the Calendar pages of *The Old Farmer's Almanac* a column headed "Farmer's Calendar" has always appeared. These Farmer's Calendars are short essays on almost every conceivable subject in a style quite their own. In one sense, they represent the editor mounting the rostrum and holding forth as a country preacher would before his flock. In another way, they show the editor as a kindly country doctor on his visits up and down the country roads; they become the afternoon call of a friendly and wise neighbor and the good talk before a roaring fire. Whatever they may be, however, these Farmer's Calendars are the main strand running through the *Almanac*, the one which gave it its place beside the old family Bible, and in recent years helped to keep it there.

OF THE SPIRIT

Our churches, and, in a sense, our religions, are a communal thing, a social binder for the order and decency of our community as well as a kind of pious proof of ourselves as solid citizens. But deeper within us lies our special worship and wonder. We mean *our* solitudes, the almost pagan beauty of sunsets and sunrises, the disturbing influence of the wandering moon, and the pity and love we keep to ourselves. These are our second religion, ours alone as we seek to reach God through them. Here is a strange, and lovely, and troubled world that we must explore through God—and through him, we seek ourselves.

The pages that follow, I think, contain here and there the essence of this inner religion—God speaking to men, almost secretly, for each man hears and interprets the word of God for himself.

And then there are the other things of the spirit that we can never completely share with others. There is the happiness of love for one's wife and children, and the sorrows that walk with this love. There is charity of the heart—as well as of the purse—and such philosophy and steadfastness as we shall find through them.

Religion

RELIGION is the best armor in the world, but the worst cloak.

1795

⌘⌘⌘

FROM quack lawyers, quack doctors, quack preachers, mad dogs, and yellow fever, good Lord, deliver us! This is my sincere prayer, let others do and say as they will. A respectable attorney is an advantage to a town and ought to have the esteem of his fellow citizens; but a meddlesome pettifogger deserves the treatment of any other sneaking puppy that runs his nose into your closet. As for strolling preachers, "O ye generation of vipers!" I would bear any evil far better than the gabble of one of these intruding boobies. Yet how many forsake all business and pleasure that they may enjoy the ecstatic bliss of listening to their empty, disgusting, and blasphemous nonsense! It is a serious misfortune to have a woman, a head of a family, yet bewitched by one of these fellows. Whenever this happens, farewell to all business, to all comfort! No more dairy, no more spinning, or weaving, or knitting, or sewing. Forenoon, afternoon, and evening, nothing but attending lectures to hear the charming, the pious, the godly Mr. Bitemslily—totally regardless of that text of the sacred volume which says, "Six days shalt thou labor and do all thy work!"

1813

⌘⌘⌘

MAY no war or battle's sound attend you, and may no system of tyranny, despotic knavery, or superstitious idiotism ever oppress you. Yours is the God of Peace, and yours the God of Plenty, Liberty, and Independence. Crowned with the sheaves of Ceres and the clusters of Pomona, the farmer walks forth amidst the music of his lowing herds and bleating flocks, a distinguished proof of the wisdom of that primeval sentence pronounced by Him who created the heavens and the earth and the beasts of the earth, and everything that creepeth upon the earth, and last of all Man—that sentence so often and so emphatically denounced a curse, but which in truth seems to be a most divine and eminent blessing: "In the sweat of thy face shalt thou eat bread till thou return unto the ground!" Go on then, thou lord of this beautiful creation, and improve this blessing.

1829

⌘⌘⌘

IT IS sometime said that women go to meeting on Sunday to look at each other's dresses and bonnets. That's scandal! They go to show off their own.

1839

⌘⌘⌘

IF RELIGION was not wanted to keep bad men in check, it still would be wanted to keep good men from despair.

1851

⌘⌘⌘

THOMAS AP-MORGAN, the Welsh preacher, says, "We must look out for the devil"; for if he finds anyone idle, he will set him at work; and who wants to do the *devil's* work?

1854

⌘⌘⌘

SAID a city pastor to a young member of his flock, "We are always pleased to hear you speak in the prayer meeting, and we hope you will continue to do so; but I would advise you to be as brief as possible, and, if the brethren think you are *too brief*, they will tell you of it."

1857

⌘⌘⌘

A CLERGYMAN was once asked whether the members of his church were united. He replied that they were perfectly united—*frozen together.*

1865

Two deacons in a country town were disputing about a graveyard.

"Well," said one of them, "*I'll* never be buried in that graveyard so long as *I* live."

"What an obstinate man!" replied the other. "If the Lord spares my life, *I* will."

1866

MEMORIAL DAY

For over sixty years the people of our nation have held this day sacred to our soldier dead.

Let us cling to the custom of decorating the graves of those that have given their lives that we may live in peace. Too often the day is spent as a gala holiday and not a thought given to these dead heroes.

1931

⌘⌘⌘

A clergyman wrote to a wealthy and influential businessman requesting a subscription to a worthy charity and soon received a curt refusal which ended, "As far as I can see, this Christian business is just one continuous Give, give, give." Replied the clergyman, "I wish to thank you for the best definition of the Christian life that I have yet heard."

1939—*Rev. W. F. A. Stride*

OLD PRAYER

God grant me the serenity to accept things I cannot change. The courage to change things I can. And the wisdom to know the difference.

1950

We would pray at this season that there may be a truce to all mankind—the forerunner of everlasting peace—and assurance of warmth and shelter, a brimming ration of love and kindness to men everywhere, even our enemies; and we pray that home fires may again be lighted for those who are homeless and forsaken.

May this be a prayer truly from our hearts, or it is no prayer at all. And may our grace on Christmas Day be humble, for we are the fortunate ones. We want no fat graces now—fork in hand and an eye to the feast. May we in humbleness of spirit, in earnestness of prayer, reach out beyond our pleasant, tidy world, to the world of agony.

1952

Happiness

Say to pleasure, "Gentle Eve, I will have none of your apple," and depend upon it, you will have sweet fruit all your lifetime.

1802

⌘⌘⌘

Seneca says, "The way to be happy is to make vice not only odious, but ridiculous, and everyone to mind his own business." Now if you want your fingers in every man's pie, ten to one if you do not get them confoundedly burnt now and then. Let us attend to our own concerns, such as cutting scions for grafting, shelling seed corn, etc.

1807

⌘⌘⌘

Hark! what delightful sounds: they come from the cottage of Felix, the farmer. His daughter, Mary, having ended the business of the dairy, and other cares of the family allotted to her charge, is chanting a sweet hymn of gratitude to that Being who hath promised that *seed time and harvest should not cease* to the tune of "Hotham," with the soft accompaniment of her brother William's flute. This is, in fact and in truth, *rural felicity*.

O ye musty heads, and ye rusty heads, and ye crusty heads, do ye seek happiness? Then call on Farmer Felix, and there you will find as much as this dirty world will afford. He has the secret to make happy; carries it continually with him, and keeps it bright with use.

Industry is its name, and it will not only make happy, but will make rich. Felix never fails to attend meeting, let who will preach. His whole family are also brought up in the same habit. Some have given him the name of Farmer Joshua, from his frequently quoting the saying of that pious patriarch, "As for me and my house, we will serve the Lord."

1817

⌘⌘⌘

YOUNG farmers, if you wish for happiness, do not turn land jobbers, and leave your digging and hoeing, your planting and sowing, your raking and mowing. Remember that agriculture is the best of culture, and he that follows the plowing is engaged in an employment that would not disgrace a king.

1836

⌘⌘⌘

One ounce of mirth is worth more than ten thousand weight of melancholy.

Can a farmer be gloomy at this season, when Nature begins to show her fat cheeks with laughter? It would seem that one engaged in such employment might ever be cheerful. To be continually cheerful is an "implicit praise and thanksgiving to Providence under all its dispensations." No man can be fit to carry on business who is ever in a moping and spiritless mood. "Such a one on a farm," said my uncle Jonas, "is not worth the gizzard of a trifle."

1843

⌘⌘⌘

THE thirty-first of December, 1850, ended the first half of the nineteenth century; and I hope, if you had then any old grudges, you have not let them lay over to spoil the beginning of new years that should be happy, and new half centuries that need not allow any "bygones" to mar their comfort.

1851

⌘⌘⌘

If you know anything that will make a brother's heart glad, run quick and tell it; and if it is something that will only cause a sigh, *bottle it up, bottle it up.*

1854

⌘⌘⌘

Encourage the boys to get up a sugar party. The few pounds of sugar it will require are nothing compared to the happiness which such a party will give the young people. If the boys are to be kept on the farm, and the girls made contented and happy, they must be encouraged to hold frequent social gatherings.

1891

⌘⌘⌘

In youth the absence of pleasure is pain; in old age the absence of pain is pleasure.

1892

⌘⌘⌘

A joyous smile adds an hour to one's life; a heartfelt laugh, a day; a grin, not a moment.

1895

⌘⌘⌘

This is the philosopher's month—good for pipe smoking in the Boston rocker—excellent for feet warming. Ma's activities will be about the same as usual, likely stepped up some—you being under foot or sick-a-bed from house drafts.

But if you have figured out your taxes and how to pay them, then you may relax and think backward and forward on this farm business of yours. You may ponder the days when you and your dad and your brothers did all the milking by hand, when there was no such thing as electric milkers, hay balers, and a bubbler for each cow—when soil analysis, contour plowing, crop rotation, and county agents were just newfangled ideas (or not ideas yet)—when your horses or your oxen pulled your machines—when you had a lot of sheep and a collie to drive them—when you had strong sons growing up to help you and sturdy daughters who would someday raise their own farm families.

You will reflect your sons didn't stay on the farm because all the new machinery you got sort of took their places. Maybe they did better off the farm—maybe they didn't—but anyhow you didn't lack too much for help, and you've been turning out two or three times the crops and milk with less labor than in the old days. Things are pretty good with you, though there is an ache behind it—your farm as a family unit is gone forever.

1953

Charity

REMEMBER, ye wealthy and affluent, the sons and daughters of affliction and distress! Think of those into whose shattered dwellings poverty enters to increase in inclemency and the horror of the present season. Distribute bread to the hungry, and clothes to the naked.

1796

⌘⌘⌘

Now, when your cellars, your granaries, and your barns are all full, let your heart also be full of gratitude to Him who gave you this abundance. But amidst this profusion of goodness, forget not the poor and needy. Shall the widow and the orphan famish while you revel in plenty? No, let their cries awaken your humanity; alleviate their distress by sending them a portion of your store, for "happy is the man who hath sown in his breast the seeds of benevolence."

HAVE you cultivated your mind as well as your farm? Have you done your best endeavors to promote temperance, prudence, gratitude, modesty, humility, justice, sincerity, diligence, benevolence, mercy, peace, religion, and CHARITY? Here, my friend, if you have been a faithful farmer, you will have stores laid up in the granary of Heaven, a supply sufficient for a life everlasting; where no moth shall corrupt, or thief break through and steal.

1817

⌘⌘⌘

NEED makes the old wife trot. Yes, yes, necessity makes us all scamper. Not only the young and lusty, but the old, decrepit, and crippled are obliged to bestir their stumps and budge off at her call. Snow, rain, hail, wind, and tempest, what are they to a poor starveling?

Hark! who knocks at the door? I hear the voice of Jeremy! "Friends of humanity, 'tis an old soldier of the Revolution who seeks a shelter from the tempest, and begs a morsel from your plenteous board to stay a hungry stomach. I bled at Brandywine and Monmouth when ye were younkers. Yes, while ye were scouring for jays and boblincons, and your granddaddies were contending amidst bayonets, bullets, and bombshells."

The door is opened and old Seventy-five partakes of generous hospitality.

1821

⌘⌘⌘

CHARITY is the greatest of the social virtues. Through the medium of charity we anticipate the joys of Heaven. Charity is a continued current of benevolence and compassion. It feels for the woes of the wretched, casts the tender veil of forgiveness over the faults and foibles of its fellow creatures, and condemns not to disgrace and infamy for one fault only. He that lacketh this godlike virtue lacketh the essence of true Christianity.

Charity, my friends, is the golden chain that binds Heaven to earth! 'Tis the bright galaxy that leads mortal man up to the celestial dwelling of the Rock of Ages!

1823

⌘⌘⌘

WINTER gives a blessed chance to get in closer touch with the wife and children. Is there a sick neighbor whose woodpile is running low, or are there any other things on his premises badly needing attention? Perhaps you can give him a quiet little boost. It takes good neighbors to make a good neighborhood.

1911

Philosophy

AT this season the farmer indulges himself in ease and plenty; but I would remind him that economy and frugality are never more essential.

1795

⌘⌘⌘

HE that makes himself an ass, must not take it ill if men ride him.

1795

⌘⌘⌘

GOOD dancers have mostly better heels than heads.

1795

⌘⌘⌘

CRAFT must have clothes, but truth prefers to go naked.

1796

⌘⌘⌘

WHO keeps company with the wolf will learn to howl.

1797

Pains to get, care to keep, and fear to lose, is the best way to make an easy bed for old age.

1802

⌘⌘⌘

Though we may give advice, we cannot give conduct.

1802

⌘⌘⌘

I wish you a merry Christmas; aye, and merry life; healthy children, and enough to give them. But the best gift is good education, a love for each other, and a reverence for religion.

1802

⌘⌘⌘

If men, with minds as cool as the evening, will lay out the work of the day, they will be able, in this leisurely January month, to lay plans for a life of prosperity and happiness.

1803

⌘⌘⌘

It is with narrow-souled people as with narrow-necked bottles—the less they have in them, the more noise they make in pouring it out.

1803

⌘⌘⌘

It is wise not only to make hay while the sun shines, but to keep your temper till the dew falls; and then an industrious man finds his bed the best place.

1803

⌘⌘⌘

A merciful man will be merciful to his beasts, nor work them beyond their strength, nor keep them sparingly.

Look to your fences; and if your neighbor neglects to repair and keep in order his half, do it yourself; you will get your pay.

1804

A WISE man will desire no more than what he may get justly, use soberly, distribute cheerfully, and live upon contentedly.

1805

⌘⌘⌘

He that lives according to reason shall never be poor; but if you give fancy the reins, she will drive you to destruction.

1807

⌘⌘⌘

KEEP clear from quarrels, and do not plague your brains about politics; for he who quarrels himself into notice, will be sick of his bargain.

1807

⌘⌘⌘

To crow well and scrape ill is the Devil's trade. If you have a bragging, noisy, quarrelsome neighbor, take no notice of him; but mind your own business, and he will soon be off.

1808

⌘⌘⌘

When it rains pottage, hold out your dish.

1809

⌘⌘⌘

'TIS an old Italian proverb, "*An idle man is a bolster for the devil.*" Then spur up, for if the old fellow once gets you under his head and horns, you are gone, my friend!

1809

⌘⌘⌘

DISBELIEVE two-thirds of the stories you hear in the neighborhood, and say nothing about the rest.

1810

⌘⌘⌘

Do nothing in great haste, except catching fleas and running from a mad dog.

1811

Love thy neighbor; yet pull not down thy hedge. That is to say, be courteous, friendly, and neighborly, but never lay yourself open to exposure to anyone.

1811

⌘⌘⌘

He who once hits will be ever shooting. This is literally true, for I have known many a foolish fellow spend much time and money in shooting to no purpose, because he happened one day to hit a turkey by chance.

1811

⌘⌘⌘

He who would have what he hath not, should do what he doth not.

1811

⌘⌘⌘

If you find near your house a gully in the road or a small hole in the bridge, do not wait for the surveyor or selectman to give orders, but hasten and repair the breach. Some men are so very particular in these matters that they will run the hazard of killing their cattle and breaking their own necks before they will give a cent to the public! No, they must be paid for it, and the selectmen must be called together to draft a town order, which is no sooner done, than away it goes to the landlord for a little stimulus. Whenever you are called to work on the highway, be diligent, for he who thinks he may loiter without wrong is in a most egregious error.

1811

⌘⌘⌘

Beware of a backbiter; above all things he is most to be despised. This character often unites with that of the miser and then the possessor becomes detestable. The neighborhood is kept in continual ferment by his groundless stories and underhand insinuations.

1813

Wilt thou hunt? Kill no more squirrels than you want for your pie, nor more partridges than you want for your spit. To slay these little innocents for mere sport is a waste of time, money, and morals; your boys had better be collecting materials for making manure, which will make your farm rich, and stop the cry of "short crops, small potatoes, and hard times."

1817

⌘⌘⌘

Avoid wrangling and law fighting. It is never worth your while to go to law at the expense of five hundred dollars about ninepence; but should you ever be forced into a lawsuit, take the advice of respectable counsel and then keep your tongue within your teeth. If you foolishly blab your case to your neighbors, they will all, men, women, and children, become prodigiously wise and knowing. They will talk Law at a great rate, and distress you with their wisdom.

1818

⌘⌘⌘

Why do you conjure up a thousand frightful monsters to torment yourself, when there are enough of real evils? Some seem to think that there is a ghost in every gust of wind. Away with such vain illusions of the imagination! Strange it is that a courage that never startles at real dangers should shrink at even the thought of an empty chimera! Signs and omens and prognostics continually fill the minds of some. "Ah, husband, I know our crops will be short next season," said a silly old woman, "for the brine has all leaked out of the pork barrel!" She happened to get a first sight of the new moon over her left shoulder, and it made her sad and glum through the month. She once dreamed of a black cat, and this so bewitched the cream that no butter could be made! Farmer Bluejoint has nailed an ass's shoe to his hogsty to keep the evil spirit from his herd of swine; for it is said that Old Splitfoot has always hated asses since the affair of Balaam. The rats by thousands destroyed his grain. So he got his daughter, Dolly, to write them a threatening letter, which he placed in his corn crib. The consequence was that every varmint of them immediately evacuated the place! What power has superstition!

1830

⌘⌘⌘

When men speak ill of thee, live so as nobody will believe them.

1832

⌘⌘⌘

None but the contemptible are apprehensive of contempt.

1835

⌘⌘⌘

The carpenter's hammer awakes us in the morning with its rap; the merry cooper sings to the rattle of his driver; the factory bell rings, and the spinners and weavers are all hying to their wonted labors! What then, shall the farmer lie still amidst all this note of life and activity? No, no, no!

1835

⌘⌘⌘

If a man cannot find ease in himself, it is vain to seek elsewhere.

1836

⌘⌘⌘

Who has no friends nor enemies is without talents or energy.

1836

⌘⌘⌘

"Go ahead!"— aye, go ahead in your well-doing. There are not a few, however, who are overzealous to go ahead, right or wrong. To *drive business* is all their end and aim.

1837

⌘⌘⌘

Judgment is the throne of prudence, and silence is its sanctuary.

1839

Open your door to a fair day, but make ready for a foul one.

1842

⌘⌘⌘

Some know just enough to excite their pride, but not to cure their ignorance.

1844

⌘⌘⌘

Never sign a writing till you have read it, nor drink water till you have seen it. An inch in a man's nose is, comparatively, no small affair. Now Farmer Rakins was furnished by nature with a proboscis not to be sneezed at for its diminutiveness. On a certain very warm day, while hard at work, he became extremely thirsty, and, hastening to the brook, he clapped down and sucked away. A hungry trout, thinking it a savory bit, instantly grappled his nose, as its point sunk beneath the surface. Up came the farmer's head, and out came the fish upon the bank! No ill was the consequence; for Rakins had a good drink from the brook, and a good dinner from the fish. But not so at another time, when, in like haste, he swallowed down about a half dozen polliwogs, which caused no small revolution and difficulty in his stomach. We ought to look to the bottom before we begin to sip.

1844

⌘⌘⌘

"Love thy neighbor as thyself." What is the meaning of this? I will tell you, friend, what I conceive it to mean. It is this—*take not too much toll in your dealings.* Act the good Samaritan, and hope for heavenly rewards.

1847

⌘⌘⌘

Do you weed carefully upon your side of your moral as well as artificial fences?

1848

WHEN conscience has dictated one course and passion another, did you ever regret following the injunctions of the former?

1848

⌘⌘⌘

SILENCE is said to be "a gift without peril, and a treasure without enemies."

1850

⌘⌘⌘

BEFORE you "go ahead," had you not better see how far you have got a head to go?

1850

⌘⌘⌘

CURIOSITY is looking over other people's affairs and overlooking our own.

1851

⌘⌘⌘

IT will not injure you to know enough of law to keep out of it.

1851

⌘⌘⌘

IF you pride yourself on saying what you like, you will often be mortified by hearing what you don't like.

1858

⌘⌘⌘

How many thoughts we waste, how much care and anxiety we expend, in forming plans to meet emergencies that never occur!

1858

⌘⌘⌘

THE only way for a man to escape being found out is to pass for what he is.

1858

ZEAL, not rightly directed, is pernicious; for as it makes a good cause better, so it makes a bad cause worse.

1860

⌘⌘⌘

THE devil tempts all men; but the idle man tempts the devil.

1865

⌘⌘⌘

A HANDFUL of common sense is worth a bushel of learning.

1865

⌘⌘⌘

A GRIM, hard-headed old judge, after hearing a flowery speech from a pretentious young barrister, advised him to pluck out the feathers from the wings of his imagination and stick them in the tail of his judgment.

1868

⌘⌘⌘

"How many people," said Jeremy Taylor, "are busy in the world gathering together a handful of thorns to sit upon!"

1877

⌘⌘⌘

THERE is one thing about hens that looks like wisdom—they don't cackle much till they have laid their eggs.

1878—*Josh Billings*

⌘⌘⌘

WHILE the word is yet unspoken you are master of it: when once it is spoken, it is master of you.

1878

⌘⌘⌘

MICHELANGELO was one day explaining to a visitor at his studio what he had been doing to a statue since his previous visit. "I have retouched this part, polished that, softened this feature, brought out that muscle, given some expression to this lip, and more energy to that limb."

"But these are trifles," remarked the visitor.

"It may be so," replied the sculptor, "but recollect that trifles make perfection, and perfection is no trifle."

1878

⌘⌘⌘

Some men acquire that tired feeling from looking for an easy job.

1902

⌘⌘⌘

The man who never makes any blunders is a very nice piece of machinery—that's all.

1903—*Josh Billings*

⌘⌘⌘

The philosophy of one century is the common sense of the next.

1906—*Henry Ward Beecher*

⌘⌘⌘

As in a game of cards, so in the game of life we must play what is dealt to us; and the glory consists, not so much in winning, as in playing a poor hand well.

1907—*Josh Billings*

⌘⌘⌘

A man's reputation is like his shadow: sometimes it follows and sometimes it precedes him; and at times it is longer and at other times shorter than he is.

1910

⌘⌘⌘

Every man should profit by his own mistakes, but most of us would prefer to profit by the mistakes of others.

1911

THE opening of the New Year is a good time for self-communion. "Man, know thyself," is good advice and advice which for the man on the farm should be coupled with the recommendation, "Know thy farm." Concerning both self and farm, ask and honestly answer the most searching possible questions. Doing this at the opening of the New Year leads most of us to make good resolutions. It is quite common to smile at the very thought of such resolutions, but the man who does not make good resolutions at New Year's or some other time is hopeless. Many of these resolutions, it is true, are broken; it is impossible to realize ideals fully. But we can at least resolve in what direction we will move during the coming year.

1912

⌘⌘⌘

CONVERSATION enriches the understanding, but solitude is the school of genius.

1914—*Edward Gibbon*

⌘⌘⌘

SOME folks don't let the grass grow under their feet fur the reasons that they never move out uv their tracks.

1917—*Joe Cone*

⌘⌘⌘

WHAT is more powerful than armies and more destructive than high explosives? In our country there is something which steals millions of dollars each year. It brings sickness. It maims, crushes, and destroys. It is relentless. It gives nothing, but takes all. It is one of our worst enemies. It is everywhere: on the street, in the factory, and in the home. It exacts a tremendous toll on the farm. It is a monster of frightful mien. Its name is CARELESSNESS.

1933

Some wag has described a philosopher as a blind man in a dark room looking for a black cat that isn't there.

To eat is human, to digest divine.

1936—*C. T. Copeland*

FLIES AND HONEY

Of all the quaint old Yankee sayings that I love, none is homelier in its original than the admonition that you can catch more flies with honey than vinegar. It instantly recalls the chipped and shallow saucers, filled, respectively, with sweet and sour substances, that were set out in sunny kitchen windows from dog days to the first frost.

"Seems like I catch more flies with honey than vinegar," the farmer's wife, taking a fragrant pie out of the ample oven, would say to her husband as he came into the kitchen for supper after his chores were done. "Well, yes, I guess maybe you do," he would reply thoughtfully.

The children who heard this and saw this happen have seldom forgotten it. Thomas has not reached his present state of prosperity by sharp dealings; he has been genial and generous in his business relations. Jane's happy marriage is not based on a tart attitude toward the male race; it is based on gentleness and lovability. Both of them have gone steadily forward on the principle that where acrimonies fail, amenities succeed.

1941—*Frances Parkinson Keyes*

OF THE HOME

So much is written about the weather and religion and social strife and war—and home—that we sometimes think of these subjects as old and tired. Ideally, home means security and love, happy memories of childhood, the philosophy of oldsters beside the hearth, generations long gone, and the fresh patter of little feet—all against a Currier and Ives backdrop. But home can be a bundle of skins carried from place to place and set up at night, an igloo, or something just built with new hope looking out a picture window at its duplicate across the way. It does not matter as long as it represents a dwelling for the heart.

Health

FOR CORNS

SPREAD the yeast of beer on a linen rag, and apply it to the part affected. Renew it once a day for three or four weeks. It will cure.

1793

TO TAKE OFF FRECKLES

TAKE bean-flower water, or elder-flower water, or May dew, gathered from corn, of either, the quantity of four spoonfuls, and add to it one spoonful of oil of tartar. Mix it well together, and often wash the face with it, and let it dry on.

1793

⌘⌘⌘

RETIRE to bed in season, and rise early; this will save your health, as well as wood and candles.

1794

⌘⌘⌘

'TIS an old custom at this season to wish our friends a Happy New Year; I wish mine many, and particularly through the present inclement one, in comfortable fires, without smoky chimneys, sleigh rides without overturning, heavy purses with a liberal hand, full tables with generous hearts, and social enjoyments without contention.

1800

⌘⌘⌘

"HEALTH is the laborer's right hand"—let him not lose it for want of caution. The healthy and ambitious too often give a strong constitution a mortal wound, while they suppose it invulnerable. The restoration of health is difficult and expensive—the art of preserving it, cheap and easy. A celebrated physician has comprehended it in three concise maxims: "Keep your feet warm, your back straight, and your head cool."

1800

⌘⌘⌘

To avoid dysentery and fall fevers, eat moderately, drink sparingly, lie not down on the damp earth, nor overheat yourself; but keep your temper, and change your clothes as the weather changes.

1802

Go not to your doctor for every ail, nor to your lawyer for every quarrel, nor to your pitcher for every thirst.

1802

⌘⌘⌘

"Health without any money is half sickness"; but we trust that every industrious farmer has now a little cash in his pocket, after having sold his produce and paid his taxes and small debts. He can now afford to take a little bit of a sleigh ride to visit his friends, and partake of a good roast turkey.

1804

⌘⌘⌘

Pin your faith upon no man's sleeve.

1804

⌘⌘⌘

A good library in town could now be enjoyed.

1804

⌘⌘⌘

"There are a great many asses without long ears." Quack, quack, went the ducks, as Doctor Motherwort rode by with his saddlebags stuffed with maidenhair and goldenrod.

1806

⌘⌘⌘

Take care that you do not kill yourself with cold water. Keep the boys from running to the ponds and rivers to bathe. This month keeps the haymakers and reapers attentively employed; the females, we hope, will not be neglectful of their care. Dolly, my dear, you will be kind enough to send out the drink, and the luncheon.

1809

⌘⌘⌘

Health is the daughter of exercise and temperance.

1810

A WHEELBARROW is a very convenient thing on a farm, which many had rather borrow than buy, and it will not be amiss for you to have a garden rake of your own. Furthermore, one thing is perhaps of still greater importance: I mean a good *hone,* for what can be worse than a long beard and a dull razor? Many however may make up wry faces at this, and say it is extravagance, that a whetstone or brick jamb is equally as good. Let such shave themselves their own way.

1811

⌘⌘⌘

"BED bugs as big as turtles! By jingo, I have not slept a moment all night," cried Tom Testy. "Pray, Mr. Weatherwise," said the Widow Wonderful, "can't you give us a receipt to cure bed bugs?"

"Oh, yes, madam. In the first place, on the last Friday in May, when you go to bed, take the tip end of a mouse's left ear, wrap it in a four-leaf clover. Fold them in a clean linen rag; then place the rag in some secret corner or niche in the house, where it will remain undisturbed. Next, take care to have your bedsteads well scoured and cleansed, and kept so during all summer, now and then rubbing a little ungentum with a feather into the holes. It is said this is a certain cure, and I have no great doubt of it."

1818

⌘⌘⌘

MAY DAY is generally too chilly and rough to find pleasure in the fields, as some pretend to; and but a few flowers will deign to show their tender petals. Yet see how the girls are on the wing at dawning, scrambling "over hill, over dale, through bog and briar," all in ecstacy with the *idea* of going a-Maying! Idea, indeed, for our sweet bonny lass too often returns, like the tired angler, catching nothing but a *cold.*

1851

⌘⌘⌘

GATHER herbs while in bloom. This business is generally thought to be of little or no consequence; but I tell you, friend, it is often the case that a bowl of herb drink, with a good nurse to attend you a few hours, saves *you* from a fever, and your *purse* from a doctor's bill. Good doctors, though, honestly earn their fees; and speaking of them and of sickness reminds me that a little ripe fruit or a few flowers sent to your sick neighbor will cheer him up. If you call to see him, carry no unpleasant news with you.

1857

⌘⌘⌘

WHY don't you clean out the well? The air and the water of the farm must be kept pure, you know, cost what it will. A well ought to be cleaned out once a year, at least, if you want to have water that's fit to drink.

There's a waste in most of our drains that ought to be stopped. They are apt to taint the air, and bad air goes to swell up the doctor's bill. A "dispensation of Providence" is more'n half the time nothing but foul air to breathe, and tainted water to go into the teapot. It's our own fault.

Let us take care of the pigpen, the cowyard, the sink drain, the outhouse, and stop the leaks in them all, if we want to live to three score and ten.

1881

⌘⌘⌘

IF the farmer neglects to keep everything sweet and clean in and around the house and farm buildings during the hot weather, he may expect that some of the family will be out of health, and perhaps have diphtheria or scarlet fever from breathing bad air.

1892

ART OF FLOATING

A HUMAN being who will have the presence of mind to clasp the hands behind the back, and turn the face toward the zenith, may float with ease, and in perfect safety, in tolerably still water—

aye, and sleep there, no matter how long. In not knowing how to swim, if you would escape drowning, when you find yourself in deep water, you have only to consider yourself an empty pitcher; let your mouth and nose—not the top part of your heavy head—be the highest part of you, and you are safe; but thrust up one of your bony hands, and down you go—turning up the hand tips over the pitcher.

1892

⌘⌘⌘

A SIMPLE and harmless remedy for sunburn is to bathe the face in buttermilk.

1898

⌘⌘⌘

AFTER touching poison ivy, wash the parts exposed in alcohol and avoid anything greasy.

1903

⌘⌘⌘

To get comfortably fitting shoes, buy them in the afternoon when the exercise of the day has stretched the muscles to their largest extent.

1903

⌘⌘⌘

THE fact that a farmer's occupation is most healthful will not excuse his neglect of sanitary conditions in and about the home. In locating the dwelling, if possible, select a southern exposure with protection from the cold winds. Good drainage is of the greatest importance; a damp cellar is a constant menace to the health of the family. Shade trees should not be permitted within fifty feet, at least, of the house. The direct rays of the sun are destructive to harmful germs, and thus a preventive of disease.

1907

⌘⌘⌘

AFTER a hard day's work in a dusty field, nothing is more valuable than a bath. Perhaps there is a good swimming hole handy by, which should be patronized by all hands. But in these days every farmhouse ought to have at least one good-sized bathtub with a plentiful supply of water.

1913

⌘⌘⌘

REPORTS of the United States Public Health Service show that while life expectancy during infancy and childhood has increased owing to preventive remedies, more sanitary living, and other causes, yet at the age of forty the expectation of life is less now than it was thirty years ago. This lessening of life expectancy in advanced years is laid in part to the decreased physical and the increased mental work that is required nowadays. Outdoor exercise is recommended to overcome the existing tendency to degeneration of the vital organs. Strenuous athletics are considered harmful. It is advised that exercise be of a kind that is pleasant and congenial. Even then it should not be taken when one is tired or hungry, and one should always stop short of fatigue. For persons who are along in years and who enjoy agriculture and horticulture, work in moderation on the farm or on the country estate would seem to comply admirably with these recommendations.

1917

RULES FOR HUMAN MOTORS

HERE'S a new way for putting some well-known rules of advice, which we believe will appeal to every motorist who thinks as much of himself as he does of his car.

Pull your machine up alongside a filling station regularly three times a day and put into it high-test fuel, such as leafy green vegetables, fresh fruit, milk, dark bread, and real butter. Do not use substitutes—you wouldn't do it with a limousine. This high-test fuel is remarkable in that it builds up your automobile as well as puts pep in your motor.

Run your human automobile into the garage each night for

eight hours of rest. Remember to turn on the fan by opening windows and getting plenty of fresh air. This will prevent flat tires.

Run your automobile body onto the wash rack daily.

Keep the chewing apparatus clean. Brush it night and morning.

Give your human car plenty of water to prevent a dry radiator.

Visit expert mechanics regularly (the doctor once a year and the dentist at least twice a year). They can help you overhaul your machine and discover a little knock in the motor before you even hear it.

1931—*The City Health, Northampton*

⌘⌘⌘

THE physician has this advantage over other salesmen: namely, that he always encounters his clients in a moment of weakness.

1939

⌘⌘⌘

KEEP the very young children and your dogs apart during the hot sultry weather. The only way Buster can talk, you know, is with his teeth.

1942

⌘⌘⌘

'FEARED of dying? Were you 'feared of being born?

1943

⌘⌘⌘

COMMON mud is still the best remedy for bee or wasp stings.

1943

⌘⌘⌘

IF your town has a good doctor, encourage him in every way to stay—especially by paying his bill promptly. Rural areas have 48 per cent of the population but only 31 per cent of the doctors.

1943

DON'T let the dog days get under your skin. Keep busy and you'll forget how hot it is. It's the fellow who mops his brow in the shade with an eye to the thermometer all day who really suffers —with everyone who has to listen to him. It's a good plan to restore your energy with salt tablets. Hot tea will pep you up and cool you off as well as, or better than, a cold drink.

1945

⌘⌘⌘

DON'T spend all your time figuring. January's full of "miseries" and "aches" if you don't keep active. A little essence of the ax handle in the wood lot will do a heap more good than the doc's prescription (if he has time to give you one). For your health's sake, reach now and then into the apple barrel... one's own "Mac's" and "Baldwins" always taste better.

1945

⌘⌘⌘

APRIL is the month of showers (or snow flurries), sandwiched haphazardly between the gales of March and the languors of May. With one foot on the threshold of spring and one at the back door of winter, it hangs uncertain which way to fall—and it's never what it's cracked up to be. However, it has just enough promise of something better in it, after something so very much worse, that it relaxes us willy-nilly. We get what is known as "spring fever," a misnomer if there ever was one. We aren't feverish at all and the "spring" is all out of us for certain. We may yearn and intend and plan but we do nothing willingly, or, rather, we willingly do nothing. When the breath of life is on all the world, we lie torpid.

1946

⌘⌘⌘

UNLESS you take care, the sun will pin you down. Put a hat on that foolish head of yours when you go out into the fields.

1948

Food

BEGIN to fat turkeys, especially as Thanksgiving is appointed as early as the seventh of next month.

1794

⌘⌘⌘

OLD EXPERIENCE says (and she generally speaks the truth) that pork killed about this time will always come out of the pot as large as when it was put in.

1803

⌘⌘⌘

MY homemade maple sweetening affords me much consolation to reflect that it possesses no mingled tears of misery; no desponding slave ever groaned over my caldrons or fanned them with his sighs. No; this little lump in my hand is the reward of my own labor on my own farm.

1804

⌘⌘⌘

THE farmer who has attended to his vegetables has now a most excellent table. What meal can we sit down to better than a dinner from the garden at this season, made up of peas, beans, carrots, beets, young potatoes, turnips, cabbages, etc., with a little pork, if you have it.

1806

⌘⌘⌘

Fat paunches make lean pates. That is to say, if you eat and drink to excess this hot weather, you will destroy both wit and understanding. Your brains will lie in your belly.

1807

⌘⌘⌘

PIES, puddings, and pancakes are best with sweetening, and as sugar is as cheap and agreeable an article as we can find for this use, we had better be attending to our caldrons. Heaven has been extremely propitious to our country in causing the growth of this valuable tree: the maple.

1808

⌘⌘⌘

FAIR words butter no parsnips.

1808

⌘⌘⌘

DO NOT let the women fret for want of oven wood. I hope, too, that sister Tabitha will pay all attention to the bread trough. I cannot bear to eat lead and clay when good, sweet, light bread is just as easily made.

1811

⌘⌘⌘

THERE is now more reason than ever for attending to making sugar from the maple tree—as we are deprived from obtaining it abroad [because of the War of 1812]. Those, therefore, who have the means will not neglect to manufacture this all-important article.

1814

⌘⌘⌘

COFFEE is now considered as one of the necessaries of life. The price is nearly double to what it was in the year 1811 [owing to the War of 1812], and continues to rise. Many articles have been tried as substitutes but, not answering the purpose, have been relinquished.

The potato is found to resemble coffee in taste, smell, and color more than any substitute that has been tried. Few persons can distinguish one from the other. It is one of our cheapest and most plentiful vegetables. We are not dependent for it on foreign commerce. It sits light on the stomach, is nourishing and easy of digestion, and does not irritate the nerves of weak persons or cause watchfulness.

Wash raw potatoes clean; cut them into small square pieces of about the size of a hazel nut. Put them into a broad dish or pan; set them in a temperate stove, or in an oven after the bread is taken out; stir them frequently, to prevent them from sticking together. When perfectly dry, put them into a dry bag or box.

When used, they must be roasted the same as coffee, and ground in a mill.

1815

❊❊❊

"Music, there, music!" Aye, boy, the music of the flail and cider mill, you mean. Well, John, let's put things in order, that we may give them the farmer's concert. Let the cider mill scream the treble—Caleb and Jo shall slam-bang the tenor with their flails; neighbor Flatstall's bull will keep up the fundamental bass; while Ben Bluster will hollow the counter with "Kid up, old Dobbin! Whoa, gee, Spark! Come in there, Berry! All together now, I say!"

1816

❊❊❊

Collect your apples, and be sure to house them until they become mellow, that your cider may be rich both in flavor and color. Some will insist that slovens make the best cider, and also that sluts make the best butter and cheese. But I cannot possibly be made to believe that tobacco spittle, hen dung, or dead rats add to the excellence of good cider, of which I am very fond; and I hope my lovely dairymaids will excuse me for saying that "I dare venture to hazard a guess" a snuff-stained nasal pearl, dropped ever so delicately into the churn and cheese tub, tho' it may enrich the color, "by no manner or means" can brighten the flavor of your milk meats.

1816

❊❊❊

The best churn now in use is supposed to be what is called the "cradle churn." It is rocked regularly not faster than the pendulum of a clock, and answers the purposes of making butter uncommonly well.

1820

⌘⌘⌘

"WHAT, parsnips for dinner at this time of the year? Where, Mr. Simpkins, did you get them?" "Get them? Why, I brought them up from my cellar, where I put them in the sand last fall. By digging them in the fall, you see, we have the use of them all winter, and certainly in the greatest perfection, possessing all their richness and nutritious qualities. If you take yours up in the spring, they are sprouted and the inside is hard as a stick. They are also strong and unsavory as the sack of a polecat; and I should as soon think of eating a rotten cabbage stump."

1825

⌘⌘⌘

ONE day last June I visited the dairy room of my cousin Susan. It was a part of the cellar of the dwelling house, and a neater place mortal man never set eyes on. It was well ceiled with plaster to prevent the dirt's descending. The top and sides were whitewashed, to increase the light, and not a hole or chink could be seen for insects to harbor in. The floor was of stones, and she told me that she often washed it in summer with the coldest water, to keep the air as cool and sweet as possible. On the northern side were two windows, and on the western, one, which could be opened and shut at pleasure. In a corner was a little stove, where sometimes in winter she burned a few coals to keep the room of an equal coolness. So her milk never grows sour in hot weather, and never freezes in cold; of course there is no obstruction to the rising of all the cream. She has a little thermometer in the room, and endeavors to keep the air at about 50 or 55 degrees. The moment a spider spins his web there, it is death.

1826

THE MEAT TUB

GIVE me a good sweet barrel. Take 4 quarts of salt, 8 ounces of saltpeter, and 5 pounds of brown sugar. This will preserve my beef well, rich and sweet. The juices will make brine enough, if it is well packed.

For pickling beef, for 100 pounds take 16 pounds fine salt, 2 pounds brown sugar, 4½ gallons water, and 6 ounces saltpeter.

1826

⌘⌘⌘

INDIAN corn is the basis of our breadstuff and gives deserved reputation to two great staples, *beef* and *pork*. If you have no pork in your cellar and no corn in your garret, you may be compared to a bank without specie, or an egg without yolk.

If you love to feast it in this way, as I do, you must know that the rich, golden corn makes the best *hasty pudding*. It is more sweet to the taste and certainly more pleasant to the eye. Give me none of your wan and vapid stuff upon my table for a pudding, made of smutty white, perhaps, and would almost throw one into a consumption to look at it. No, no, the lovely *yellow*, that's your sort.

1831

⌘⌘⌘

WHAT say, Aunt Eunice? How goes the dairy in dog days? Now and then a fly's leg in the cream? Oh, gracious! and there's a curious insect in Mother Runlet's butter! Many people, of delicate stomachs, are somewhat squeamish at seeing these little triangular spindleshanks upon their toast and johnnycake. But they don't consider that, at each breath we draw, down goes an army of animalcula into the windpipe! Did you ever look at a drop of pure, spring water through a microscope, and see what queer creatures are there, all on the riggle?

1846

"FIDDLESTOCK on your butcher's and baker's bills," Uncle Jeremy cries again. "Go down cellar to your own barrels for your meat, and as to bread—patronize and protect your wife's manufacture."

1849

⌘⌘⌘

"GOOD bread and butter is good enough for anybody," said my friend Bonce, who, I believe, likes good munching as well as any of us. He, at another time, added to it sweet apples and milk.

People's tastes and notions about butter seem to differ. When I see Mother Drizzle kneading johnnycake or patting her butter with a pinch of "old Scotch" 'twixt thumb and finger, I cannot agree, on any condition, that her bread and butter are good.

Now, butter makes me think about cooking, which also brings to mind how they cook in the Western states. The *Prairie* paper says that they *fry* all there. Bacon, pork, veal, chicken, mutton, and fish, and what not, are all fried—often cooked to the hardness of old junk. They eat warm bread, and fried meat, and drink strong coffee. Enough to give a hog the dyspepsia.

1850

⌘⌘⌘

THIS is the great month [August] for the growth of corn. The hot nights of July and August make the crop sure. I hope you don't give up the corn crop. Did you ever think what a universal food it is? Cows and calves, oxen, horses and colts, pigs and poultry, and even dogs, like it when it is fixed right. It is good in brown bread, Indian puddings, corn cakes, corn fritters, corn starch, and a thousand other forms; and then the leaves are eaten by cattle, and when dried, leaves and husks make the best of paper, for which they are getting to be very largely used.

1874

HAVE you an icehouse? It is handy to have plenty of ice in the house in the hot days of summer. We can't do without ice. It is worth its weight in the fruits of the tropics any hot day.

1880

⌘⌘⌘

ANY flavor that may be desired can be given to the flesh of cattle, sheep, pigs, or poultry. Acorn or beechnuts, fish scraps, etc., fed to pigs will give the pork their oily flavor, unless the animals are put upon a corn or other grain diet a few weeks before slaughter. Feed chickens on chopped onions for some time, and not only the flesh but the eggs will have the onion flavor. Feed them upon chopped truffles and they will give their flesh a finer flavor than stuffing or larding them with truffles in cooking. Waterfowls that feed on fish have the fish flavor. Wild deer living on the wild aromatic plants and shrubs that abound in the forests yield a peculiarly flavored flesh known as venison; but domesticate the wild deer and feed him on the cultivated grasses, and his flesh loses its venison flavor in the second generation. It is clear, therefore, that the food of animals permeates the whole system and gives the quality to the flesh.

1884

⌘⌘⌘

TO PACK corn in a silo does not add to its nutritive value, but just keeps its juices in their normal state. To some extent it may be said to carry June into midwinter. Strawberries well preserved are the next best thing to strawberries fresh.

1885

⌘⌘⌘

A DELICATE and fine flavored butter may be made by simply wrapping the cream in a napkin or clean cloth, and burying it a foot deep or so in the earth, from twelve to twenty-four hours. The experiment has been repeatedly tried with complete success. The butter will come out sweet and palatable, but destitute of the yellow or straw color common to most butter in summer. Of course it requires to be salted to the taste as much as butter made by any other process. A tenacious subsoil loam would seem to be best for such an experiment. After putting the cream into a clean cloth, the whole should be surrounded by a coarse towel.

1889

⌘⌘⌘

One of the best cosmetics for bicycle riders or persons upon the water is fresh cucumber juice. To extract the juice, first peel the cucumber, then cut it into thick slices, and press the juice out with a lemon squeezer.

1898

⌘⌘⌘

Lemons should be kept in water until they are wanted for use, and the skin will not only be kept from hardening but their flavor will be improved.

1905

⌘⌘⌘

Making mince pies is a serious matter, and not to be lightly undertaken. All the materials should be of the best quality, each ingredient have its due proportion, and the aggregate be blended into a harmonious whole. It's the devoted housewife alone who can bring them to their best estate. Time, experience, and skill, such as she applies, are necessary to the creation of the mince pies we have in mind, whatever other sorts of things may go by that name.

1907

⌘⌘⌘

To make apple butter, fill a large kettle with cider and boil until reduced nearly one-half. Skim, and to four gallons of the boiled cider allow a half bushel of good, juicy apples cored and quartered. When they are cooked soft and begin to settle, stir continuously and cook until the butter is mahogany color and the consistency of marmalade. If desired, cinnamon and nutmeg may be added to taste.

1914

MAKING corned-beef hash involves something more than assembling chunks of corned beef and potatoes and heating over the fire. The meat and potatoes, and other vegetables if any, after being chopped to the proper degree of fineness, should be blended into a composite in which any one of the original elements will be hardly distinguishable. The crust should be delicate, and not hard, dried up, juiceless, and indigestible.

1915

⌘⌘⌘

THIS is the month when the children start in school and many of them have to carry a lunch. Children's lunches, and indeed all their meals, should consist of a balanced ration, providing all the material necessary for work and for growth. Such a ration should consist of some food from each of five groups. First is the *protein-rich* group of milk, cheese, fish, meats, ripe beans or peas, and peanuts or other nuts. Second are the *starchy foods:* breads, cereals, rice, macaroni, tapioca. Third are *fats:* butter, cream, salad oils, bacon. Fourth are the *vegetables* and *fruits:* potatoes, carrots, and all green or canned vegetables, with all fresh fruits and those which have been cooked or dried without much sugar. Finally are the *plain sweets:* cakes and cookies which contain little fat, simple candies, sugars, chocolate, jellies and preserves, figs and other dried fruits whose percentage of sugar is high.

If some of all these groups are represented in each lunch, the child will benefit by its variety and its completeness. A meal made up from one or two groups only will, on the other hand, overload the system and many meals of the kind will prevent proper development. Therefore, the child should be required to eat his own lunch instead of exchanging with his neighbors.

1920

⌘⌘⌘

IT is now believed by many that fruit in some form should form a part of every meal. If not fresh fruit, then dried, canned, or otherwise preserved. Home-grown fruit is most desirable because it reaches the consumer in the freshest condition, and also because families get fruit of which they would often be deprived if it had to be purchased. The growing of fruit, besides being profitable, becomes often a recreation and a joy itself.

1921

⌘⌘⌘

IF A cream pitcher is likely to drip, it can be prevented by placing a small piece of butter beneath the lip.

1922

⌘⌘⌘

HONEY is one of the best of our high energy-producing foods because it is composed almost entirely of simple sugars which are easily assimilated. Because of this, honey is a valuable food where normal digestive activities have been impaired by disease or old age. It is also recognized as a highly suitable food for babies and children.

1932

⌘⌘⌘

MELONS should not have ice placed on the edible portion. They should be cooled either by setting them on a bed of ice or by placing in the refrigerator. If they are wrapped in wax paper the odor and taste will not permeate other foods.

1933

⌘⌘⌘

WHEN two glass vessels get stuck together, so that there is danger of breaking them in getting them apart, put cold water in the inner one, and hold the outer one in warm water and you will find that they will separate at once.

1933

BEANS

I KNOW a woman who makes exceptionally fine baked beans—the kind that are full of double distilled sweetness—who always says she can tell what sort of an output is to be pulled off by the sound of the beans as they bake.

We would not eat a bean in Maine, if we could help it, that is not served direct from the bean pot. That bean pot must be enthroned at the head of the table and, for exotic purposes, may be surrounded by any old-fashioned garden flowers—aster, sweet Williams, forget-me-nots.

You remove the cover; take a large spoon; stand up; break gently the crispy black surface of the covering of pig-pork; and plunge the big spoon to the heart of the colony. They turn up and turn over with a song of joy. The juices, alive with the fire of love, sweep to the surface. You ladle out a neighborhood of highly individualized, yet completely co-ordinated, beans and put them on a heated plate. Some of them roll over on their sides and laugh; others leap around as if it were for joy; all are sizzling and singing—community singing.

With each helping, you give out a fine piece of pork. Even if the party does not eat pork, give it to 'em. It is as improper to serve beans without pork as it is to serve goose without apple sauce.

1941—*Arthur Staples*

⌘⌘⌘

ABOUT this time of year we hunger for something that's fresh and green and sprouty and that we can see growing. We would browse like the kine, if we were made for browsing, but the instinct to get something lush between our teeth is just the same as theirs.

This leads many people to eat weeds—such as dandelion, mustard, and wild turnip—or nibble at bittersweet, or root through the woods for "fiddleheads" (the new curled shoots of a certain kind of fern which none of us recognize). Many find pleasure in chewing the twigs of black birch and sassafras.

The violet, as a salad delicacy, has its advocates (the same, we believe, who eat rose petals later). Then there are those of the chive and garlic school who like nothing better than a dish of skunk cabbage. But, no doubt, the digestive organs of these gourmets are greatly exaggerated.

This, of course, is but a small list of the edible inedibles to be found in our woods and fields this time of year, but still it is long enough to be dangerous. Few, if any of us, know what we're looking for and so are likely to browse on the Lord knows what. It's a lot safer to go back to the old diet of beans and spinach till the radishes come up. By then the madness will have left us.

1946

⌘⌘⌘

So YOU are thinking of good resolutions? That reminds us of a certain old lady reputed to be the greatest jam maker in the county. She has shelf on shelf of every kind of jam—peach, beach plum, raspberry, wild strawberry, cherry, etc.—they are there, the whole mouth-watering list. But no one ever gets to taste "Auntie's" masterpieces. She just keeps them on the shelf to be looked at. Well, those jams of hers seem to us like most of the resolutions you and I make. They're mighty pretty things, but we just keep them on the shelf.

1947

⌘⌘⌘

MOTHER's kitchen business really got into swing this month. And that business was, of course (besides the three square meals a day when the menfolk got called in), the matter of preserving and canning. June was the month for wild strawberries, and if us kids were up and coming in our picking and hulling, there would be wild-strawberry jam for the next twelve months. And if there was ever anything better than Mother's wild-strawberry jam mounded up and oozing over on a slice of homemade bread, we have never known it—unless it were her raspberry jam and "plum-rum" (to come later in the season) or the sweet cherries in their Mason jars, or the small-fruits jam (strawberries, raspberries, cherries, currants), and rhubarb and strawberry for pies.

Of course, all these were but the first perceptible swelling of the pregnant shelves. Later there would be such solid stuff as beans, peas, corn, chicken, chicken soup, plums swimming in their scarlet liquid, blueberries, golden jars of pears, a phalanx of mince-meat (made from venison), grape juice, and tawny "Christmas" squash waiting only hot crust and spices.

1952

Drink

THIS is a busy time with the industrious husbandman, and he will frequently have occasion for nourishing liquor, which should be beer, cider, mead, and other fermented liquors; but avoid distilled spirit of every kind, except in wet weather or after violent exercise.

1794

※※※

AS THOU soweth, so shalt thou reap. To this every industrious farmer can now say, *Amen.*

1801

※※※

THOSE who are fond of sweet and sound cider must be careful their fruit is not rotten ripe, or pressed during a heavy rain. Let your barrels be rinsed with warm water, and smoked with brimstone, if they smell musty.

1801

※※※

DO NOT visit the dramshop, that is no place to learn morality or politics; but stay at home with your wife and children, and enjoy the felicity of making them cheerful and happy. Peradventure you are a bachelor—oh, haste then and be married, for "he who hath no children [nor wife] doth not know what love means."

1805

⌘⌘⌘

"I told you so," says Dorothy, *"I told you so."* "John, where's the plow?" "I ha'nt seen it since last fall." "Bill, what's become of our hoes?" "We left them in the field, Father." *"I told you so,"* says Dorothy; *"but you would be at the tavern, and let the boys go a-fishing."* Who would not choose to avoid the dangerous habit of tavern haunting, to stay at home and keep himself and family in business, rather than be perpetually tormented with that mortifying cant *"I told you so"*?

1805

DISTILLATION FROM POTATOES

Potatoes yield by distillation a vinous spirit of the most exquisite quality, superior to the finest brandy, and in the quantity of about five quarts, highly rarefied, from seventy pounds. The potatoes are boiled to a thin pulp, which is diluted with hot water and strained. The mass is then fermented with barm [yeast] for about a fortnight, and then distilled in the usual way.

1805

⌘⌘⌘

When I pass by a farm and see it poorly fenced, run over with bushes, a shabby barn, and no wood at the door, I set this man down as either a horsejockey or a tippler. If you have any business with him, you possibly may find him at home on Sunday: surrounded by a disconsolate wife and hungry children, and about half a dozen starving dogs.

1811

Spruce beer is a most excellent beverage; and if you are as fond of it as I am, you will take this opportunity to cut and gather a suitable quantity of spruce for your family drink through the summer.

1811

⌘⌘⌘

"Heigh-ho-hum! Here, John, take the jug and run down to Squire Plunket's and get a quart of new rum. Tell him to put it down with the rest and I'll pay him in rye, as I told him. Come, Eunice, hang on the teakettle and let us have some sling when John gets back. Wife, how long before breakfast?" "Alas, husband, where is this to end? Our farm is mortgaged, you know; the mare and colt both attached, last week the oxen were sold, and yesterday the blue heifer was driven away; next goes our grain and at last, I suppose, I must give up my wedding suit, and all for sling! A plague on the shopkeepers—I wish there was not a glass of rum in the universe!"

1812

⌘⌘⌘

My neighbor Freeport had a knack at telling a story, cracking a joke, and singing a song, and these talents made him a favorite of his townsmen. Every town meeting and training was sure to gather round him a crowd of jovial fellows, and my neighbor pretty soon added to his other acquisitions that of handsomely swigging a glass of grog. The demands for stories, jokes, and songs increased with the reward he received for them; and Freeport had not a heart to refuse either, till the tavern became his common resort. But while Freeport was so musical at the tavern his affairs got out of tune at home. His wife took a high pitch, and often gave him an unwelcome solo. Her stories had much of pith, and her sarcasms were of the keenest sort. She insisted that their affairs were going to rack and ruin. Sometimes the neighbor's cattle had broken into the corn, the rye had been ruined by laying out in the storm, the hogs had broken in and rooted up the garden, the hay was half lost for want of attention, the fences were broken down, etc., etc. And then the children were shoeless, coatless, and heartless; for they had become the scoff and sport of their little companions by reason of their father's neglect to provide them with decent and comfortable apparel. They were unable to read, for they had no books. The sheep—here the poor woman sorely wept—were sold by the collector to pay taxes. So there was no chance for any wool to knit the children's stocking. No flax had been raised and of course they could have no shirts. To hear all this and ten times more was not very welcome to the ears of Freeport, whose heart was naturally tender and humane; so to get rid of it, he used to return to the tavern like a sow to her wallowing. His shop bills ran up fast, while his character was running down. In this way he went on about two years, till old Scrapewell and Screwpenny got his farm; for all this time these usurers had been lending him money, and thus encouraging him to pursue this dreadful course.

Old Captain Gripe also came in for a share of poor Freeport's estate; and there was Plunket the cobbler, he had lent him nine-pence several times and now had cobbled it up to a court demand. Bob Raikins had swapped watches with him, and came in for the boot. The Widow Nippet had lent him her mare twice to mill and once to a funeral, and had sold the boys an old tow jacket for a peck of whortleberries, and also given them a mess of turnips, and so she made out her account and got a writ. Tom Teazer, well known at the grogshops for a dabster at shoemaker loo, old Jeremiah Jenkins, Stephen Staball the butcher, and all the village moon cursers came in for their portion of the wreck. So poor Free-port gave up vessel and cargo to these land pirates, sent his disconsolate wife again to her father with one of their babes, the rest were provided for by the town; and as for himself, miserable wretch, he became an outcast, a vagabond, and died drunk in the highway!

1813

A CHEAP BEER

Take two ounces of good hops and boil them three or four hours in three or four pailfuls of water. Then scald two quarts of molasses in the liquor and turn it up into a clean half barrel, boiling hot. Then fill it up with cold water. Before it is quite full, put in your yeast to work it. The next day you will have agreeable, wholesome small beer that will not fill with wind as that which is brewed from malt or bran, and it will keep good till it is all drank out.

1815

⌘⌘⌘

Cider is a very good beverage, if used with discretion, but to swill it down as some do will keep one's brain in a continual fog. Old Captain Red Eyes takes his mug every morning before breakfast, as I am informed; and toddy blossoms, it is said, are making their appearance on his nose and cheeks. Alas, Captain, look out! or I fear you will ere long find yourself to be *sans eyes, sans nose, sans farm, sans reputation, and sans everything.*

1817

⌘⌘⌘

Uncle Jeremy was brought up in the good old charter style. He never turned up his nose at a bowl of bean porridge, or despised a draft of Yankee small beer. In days of yore, when girls spun and wove their own petticoats, and knit their own stockings, and wore a goose quill and eelskin in their hair, instead of the modern five-dollar turtle shell, I say, in those halcyon times, how slick everything went on at Uncle Jeremy's!

The whole family were out of bed before sunrise. The cows milked—the hogs fed—breakfast on the table in due season, and all was active and lively!

Away went the haymakers whistling to their duty.

The boy at eleven brought out the luncheon. And at four in

the afternoon, that black bottle was passed round right jollily; but this indulgence was never allowed except in haytime!

Oh, how changed is the scene! Now all is sluggish and slothful! And what is the cause of this? Uncle Jeremy went to Boston, and brought home a *gin case*.

1822

⌘⌘⌘

TAKE the whites of six eggs with a handful of fine beach sand, washed clean; stir them well together, then boil a quart of molasses down to a candy, and cool it by pouring in cider, and put this together with the eggs and sand into a barrel of cider and mix the whole together. It will keep for many years, and be good enough for kings, emperors, and presidents.

1826

⌘⌘⌘

HE WHO peeps through a hole may see what will vex him.

This peeping disposition is not characteristic of farmers; it belongs to the loafers, that set of do-nothings. You will find them, at all times, winds, and weathers, lounging at their rendezvous, which may be a drug shop, where the ardent is sold only as a medicine; or, peradventure, the barroom of a miscalled temperance tavern, to which is attached a striped piggery, where none but those of the lodge are admitted. Here you will find them, killing time over a checker board, and enveloped in gin slings and smoke.

1845

SMOKING

CRACK, Wallop, and Dasho. These three merry grigs are farmers' sons, trained up in the way they should *not* go. Obedience to parental authority—what have they to do with? Alas! nothing at all. They go and come as they please, leaving their fathers to solitary employment in their respective field, while they, reckless of consequences, fill up their idle hours in folly and regalement. Should a father, at any time, attempt to command his son, "Mind your own business, old Buzzard!" is the reply. This comes from lax family government, and the want of energy and decision, which has become very fashionable. Suasion and suavity, I know, some will have it, are the most proper means to be used in this case. "Tommy shall not have his genius cramped by any compulsory course." Look, now, at those spoiled younkers in the grog room. How they puff, puff, puff the stenchy narcotic! whiffing it out at the corners of the mouth as a cuttlefish sends out his cloudy liquid! Now a julep, or Tom and Jerry; and anon the big swell, followed by such a mammoth oath, as would make Tom Belcher, Cribb, or Molineaux cower! This is serving the father of mischief *gratis*, sure enough!

1851

⌘⌘⌘

THE surest way to destroy your own health is to be constantly drinking that of other people.

1860

⌘⌘⌘

A SOUR-FACE wife is the liquor dealer's friend.

1872

⌘⌘⌘

JUDGE EMORY SPEER, of the southern district of Georgia, had before his court a typical charge of illicit distilling. "What's your name?" demanded the judge.

"Joshua, jedge," drawled the prisoner.

"Joshua who made the sun stand still?" smiled the judge, in amusement at the laconic answer.

"No, sir. Joshua who made the moon shine," answered the quick-witted mountaineer.

1929

SOMETHING more about good resolutions. If they're really good, they not only have to be used but they aren't made with loopholes you can wriggle through now and then. Which brings up by way of example the story of the old soak who swore off drinking the morning of January first, with the solemn vow, "I shall drink no more." In a few hours, however, he was again in his cups, and on being asked if that was what he meant by drinking "no more," replied, "It sure is—no more than I used to."

1947

Wood

SIT not too near the fire, lest you burn your shins.

1797

⌘⌘⌘

PAY more attention to sledding than to sleighing, until you get a sufficient woodpile. I have said much about woodhouses, and shall continue to harass you with my clamor, until you are wise enough to get one.

1807

⌘⌘⌘

"NEVER make two bites at a cherry. None of your piddlers for me," said Farmer Simkins, when he saw Captain Dolettle carry home three feet of pine wood at a load.

1820

⌘⌘⌘

SO THEN, you have a cooking stove! This is economical, saving much in wood and labor. I know it by experience. But many people are so prejudiced against them that they will scarcely look at one. Wood has become a cash article nowadays in my neighborhood. I have procured me one of Rich's cooking stoves, and think I save half my wood by it nearly. My wife and the girls would not be deprived of it on any account. It furnishes us every morning, if we wish, with baked potatoes, warm biscuit, flapjacks, muffins, crumpets, etc., etc.

1823

⌘⌘⌘

A GOOD farmer will take good care of his woodlands, and keep them well fenced, that the trees may increase, and that cattle may not injure them by browsing. It is the practice of the French not to cut off their woods oftener than once in twenty or twenty-five years; and then the owner cuts all smooth, in order that the new growth may start together. It is a poor plan to cut down trees in a scattered manner, as the practice of many is. The growth next following must remain forever feeble.

1830

⌘⌘⌘

THE demand for wood yearly increases. Fire and smoke seem to be the order of the day. Look which way you will, on land or water, you behold the all-devouring monster, driving ahead, in his puffing and snorting majesty! His huge jaws are ever gaping and craving more fuel! more fuel! so that "Wood Up" is the cry of the fire tender every now and then. The farmer of forethought and forecast will watch the change in the business world, and shape and regulate his own affairs accordingly.

1842

⌘⌘⌘

WIT is brushwood, judgment is timber; the former makes the brightest flame, but the latter makes the most lasting heat.

1854

⌘⌘⌘

IF YOU want your name to be held in grateful remembrance, plant trees; if you want to improve the roadsides in your town, plant trees; if you want to add to the beauty of the surroundings of your dwelling, for your own and your friends' eyes, plant trees;

if you would have your house and grounds more valuable, to keep or to sell, plant trees; if any of your land is not well adapted for cultivation or pasturage, cannot you plant trees? If you want property that, like money at interest, will be "growing while you are sleeping," plant trees.

1860

⌘⌘⌘

TIMBER cut during the months of February, March, and April is nearly worthless compared with that cut earlier, on account of worms which infest it. Did you ever notice the woodwork inside a house or barn, full of wormholes or powder post, as it is sometimes called? This is the result of cutting the timber at the wrong season.

1901

⌘⌘⌘

A GOOD business might be built up by some young man by spraying trees, as most individuals would sooner pay a fair price for this work than undertake it themselves, as it is expensive when done as individual work.

1901

⌘⌘⌘

A FEW shade trees in every pasture are desirable, that the cattle may have shelter from the hot sun. If there are none in the pasture naturally, it is advisable to set out a few deciduous trees; these are preferable, because evergreens, at least in clusters, may kill the grass beneath them.

1902

⌘⌘⌘

CHRISTMAS trees are getting to be in great demand, immense numbers being used each season. But the farmer seldom gets more than three cents apiece for them. There is more money in growing such pasture spruces for timber than in selling them thus.

1904

Arbor Day is not so generally observed as it should be. The man who plants a tree and takes good care of it afterward is a public benefactor, and deserves well, not only of the present, but of future generations. Nothing adds more to the appearance and the comfort of the home than well-selected and well-cared-for trees and plants.

1906

❋❋❋

Are you going to keep a tidy woodshed? Have handsome logs for the open fires and neat-looking sticks of kindling that it will be a pleasure for the womenfolks to use. At any rate, don't bring in a mess of old, earth-rotted shingles and boards with its contingent of earwigs and sow bugs. Gather such and other like trash out of doors, burn from time to time in some place protected from the wind, and save the precious ashes for soil improvement and the encouragement of plant growth. Yes, it does involve some trouble, possibly a little expense; but isn't the gratification of having the woodshed wholesome and attractive a much more than adequate recompense?

1910

❋❋❋

On one of these clear, cold mornings, when the kine's leisurely breaths come in steam, when the frost is thick and sparkling on the spare-chamber windows, and the cat is plumb full of electricity—on such a morning, harness old Major into the sled and take the men and boys for a day's work cutting out firewood and fencing stuff on the Wampum Hill wood lot. And about noon you'll all enjoy sitting around the wood fire eating luncheon and drinking the hot tea or coffee. Uncle Jethro used to say that nothing ever quite came up to the sandwiches and coffee he had consumed in the winter woods.

1911

❋❋❋

Have you considered the possibility of getting fuel and lumber as you may need by making selective or improvement cuttings?

This course has great advantage, since inferior kinds and such trees as are crowding or threatening to crowd more desirable individuals can thus be removed, not only without damage but with positive benefit to the forest as a whole. If this course be followed, the value of your woodlands as a source of income can be greatly increased. Instead of a crowded growth with a large proportion of inferior kinds, it may be made to produce trees valuable for lumber and the better varieties for fuel. If you do not understand how the improvement cutting should be made, consult your State Forester or Agricultural College.

1912

⌘⌘⌘

NUTS are being increasingly recognized as a wholesome food, but unaided nature can less and less be depended upon for this bounty. The native chestnut formerly so abundant has been nearly exterminated in the Northeastern states. Shagbarks, butternuts, and other native varieties are scarce. It is quite time that man should lend his aid. Japan chestnuts begin to bear in very few years after setting and are blight resistant. The Italian varieties are also less susceptible than the native. New varieties of English walnuts believed to be hardy as far north as about 42 degrees are worth trial.

1918

⌘⌘⌘

KEEP the woodpile replenished. The farmer with a wood lot is not bound hand and foot to the coal trust. The price of coal looks likely to go higher and higher. Wood is great fuel for health. The open wood fire is benefit and luxury combined. There is no more healthful exercise than woodcutting, and cold weather is the time to chop wood economically.

1918

⌘⌘⌘

"YES, those are fine black walnut trees. We think more of them than you realize. With every tree we associate either family or friendly ties. That magnificent tree, three feet in diameter and thirty feet to its first limb, was planted by my father. Every walnut tree on this farm is descended from it.

"In October, each member of our family places three walnuts in tins, covers them with ground and with wire to protect from squirrels. In spring, the seedlings are carefully transplanted. Yes, the womenfolks do their own planting.

"No, not all of the walnuts sprout. We usually have one or more for everyone on the farm when our family observes Arbor Day. The name and the date of planting are recorded on our chart. That irregular tree was planted by the parson, but it is no reflection upon that good man.

"We have not decided what will become of the trees. Yes, Mother's tree was injured by a storm and the boards were used for tables patterned after my mother's table. I allow not one of those tables is for sale. No, stranger, you cannot cut any of our walnut trees. We wish we had many more of them, and someday we probably shall. Yes, we eat and sell the nuts, but in October we'll be glad to give you enough to grow your own trees."

1923

⌘⌘⌘

THE seven best woods for fence posts in the order of their durability are: Osage orange, locust, red cedar, mulberry, catalpa, white cedar, and chestnut. Other good woods are walnut, oak, and black ash.

1925

⌘⌘⌘

IT IS important when planting a tree to make sure that the roots extend radially and that none is laid in such a way that it may circle the base of the tree. It is said on good authority, "Trees commit suicide by winding their roots about their stems, usually just below the surface of the ground, and gradually strangling their own life blood." The most common tree to do this is the swamp maple.

1930

CHRISTMAS can, of course, be as happy in a hotel room, city mansion, or tenement, on sea or land anywhere, as here with us in these frozen hills. But we who have always known country Christmases couldn't find it so. Just take the matter of the Christmas tree. Christmas wouldn't be the same if we had to walk a city pavement and *buy* a tree at the corner store. To us, getting our own tree on our land is a mighty pleasant business. In truth, it's a business that usually starts with us some time in the summer when we spot our tree "for next Christmas," while we are out picking blueberries.

And as for Christmas wreaths. We make them here in the house and put them on the same frames year after year. What more Christmasy smell (unless it be plum pudding) than in the making of those wreaths—when the whole house is redolent with the clean tang of spruce and balsam? And it almost seems as if the ground pine and the red berries gave forth their own faint earthy aromas, too.

One of my neighbors leaves her Christmas wreath on the door till almost town meeting. She says it makes Christmas last longer. All of us would be sorry if she took it down a mite sooner than that—for we, too, feel that it keeps Christmas in our hearts all winter.

1951

Women and Marriage

A GOOD wife should be like a snail, always keep within her own house; but she should not be like a snail, to carry all she has upon her back.

She should be like an echo, to speak when she is spoken to; but she should not be like an echo, always have the last word.

She should be like a town clock, always keep time and regularity; but she should not be like a town clock, to speak out loud that all the town may hear her.

1796

A MAN hurrying home from purchasing a hat for his wife was stopped by a friend.

"What is the hurry?" the friend asked.

"I want to get this hat home before the fashions change."

1807

⌘⌘⌘

SHE that is born a beauty, is half married.

1797

⌘⌘⌘

HE THAT marries a widow will often have a dead man's head thrown into his dish; unless he has been a widower and then it is "tit for tat."

1802

⌘⌘⌘

NOW is an excellent time for old bachelors to visit old maids, as the sun is in Libra, which promises a balance of affection to the wedded pair.

1803

⌘⌘⌘

HE WHO gets a good husband for his daughter, hath gained a son; but he who meets with a bad one, hath lost a daughter.

1805

⌘⌘⌘

"A GOOD wife is the workmanship of a good husband"—mind that, Cousin Ned. Come, see, Dolly is up before you! Why will you lie and doze while the redbreast sings at your window, and warns you to your work?

1806

⌘⌘⌘

ALL things must give way to necessity; yet what need is there for a woman to leave her domestic concerns, go into the field, and like an Amazon wield the pitch fork and the rake? 'Tis abominable! Is this the duty of a wife? Is such the tenderness of a husband? Remember she is the mistress of thy house; treat her therefore with respect, that thy children may, also. Consider the tenderness of her sex, and the delicacy of her frame.

1809

⌘⌘⌘

THE farmer's wife—how pleasant it is to see her hasten to meet her husband as he returns at night from the field. Careless of his dust, she takes him by the arm, and with tender concern and smiles of heavenly affection, supports him to his happy cottage.

1809

⌘⌘⌘

YE cold and barren sons of celibacy, behold the delightful regions of matrimony. Leave your frigid abodes, and come and dwell in society, and taste the rational pleasures of a connubial state.

1810

⌘⌘⌘

DELIVER me from a shabby horse and a sluttish wife.

1810

⌘⌘⌘

THERE is much bluster out of doors this month; then for mercy's sake let us have peace within. Oh! 'tis enough to make a man sick of living, even in the highest state of prosperity, to have a noisy, bawling Xanthippe in the house. I tell you, my dear Nabby, I had rather go hungry, cold, naked, moneyless, and almost friendless than to be scolded at by my wife. Yet how many poor souls there are, who endure it with the submissiveness of a religious devotee! On the contrary, the man that abuses his wife, who is the partner of his joys and the partaker of his afflictions, is a brute of the lowest description.

1812

It was a fine day for plowing, and Tom Lifeless was engaged in that healthy and pleasant employment, when Dolly came into the field.

"I must have the mare," said she.

"No, wife," said Tom, "you see I cannot do without her."

"No! but I will have her!"

"But, Dolly, here's Captain Clacket come to help me, and if you take the mare, he must go home, and I lay still, and my work behind."

"Hang you and Captain Clacket, and go to the devil with your work—I say the mare I'll have to go a-visiting, so there's an end to it."

In a twink she seized the animal, took off the harness, and steered toward the bars, leading poor Dobbin.

And now, for once in his life, did Tom feel something like spirit within him! Off in a trice went his tow trousers! And then, brave sans-culotte, with arm high pois'd in air, he with fury hurl'd them at his dear beloved!

"There," said he, "since you will have it so, take breeches and all."

They lodg'd upon her head, and that part the most delicate hung as a screen over her rosy countenance.

1822

⌘⌘⌘

It is said that a woman can throw out at the window with a teaspoon more than a man can throw in at the door with a broad shovel. It is your province, wife, to keep a good lookout, and see that Goody Waste, that old, pestiferous hag, is no inmate of our family. Keep watch, otherwise she may be dashing in pieces our crockery; casting sweet and wholesome provisions into the hog pail; cracking the window glass; spilling the oil; burning wood and coal unnecessarily; frying nutcakes and making candy, when you are away, and many other things too numerous to particularize.

1830

A WIFE who loses her patience must not expect to keep her husband's heart.

1832

⌘⌘⌘

SOME think much of going *a-Maying*. They will ransack the fields and meadows, and trample over brake, brier, and bramble; leaving a shoe in the mud, and a reticule upon the thorn bush; and tire and fatigue themselves nigh unto fainting, all for the sake of a nosegay of buttercup, hog lily, and john's-wort. Poh! What nonsense! Give me one of your ruddy farmer's daughters, who thinks more of the yellow harvest abundance than of the spring posies. A good, buxom country lass, who knows how to boil a potato, and can tell a mealy chenango from a bluenose—one that can make good brown bread, and is never afraid to be seen in the dough. Our genuine farmer girl is modest, but has no affectation. She affects not to be delighted with the effluvium of a marigold nor to be disgusted at the sight of a cow. She can make butter, as well as eat it. She can ride a trotting pony without being strapped on; and though she never cut a pigeon wing, or whirled in the mazy cotillion, yet she can leap a fence like a foxhound, and dance good old *rural felicity* to a charm. As for nosegays and garlands, she gathers them in thousands before the rising of the sun, while the pale city loungers are dreaming of coteries, waltzes, promenade, and pound cake.

1836

⌘⌘⌘

"CHOOSE your wife on a Saturday, not on a Sunday." So says a good old Spanish proverb; and surely this is good sense. Saturday is a business day, and those who are disposed to be industrious and make all suitable preparation for the "day of rest" will show it by their engagedness. To show forth in ribbons and lace on the Sabbath may be a good plan to entrap those who are "pleased with a feather, and tickled with a straw"; but let a young farmer look for some more solid qualification in a wife.

1841

IF the man is fire and the woman tow, the devil blows the coals.

1843

⌘⌘⌘

THUNDER, how tremendous! and lightning, how terrific! See it flash; hear it crack through the welkin! Yet, "guns, drum, trumpet, blunderbuss, and thunder" are naught by way of annoyance compared to the tongue of Xanthippe in a rage. My good brother farmers and darling housewives, see that you keep clear of the devil in this respect. Should it ever be the case that you lose the reins of passion, and are run away with, finding yourselves hemmed in by a thousand combustibles, then is the time to cry, "Hush, Sparkle! back, Star! steady there, both Lightfoot and Lily!" lest the busy old author of all jar and jangle come along with his friction match and blow you sky-high. Let "peace be within thy walls" at all times, if thou wouldst enjoy prosperity.

1843

⌘⌘⌘

WHAT is thrown away, in some places, would support a moderate family. Your old clothes should not be suffered to go to the moths and ruin, when there are so many that would be glad of them. Some women will turn up their noses at a patch upon their husband's coat, though they have a hole in the heel of their own stocking. Ladies, 'tis no more disgraceful to mend your clothes than to mend your ways, when needful. A good old song used to run thus:

Can she darn a stocking well?
Can she make a pudding well?
Can she stitch and can she fell,
My boy, Billy, O!

What is a wife good for that cannot do these, and a hundred more things of the kind? I tell you what, my fair ones, a good farmer's wife is beyond price. She will draw an even yoke with her husband.

1849

An old lady on Long Island said her idea of a nice man was, "A man what is careful of his clothes, don't drink spirits, can read the Bible without spelling the words, and can eat a cold dinner on washday to save the womenfolks from cooking."

1853

⌘⌘⌘

Mr. Growler, when a bill of twenty-five dollars was sent to him by the dealer in confectionery and tobacco, roundly abused his wife for being so extravagant. A careful examination disclosed the fact that his wife had purchased only five cents' worth of peppermints for the children; she had eaten only one herself; the remaining $24.95 Growler had spent principally for cigars and tobacco.

1891

⌘⌘⌘

Love letters, if enclosed in red envelopes, go through the mail in South America, half rate. Love letters, in North America, coming into lawyer's hands, sometimes cost double.

1943

Household

A FEW POINTS FROM "RULES ON FIRES"

Oblige all your servants to go to bed before you every night, and inspect all your fireplaces before you retire. Do not permit a servant to carry a candle to his bedroom if he sleeps in an unplastered garret.

If sickness or any other cause should oblige you to leave a candle burning all night, place it in such a situation as to be out of the way of rats. A house was once destroyed by a rat running away with a lighted candle for the sake of the tallow, and conveying it into a hole filled with rags and inflammable matter.

Strictly forbid the use of cigars in your family at all times but especially after night. A house was lately set on fire by a half-consumed cigar which a woman suddenly threw away to prevent being detected in the unhealthy and offensive practice of smoking.

1797

⌘⌘⌘

EVERY loose clapboard and broken window should now be attended to. Forethought is better than repentance.

1801

⌘⌘⌘

"AN ounce of judgment is worth a pound of wit." Then delay not to complete your indoor business.

1801

⌘⌘⌘

TURN out, turn out and break paths. No man of spirit and industry will lay sleeping and stewing at home like a bear in the wood, while his neighbors are wallowing midrib in snow to shovel him a road.

1805

⌘⌘⌘

THE inflammability of muslin dresses may be prevented by rinsing them out in alum water, made by dissolving the proportion of a hen's egg in a quart of water.

1805

⌘⌘⌘

TAKE care that you do not encumber the road by filling it up with carts, cart wheels, sleds, rails, boards, shingles, barrels, with a thousand other things which do no honor to a neighborhood or give travelers cross looks and sore shins.

1809

Come, let us attend to our windows, and if they are stuffed with old rags, out with them, and sell them for glass, which is now cheap enough.

1821

"GONE TO THE SOUTHARD"

Good morning, Mr. Cleverly, you appear to be right at work, and all alone, too! Where is your son John? Why, sir, he is gone to the Southard. And where is William? Ah, he, too, is gone to the Southard. Well, Joseph, I presume, has not left you? Alas, Mr. Dupy, I am all alone! I had hopes that my boys, some of them at least, would have followed the occupation of their father; but no, Tom Loosely made them a visit last June after he came from New Orleans and got them all bewitched. Every face is now turned to the Southard! Away, boys, away, boys, to the Southard we go! as the song says. And this, you know, is the way to make a pretty fine gentleman. But, fags, as I live, not a copper shall my boys have of me to carry to this Southard. There's poor neighbor Hardfare. His boy, Simon, must go to the Southard—and he was foolish enough to endorse for him—and now all is gone, gone, gone to the Southard! Here's land enough for all my boys, and when they have had enough of the Southard, I hope they will steer *homeward* to farming again.

1823

BETTY BUTTERMILK

Betty was neat, trim, and comely withal. She was one of the best dairymaids in the whole country round about, and her butter and cheese always found the readiest market. She never wanted a little more sleep, and a little more slumber in the morning; but no sooner did the lark and robin begin their caroling, than bounce came Betty out of bed! The cows were milked, the pigs were fed, and breakfast a-doing all before sunrise, and it was said on all hands that Betty would make a noble wife for a farmer; but she turned off each rustic clown and bumpkin that approached her with the song, "O prithee, no more come to woo." Betty had laid up a little money, and thought best to go to Boston and spend it; and so she did. But when she returned, alack, it was all over with poor Betty. Her head was brimful of Boston notions. She dared not milk, because she was afraid of a cow. As to hogs, they were odious creatures! And as to getting up early, it was dreadfully vulgar. Market Street and Leghorn flats was all her theme. Alas! poor Betty was ruined.

1824

⌘⌘⌘

Ah, my beautiful cornfield, torn, trampled, devoured, destroyed, ruined! and all because of Yawny's neglect to keep his fences in order. Once in a while he will pretend to be mighty exact about it, and to make everything tight and snug and secure. But how does he do it? Why, he does it by laying on a birch pole in one place, lopping a bunch of hazels in another, and then finishing out with pine boughs and bramble bushes, tucked in here and there. If his cattle then break in, oh, he is all accommodation, pliability, and gum salvo, and more than ready to make any amends—will leave it out to the lawyer, the doctor, the minister, the deacon, or anybody in the neighborhood, or the parish, or the town, or the county, or the state, or the nation to appraise the damage. And thus the matter ends and rests until another trespass. Oh, a plague, I say, on all such bad neighbors!

1830

⌘⌘⌘

For want of a little putty a square of glass in the buttery window fell out. The cat and kittens took advantage of this, and entered upon the premises; and so here was a pretty kettle of fish, you may depend upon it. In fact it was a most cruel *cat*-astrophe for Aunt Dolly: for those feline intruders had broached every pan of milk, either with tongue or tail; her cookies and knickknacks were crumbled about; and marks of buttered paws were all over the floor and shelf!

1845

⌘⌘⌘

THE uneasy farmer boy would fain go a-whaling. No persuasion could prevent his taking "a little bit of a trip" to try the pleasures and comforts of a greasy sea life upon the Pacific. And there was he tossed up and down, "like an eggshell upon the ocean." Loud roared the dreadful tempest, smiting smack-smooth the deck! Poor sailor lad! Hear him cry, "Oh, for a safe foothold in my father's barnyard!" Aye, how would his trembling heart then bounce in exultation! Ye farmers' sons, be still; be content, and away with this restless folly.

1847

⌘⌘⌘

BROTHER WHITEACRE, if you are about to build, strike not a blow till you have it all complete in your mind's eye. Be sure and consult your wife about it. Let her have a finger in the pie—'tis most proper that she should.

Women are good at planning, and study convenience and accommodation more than men are apt to do. A dwelling house, as well as a porridge pot, should be of a suitable size and construction. Your wife will want a place for everything, and then she can have everything in its place.

1854

⌘⌘⌘

STICK to the farm! Bring head, heart, and hand to the work; and you must succeed. Don't leave the old homestead! In the year 1857, at the time of the great panic, when all business matters were in confusion, how the people in trade sighed for snug farms, free from debt and danger! Farming may be hard work, but farmers have excellent appetites, pleasant slumbers, and arise refreshed.

1859

⌘⌘⌘

Keep things snug this cold January weather, and you'll weather it well. A good fire on the hearth, warm barns for the stock, and plenty of feed, is the true plan.

1865

⌘⌘⌘

A good coat of oil paint on the house saves the wood, because it keeps the water from working into it. It is good economy to keep things well painted, to say nothing of the looks.

1871

⌘⌘⌘

There is no other month [February] like this. Cold, sleet, rain, snow, and sunshine. But we must make the best of it. There is the cellar to be cleaned out. Might as well do it now as any time, and a great deal better than put it off till the spring work begins to press.

If any of the roots or the cabbages are likely to rot, get them out. Sort over the potatoes for planting. Look after the casks and tubs, and put everything to rights. See that the beef and pork are packed all safe to keep into hot weather. Sweep off the cobwebs dangling here and there, and whitewash the walls and timbers. The bottom ought to be hard and smooth, and often swept. The health of the folks upstairs depends a great deal on the sweetness of the cellar at this season of the year. You can't be too careful about the drains and the ventilation. The henhouse needs cleaning now. Eggs, and hens too, will be scarce if you let the lice get the upper hand. Wash all the roosts with hot water and soap suds, and pour it into every crack and cranny. It is a good plan to rub a little grease under the wings and over the head of fowls to keep off the vermin.

1874

A TRAVELER, describing a very quiet village, said, "It was still —very still, so still at night that I could almost hear my bed tick."

1878

⌘⌘⌘

To remove grease from wallpaper, lay several folds of blotting paper on the spot and hold a hot iron near it until the grease is absorbed.

1886

⌘⌘⌘

To use a shovel to clear the paths between the house and the barn every time it snows is not to economize labor, for with a snowplow that would take but a few hours to make, the paths can be cleared in a tenth part of the time, while, so far from bending their own backs to the work, the boys will find it fun to ride the snowplow and make the horse do the work. A workshop on the farm is worth more than its cost.

1887

⌘⌘⌘

Do not forget the waterpipes; protect them from the cold, and thus save a world of trouble when the thermometer sinks below zero. It is so easy to wait, and not prepare for winter before it comes, that too many farmers leave their late crops to gather after the cold weather commences, and their waterpipes uncovered until they freeze and burst. It is not safe to be unprepared for winter after the first of November.

1892

⌘⌘⌘

THE saying, "Keep the boys on the farm," has been the text for a good many sermons. But why keep the boys on the farm if they do not want to stay? If your boy is made for some other calling, it is not advisable to try to make a farmer of him; and why spoil a good lawyer, engineer, or mechanic to make a poor farmer? Some men make life on the farm a dull routine of work, with little or no relaxation or prospect of improvement or advancement. They seem to have no ideas except hard work and plenty of it, like the man who at the close of the day said to his help, "Come, boys, let's quit work and go to sawing wood."

1906

⌘⌘⌘

Be sure of your chimneys, unused during the summer, before you start the winter fires. Handle gingerly until you find they are all right.

1909

⌘⌘⌘

Remember that summer boarders are finicky folks—the best of 'em. But more of them are coming to the farms every year. They have money for what suits them. They come again. But they have long memories for untidy corners and slack housekeepers. And they tell their friends about those things.

1909

⌘⌘⌘

Fowls straying beyond the confines of the estate are a fruitful source of controversies between neighbors. Fortunately, they may be kept within bounds at no great expense by the use of a poultry fence made of wire netting. Whether you contemplate making use of this or some other kind of fence, perhaps your neighbor will be willing to bear his proportionate part of the expense; but if he declines, and the fence viewers will not help you out, you had better put up an adequate fence at your own cost.

1909

⌘⌘⌘

Those who in these days of telephones and free mail delivery, of granges and institutes, call life in the country isolated and narrow, forget that in cities men and women do not know their next-door neighbors and are only atoms in the big swirl.

1910

A MATTER of prime importance is the adaptability of the several articles of kitchen furniture and utensils to their most effective use and the placing of them in the way making most for convenience. A worktable, for instance, may be too low considering the height of the worker. Bending over this involves discomfort, increased effort, and earlier weariness than if the table were the right height.

1917

⌘⌘⌘

A SMALL thimble over the end of a curtain rod protects the curtain from tearing when it is being run on the rod.

1921

⌘⌘⌘

THE labor question is the one which will now present more difficult problems perhaps than any other, for since the World War the tide of immigration has greatly lessened and wages in other industries are high, tempting away from the farm; moreover, the home supply is much smaller than of yore when children, trained each to do his part, were more numerous in the substantial old houses which our fathers built.

1921

⌘⌘⌘

THE water's frozen stiff again, and you're lugging from the old well. As near as you can figure it, there's only about a month's feed left in the loft, with baled hay selling at forty dollars a ton. The last snow's busted in the henhouse roof. Ma's feeling "peckish" and the price of grain is higher than Gilroy's kite. There you are, knee-deep in chores and taxes and government regulations. Take it all in all, the world is just another dish of cold beans.

You don't know it, but somehow things are going to come around—sure as town meeting. They start with the mild spell and a sort of hankering you have to let things slide anyhow. You cut Ma an armful of forsythia branches to "force" in the parlor window. Maybe you add a few cuttings from the old apple on the sunny side of the lane. Ma perks up—and you go to Grange meeting. Your neighbors lend a hand with the henhouse roof. Then one day sap's running—and you're twice as busy as ever—but the smell of the hot, bubbling syrup makes you young again. The boys come down to help after school, and pour the syrup on the snow, and make a real spree of eating it, just as you did when you were a kid.

Before you know it you've slid right around the corner into March, and Ma's seen the first robin.

1945

⌘⌘⌘

Now is the time of the deep snows—and thrice blessed is the neighbor who will plow you out. A mug of good steaming coffee or something bracing from the bottle behind the clock will be just the thing for him when he has bucked out your drifts. A touch of neighborly kindness goes a long ways—and there'll be more storms coming.

1946

OF THE FIELDS AND FORESTS

New England is not, as this old *Almanac* has learned, by any means the whole country. Indeed, scattered across the corn or wheat or cotton belts of this continent there are fields as large as one New England state. Yet I daresay some of these pieces, dug out of the rock and granite of New England years ago, will transplant well in the West, the Midwest—and even in the South.

Soil and Plants

Sow early peas. Look well to your gardens; see to your roots of all kinds; turn up the ground that it may become light.

1793

⌘⌘⌘

A couple of smart city men, seeing a farmer planting his field, one of them called out, "Well, honest fellow, it is your business to sow, but we reap the fruits of your labor."

"It is very likely you may," said the farmer, "for I am sowing hemp."

1797

⌘⌘⌘

Let your flowers and rosebushes be protected against the frost by straw and coarse dung.

1801

⌘⌘⌘

Exotics should be taken in every day by sunset.

1801

⌘⌘⌘

Take care of your vines, and see that the bugs do not destroy them. It is good to throw water often upon them; but the most effectual method to get rid of bugs is to visit your vines several times a day, and destroy them with your fingers.

1805

⌘⌘⌘

Set cabbages in the middle of the day, first putting the top into very cold water. Hoe your cabbages in the morning.

1805

PLANT your Indian corn if you mean to keep fat hogs; but a portion of rye with your Indian is best. An Indian bannock was said to be a favorite of Washington. If he loved this humble meal as he did his country, it must have been a dainty dish to him. Come, let us copy his virtues, one of which, and a very signal one, was prudence; add to this industry, which never left him till his death.

1809

⌘⌘⌘

I NEVER suffer any of my family to kill those little innocent animals called striped snakes, for they do me much service in destroying grasshoppers and other troublesome insects. Toads are of essential service, especially in a garden, to eat up cabbage worms, caterpillars, etc.

1813

⌘⌘⌘

YOU may think that a garden is of little consequence to you, as your father before you never paid much attention to one. But, my friend, I tell you for a truth, that a good garden, well managed, is as valuable as a beef and pork barrel well filled.

1820

⌘⌘⌘

COMPOSTS are frequently made of various materials, as, several sorts of earth, lime, old mortar and plaster, green vegetables, before they run to seed, soft chalk, tanner's bark, soap ashes, dung, etc. They should be mixed as much as possible before forming the heap. A fermentation is soon excited, and the oftener the heap is turned, so much the more will fermentation be promoted.

1820

⌘⌘⌘

A FARMER must have all hands at work to make the best use of fine seasons, or he will be called an "afternoon farmer."

1830

MANURE your wet mowing lands with coarse, strawy dung, spread thin. Recollect, we do not live in Illinois or Ohio, where it is enough to work one-half the time, and sleep the rest.

1833

CONSERVATION

THIS has become a mighty fashionable word; such as we farmers, however, do not use much. I have been looking it up in the dictionary, and conclude it is about synonymous with *pre*servatism. It therefore may have something to do with husbandry. I have lately been reading an oration on this very subject, by one of our smartest scholar men. He says that the world, nowadays, is divided into Conservatism and Reform: that is, the old and the new; and just so it is in farming. Faith, as he says, goes ahead to the new; fear, with eyes behind, holds on to the old.

One man spreads his manure broadcast, another does differently, after the old fashion. The stickler for reform takes a small piece of land, puts what manure he has upon it, plows it thoroughly, tends it closely, hires but little help, and gets a good crop. The conservator, sticking to old customs, thinks the more land he has, the greater the produce; goes on scratching over his broad fields, hiring abundance of help, one-half of which are loafers, and at last don't bring buckle and strap together; that is, he comes out at the little end of the horn.

1849

⌘⌘⌘

PLOW deep with strong drafts, and drink shallow with scant draughts.

1854

⌘⌘⌘

JUNE is the month of roses—and this reminds me of thorns; and, if we don't want thorns in our sides, we must make head and hands work well this month. Fishing may be fun, but the hoe handle must take the place of the fishing pole, if we want to sing merry tunes in harvest time.

1858

⌘⌘⌘

Go over and pick up all loose stones on the mowing lots. If you take along a crowbar you can get out many a half-tight rock that will be sure to dull the scythe or the knives of the mowing machine. I've seen a mowing machine broken so as to cost five dollars to mend, to say nothing of the delay, by a stone that might have been got out in five minutes.

1867

⌘⌘⌘

The weeds must be kept down. Let them get the upper hand and they give a heap of trouble. Pull them up root and branch. That's the cheapest in the end. Keep the hoe or the cultivator going. It not only kills weeds, but mellows the soil and makes things grow. There is nothing like it.

1874

⌘⌘⌘

Corn wants a rich and mellow soil, and clean cultivation. We ought to lay out our plans to raise fifty or sixty bushels to the acre, at least. Tar the seed to save it from the birds. Pour hot water over a peck of seed and let it drain off at once. It will heat the outside, and not hurt the germ. Then turn on a pint of hot tar, and every kernel will get a thin coat of it, when it may be dusted with plaster or with air-clacked lime, and it is ready to drop, and no bird will touch it.

1877

⌘⌘⌘

Jack Frost is as smart as a good breaking-up plow, and he doesn't charge much for his winter's work. It is a good plan to give him a chance to try and see what he can do.

1888

No TEN-HOUR law on the farm. Spring comes but once a year, and it doesn't last long when it does come.

1889

❋❋❋

IF TOMATO plants are to be grown, it is time [March] to prepare the hotbed; in doing this, see that the manure is in proper condition to secure good bottom heat; to make it so, pitch it over a few days before placing it in the hotbed.

1890

❋❋❋

IT IS about time [March] for the good housewife to begin to prepare a flower garden, by planting seeds in flowerpots, and forcing the young plants in the house by artificial heat, or by planting in a well-constructed hotbed.

1891

❋❋❋

THE race between man and the creeping things of the earth is said to be very equal. As soon as man is master of one, a new one appears, more persistent in its destructive work, and more difficult to conquer, than any that has preceded it; consequently, man has to seek new and more effective poisonous compounds that will kill these enemies, and not injure the vegetation upon which they feed. Hellebore was once sufficient; then Paris green was required; now arsenate of lead comes into use to kill the gypsy moth, and other recently introduced creeping things that rapidly devour the crops in our gardens, orchards, and fields.

1899

❋❋❋

THE farmer's as well as the mechanic's home is made more attractive by having a few pot plants in the sitting room during the winter months. Geraniums are hardy and easily cared for, and, what is important, will blossom at all seasons of the year; some hardy pinks are desirable; a small orange tree with its ripening fruit is always interesting; and a few pots of strawberries are very attractive. The green leaves, the white blossoms, and the ripening fruit in midwinter afford an attraction not only to the members of the home but to all visitors.

1900

⌘⌘⌘

NEVER plant the home garden all at one time, but begin to plant peas in March, and plant a few every two weeks until the fifteenth of June. Begin to plant sweet corn the middle of April, and plant every two weeks until July.

1900

⌘⌘⌘

ENCOURAGE the boys and girls to cultivate a few flowers around the dwelling, in order to make the home surroundings as cheerful as possible. Allow the boys a plot of ground in which to raise some vegetables to exhibit in the children's department at your agricultural fair, thus stimulating them to be painstaking in their work.

1902

⌘⌘⌘

PINE needles are much better than leaves for plants like the strawberry. They lie loose, admit air, and do not cause rot. Cover roses, peonies, Dutch bulbs, etc., with strawy manure. Leaves are used over rhododendrons and azaleas and allowed to decay on the ground and become part of the soil. Leaf mold, mixed with rotted sod, sand, and old manure, is much better for house plants than the chip dirt and decayed wood from old stumps sometimes employed.

1909

⌘⌘⌘

ALFALFA is now attracting the attention of many farmers who formerly believed it to be impossible to produce it. If you have not tried it, this is a good month to begin the experiment. Select well-drained loam and a field with sloping surface so that water will never stand upon it. After plowing, lime heavily, stock the soil abundantly with phosphoric acid and potash, work it repeatedly at intervals of a few days until you bring it into perfect tilth, and about the end of this month sow the seed, which should be inoculated with a culture to supply the needed bacteria. Alfalfa would be a valuable addition to New England's agricultural assets.

1912

⌘⌘⌘

THE summer drought is now to be expected, but it need not be feared. Uncle Jethro used to say that farmers were scared to death in a dry year, but they starved to death in a wet year. The best way to meet drought is with cultivation. If the ground has been deeply prepared in the first place, it will hold a quantity of moisture. Then, if frequent surface cultivation is practiced during the summer season, this stored moisture will be conserved.

1913

⌘⌘⌘

FALL plowing now demands our attention. With minor exceptions, all the land which is to be put under cultivation next year should be plowed before freezing. It is neither necessary nor desirable to turn the furrows smooth and flat as in spring plowing. If the land is left quite rough, the action of frost during the winter will be more effective in breaking up the soil and reducing it to a fine powder.

1913

⌘⌘⌘

GET something for every month of the flowering season, and place the flowers of any one month at such intervals that every part of your bed will show bloom all summer. Such gardens are now comparatively frequent and should be carefully observed as object lessons. Annuals may fill spaces until you know just what to grow.

1918

FIRE which goes through the woods and burns not only the trees but the humus—the ground itself—is but a magnified illustration of what happens when we burn grassland. When the ground is saturated and the material to be disposed of, dry, we may well enough burn, be it grass, brush, or even decaying trees. But we must be sure we can stop the destruction just where we want to, and prevent the flames from burning too deep or traveling too far and consuming valuable possessions, whether roots, soil, fences, woods, or buildings.

1919

⌘⌘⌘

THE famous Daniel Webster plow was presented to Mr. Webster by a group of his admiring friends about 1840, and was used by him on his estate at Marshfield, Massachusetts. It is related that the noted statesman greatly enjoyed holding the handles behind four yoke of oxen and listening to the roots crack. After his death in 1852, the plow was secured by the New Hampshire Historical Society and taken to Hanover. At the opening of Culver Hall at Dartmouth in 1871, it was taken into the field and several furrows were turned by Hon. David M. Clough of Canterbury, known as the Corn King of New Hampshire.

In 1893 the plow was transferred from Hanover to Durham and has been in the keeping of the University of New Hampshire ever since.

It had not been put to actual use from 1871 until the annual Farmer's Week at the University of New Hampshire in August, 1919, when it was hitched to a tractor, and with Dean Taylor holding the handles, two furrows, 300 feet long, were turned. The plow did not even groan or creak, and it was surprising to see what a really good job it would do when turning a furrow about 10 inches deep and 18 inches wide. It is made of white oak with a wooden moldboard covered with strips of iron. It is 13 feet long, 25 inches high, and weighs 372 pounds.

1926

A VERY persistent superstition is that regarding the effect of the moon on the weather and on the farm crops. One phase of this is the belief that if the horns of the new crescent moon tip downward, it is a wet moon, portending rain. On any given date, the position of the crescent moon is always the same in places having the same latitude, so if this sign meant anything, the same kind of weather would prevail in the places of that latitude around the entire globe, which, of course, is never the case.

Still other superstitions relating to the moon are those offering guidance in farm practices such as breeding or butchering, shingling or shearing, sowing or reaping. All of these are supposed to be affected by the "dark" or "light" of the moon.

The moon has no relation to these conditions. Even the light of the full moon is not intense enough to affect plant growth.

1931

⌘⌘⌘

THE belief that plants should be removed from sleeping rooms at night is entirely without foundation.

Instead of plants being harmful, they are beneficial. During the day they give off oxygen and take on carbon dioxide. At night these processes slow down and small amounts of carbon dioxide are given off but a whole greenhouse full of plants would not give off enough to affect the composition of the air.

1931

⌘⌘⌘

DO NOT burn the leaves that are raked off the lawn. If not used as bedding for animals, add them to the grass clippings in the compost heap, where they will make valuable fertilizer.

1936

⌘⌘⌘

IN THE vast and ancient attic of the farm, in that steep tent of old, brown board which the storms of winter lately filled with so tumultuous a sound, the household herbs hang from an oaken bar.

Peppermint and spearmint, sweet tongue and penny'rile', wormwood and balm, and all a dozen more.

Herbs have a hundred pleasant uses in country life, being valuable both as green plants and as dried leaves. In the olden days, a farm without a few herbs would have been as unheard-of as a barn without a barn cat or a well without a pail. Now is a good time to begin a small garden of these delightful plants, planting them conveniently near the house and putting in first the strong perennials. Various herbs have various strains, some more agreeable than others, and it is well to search about till you find what you like. Peppermint and spearmint are good foundations, and sweet marjoram and green basil may be tried as annuals.

1938—*Henry Beston*

⌘⌘⌘

MARCH is seed catalog time. The home gardener has been studying the catalogs for some time, but the real fever comes during this month. He sends in his order, and, during late March, starts the early seeds like early cabbage, cauliflower, tomatoes, peppers, and eggplants.

1938

⌘⌘⌘

A GLASS garden is an interesting thing to watch during the winter. It does best in a north window where blossoming plants do not flourish, and it is easy to make if one can go into the woods before hard frost with a basket and trowel. The first requisite is a glass dish with a close-fitting cover. The rectangular, straight-sided goldfish tank with a pane of glass to fit the top is the perfect thing, though all shapes and sizes of glass receptacles may be used. A layer of charcoal and coarse gravel in the bottom of the dish is covered with good woods' soil and leaf mold to the depth of three or four inches, the depth depending upon the size of the container. A nice stone or two, bits of different mosses, and an uneven surface will add to the landscape effect. Then the planting may be made with tiny ferns, partridge berries, spotted pipsissewa, and other woodsy things. After planting, the soil must be well moistened with a spray. Put the cover in place and do not water again for several weeks.

1939—*Margaret S. Watson*

⌘⌘⌘

PLOW as soon as possible, but following the contours of the land rather than straight up and down hill, no matter how gentle the slope. Each year tons of good topsoil are washed away because of planless plowing. Your furrows should be water catchers, water holders, not watercourses. A dry summer will prove the wisdom of this.

1945

⌘⌘⌘

ANY plant growing in the wrong place is a "weed."

1947

⌘⌘⌘

NOW shall that wisest, most patient trouper of them all, the old farmer, go into his eternal act of juggling seeds, budget, and mortgage, beeves and plows, sows and subsidies against the winds of April—against the winds of chance.

April has her axioms: "A fair wind blows nobody good—just a weather breeder." "Only fools dig wells this month." "Look to your fences and your daughters. Spring's here."

1950

Orchard

SET trees; be sure to set that side south, which was south before, because it cannot endure the cold. Graft and inoculate fruit trees.

1793

Many a barrel of cider has been lost by nobody taking the pains to pick the fruit up as it falls.

1802

⌘⌘⌘

You surely will not neglect to set out fruit trees. Much has been said about ornamenting streets, highways, and farms with poplars and other ornamental trees; but 'tis far better to unite beauty with utility as much as possible. Then instead of poplars, elms, etc., you will surround your farm with apple and pear trees, etc., etc.

1811

THE LAW

It was a darkish night and a little stormy when Tom Trespass and Peter Pilfer beset Mr. Wellman's pear trees. Having filled their wallets, they crawled snug under the garden wall, and there sat munching their predatory booty, every bit as safe as thieves in a mill. But all at once, bounce came Ben Clincher and seized them! There was no relief! Wellman was resolved that the law should take its course, and he was justified by everyone.

This is the only way to deal with these night villains that more or less infest every neighborhood. When once you get the grab of them, hold tight, and let the watermelon law, as it is called, have full swing upon them.

"What," says Farmer Simpkins, "shall a man willingly tug, toil, and sweat over his fields and gardens through the summer for the sport of rascally and dastardly night pilferers? No, no, no, I say! When once you can put your finger upon the thievish dog who steals into your orchard, while you lie reposing and unsuspecting, and robs you of the fair fruits of your industry and toil, I say, when you have the scoundrel, hold him fast."

1824

Boys, bring the ladders and baskets! These winter apples, russets, greenings, Baldwins, and what not, of ours must every one be taken off the trees as carefully as if they were eggs. I know very well how Captain Thrasher gathers his; but his notions and mine differ. Now, if you love apple dumplings, be careful how you pack apples.

1851

HERE'S TO THEE, OLD APPLE TREE!

Yes, indeed, here's to 't! I well remember it; and who cannot say the same; and with all the feeling and veneration that Woodworth had for the Old Oaken Bucket, or Eliza Cook for the Old Armchair.

There it stood, but a little distance from the well; and under its shade was the grindstone, where, at haytime, the neighbors were wont to grind their scythes, because of its peculiar grit and texture.

The *old apple tree?* Oh, it is full fresh in my recollection, though the rude hand of barbarism hath, long since, laid it low. There the robin and the sparrow sang and built their nest; and there it was that, under its branches, at the close of day, or when the moonlight night was still, carrying out our chairs, we sat and sang, peradventure, it might be, "Sweet Home," "Bidden to the Wake," or "Bidden to the Fair," or even good old "Canterbury," my father's favorite.

1851

⌘⌘⌘

Did you tread the snow closely around your fruit trees when the first snows came? The mice'll bark 'em if you don't, and you'll find, to your cost, they've been barking up the wrong tree.

1863

Don't fail to go round your apple, pear, and cherry trees, and destroy carefully the nests of the caterpillars which will soon appear there. It is easy now, by sticking a brush upon the end of a long pole, to reach every limb, and make clean work of them.

1863

⌘⌘⌘

It is about time to be getting the garden ready and to set out fruit trees. Aren't you sorry now that you didn't set out a few pear trees, a few cherry trees, a few currant bushes, and such like, ten years ago? The quicker you set about it the better.

1874

⌘⌘⌘

Winter apples should be kept at a temperature about eight degrees above that which will freeze water; and they should not be disturbed until wanted for the market or for use. The old practice of picking over apples every week, to get the partially decayed to use in the family, was a very bad one, and has been abandoned by modern farmers as very wasteful.

1900

⌘⌘⌘

From the first to the middle of the month [April], if the season is forward, is the time for grafting trees. If you have apple or pear trees which bear inferior fruit, cut off the limbs, and graft the trees with a good quality. You can easily learn the process of grafting, which is an interesting study, so you can do the work yourself.

1901

⌘⌘⌘

Where bees swarm freely little or no surplus honey will be produced. Good beekeepers working for honey try to prevent swarming. Absolute prevention is so far impossible, but by giving the bees plenty of room, wide entrances, and good ventilation the tendency to swarm is reduced. If it is impossible to prevent swarming, hives should be conveniently ready to receive them. Strong colonies of bees will need supers when the apple trees come into blossom.

1912

⌘⌘⌘

THIS month [June] will bring many days suitable for work in the orchard. Trees possess wonderful vitality. You may have neglected those that your father planted. Their response to good treatment may surprise you. They may prove as welcome and unexpected a legacy as money found in old bags or books. Prune, spray, remove the shaggy bark, using care not to cut into living tissues, plow and harrow about them, and give them plant food. Conditions must be bad indeed, if within a year or two they do not respond generously.

Bees wintered in cellars are not infrequently set out too early. Nothing, as a rule, is gained in putting them on their summer stands previous to the date when the red maples are in bloom; and the best time of day to do the work is toward evening, when you feel confident that the next day will be warm and pleasant. Remember bees often enter the wrong hives when hives are set too near together.

1912

⌘⌘⌘

EARLY apples are usually a waste, and largely so because they are handled like hard, late-keeping varieties. Instead, they ought to be handled like peaches, the trees picked several times over, the soft fruits tenderly handled and sent to market in small packages. Such varieties as William's Favorite, Yellow Transparent, and Duchess of Oldenburg find a good market at reasonable prices when delivered in this way.

1913

THIS is apple-picking month, though if the season has been early you may have harvested your Macs and earlier apples in September. Well-picked is often well-sold. Handle your apples like eggs, but twice as carefully. Eggs don't bruise.

Pickers should know that apples are not pulled (this usually draws the stem out) but grasped by the whole hand turned back and up toward the bough till gently released. They should know, too, that fruit cannot be dropped into the picking basket, nor the basket filled too full; and that apples are taken from basket to box two or three at a time and never poured out. Great care should be used in placing of picking ladders, and in the pickers' movements in the trees. Next year's fruit spurs can be broken off at a touch. See that no tree is left until it is picked clean, even of small tight-clinging culls. Drop apples should be gotten out of the orchard as soon as possible, but never dump these nearby. The rotting pile is a sure disease breeder. Best drops bring a fair price, but run no drops in with hand-picks. Drops are bruised somewhere, and this is sure to show up late.

It's a good practice in sorting and boxing the fruit to wear clean cotton gloves. Fingernails may scar fruit, and gloves are less likely to brush off the bloom.

1944

⌘⌘⌘

IF YOU have more apples than you can winter through, why not dry some? Peel, core, and slice the smaller apples. Then hang them on stout strings, necklace fashion, to dry in the kitchen. A good old-fashioned occupation that will pay you dividends in pies and applesauce come summer.

1946

⌘⌘⌘

Now will you hear the cry of hawks and see the bluebirds in the orchards. The woodchuck will busy himself with his earth, the deer browse on the new meadow grass, the mink hunt along the little forest streams. Once again over the moonlit hill will echo the bark of the fox. Along the swamps where the fresh green ferns have begun to uncurl, red-winged blackbirds will sway and chatter and bob on the cat-o'-nine-tails. On the school bench young fry will dream of little trouts and ice-cream cones and circuses and swimming holes. Teacher will have the first pansies in front of her on the desk, just where the first red apple appears in fall. The organ and the monkey will appear and the junkman bestir himself. Some folks will spend their nooning on sunny banks, hats over eyes. Lots of others will wish they could.

Cedarwood and mothballs—thunder again and big drops on the dust of country roads—wind and crows—cheepers in the swamp—screens and old folks rocking in the sun—a snow flurry and lawn mowers—buds and frost—picnics, grass fires, violets. This will be our April with its ageless reawakenings and rebirths—as poignant and strange and hot to the blood as young love.

1948

⌘⌘⌘

HERE is a partial list of the chief hazards of the orchardist: frost, snow, or prolonged cold at blossoming time, either killing the blossoms or preventing the bees from working; fungus disease (scab) and the onsets of a number of flies, moths, beetles, and worms to be fought with sprays or dusts; drought or too much rain; hail or great winds (even hurricanes); porcupine, deer, raccoon, and other animal damage as the fruit swells and sweetens; early frost before or at picking time; careless handling of fruit by inexperienced pickers; when winter comes on and snows deepen, the girdling of trees by mouse and rabbits, and a bit later the "budding" by partridge and other birds.

1951

Crops

HARVEST your Indian corn, unless you intend it for the squirrels. If you make a husking, keep an old man between every two boys, else your husking will turn out a loafing.

In a husking there is some fun and frolic, but on the whole it hardly pays the way; for they will not husk clean, since many go more for the sport than to do any real work.

1805

⌘⌘⌘

OUR farmers seem entirely to neglect raising tobacco; and yet there is more of that article used than ever.

1808

⌘⌘⌘

Boston folks, they say, *are full of notions*—and so are country folks. By this time perhaps you think that I am a silly, notional creature. No matter for that. Perhaps it is but a notion, but I think it will be to our interest to gratify these Boston people in their notions, by raising peas, beans, beets, carrots, cabbage, squashes, turnips, and potatoes, etc., etc., for their market. If you would know how this is to be done, go and look in your old *Almanacs.*

1811

⌘⌘⌘

I BELIEVE it to be pretty well ascertained that in case the frost takes your corn before it is full and ripe, the best way is immediately to cut and shock it. This was done by many in 1816, and they made a great saving thereby.

1818

⌘⌘⌘

MAKE your hay so dry as to prevent its heating; but look out that you do not make it a mere parched straw, without any of its natural juices. Cut close and even at the bottom, for remember that an inch at the bottom outweighs many at the top.

1828

⌘⌘⌘

THERE are two main points to be particularly attended to in mowing: point *in* and point *out*. Captain Tidy swings the clipper for me. How steady, how true, and how even he moves! He is neither banger nor boaster, but his arms move like the swinging of a door on its hinges. Now he points *in* and now he points *out*, and the ground behind him is as level as a bowling green! He is on the spot by times, and the music of his scythe, as it sweeps through the dewy herbage, mimics the sweet matins of the merry lark!

1832

⌘⌘⌘

CUT your grass while the dew is on, if you would have your scythe move slick and smoothly. In this way there will be no chopping, but a regular, gentle sweep from right to left.

1835

⌘⌘⌘

THE Harvest Moon and the Hunter's Moon—the first occurring in September and the latter in October—it may not be amiss to explain to our younger readers here. In the month of September the moon rises on six or eight successive nights apparently about the same time. This annual peculiarity in the moon's rising was observed by the ancients long before astronomers were able to explain the cause. On account of the convenient light it afforded them in harvest time, it was called the *Harvest Moon;* and that in October —for a similar peculiarity is then observable—the *Hunter's Moon.*

1858

⌘⌘⌘

HAVE you tried the haycaps yet; or had you rather have your hay spoiled than try "new notions"?

1859

I'VE reaped many an acre of as fine wheat as ever stood outdoors, but the reaper takes me right down. It's no use to stand out against facts, might as well knock under with a good grace. So keep up with the times. A good mower in the hayfield, and a good horse rake to follow, will put through the work of July in double-quick time, and give time to do a little draining over there in the swamp, and to spruce up a little about the place.

1862

⌘⌘⌘

THESE labor-saving machines in the field, in the workshop, and the house are helping on the civilization of the nineteenth century at a rapid rate. A good and substantial sewing machine in the house is as much help all the year round as a Manny's mower or a McCormick's reaper in the field in summer.

1862

⌘⌘⌘

DON'T you think we let our grass stand too long? I've been thinking it would be better to cut earlier. If we didn't get quite so much, it would be worth more, and go farther. It is the juice we want—the real heart—and not the dry crisp of a stalk; and you know the best of the grass is just when it is coming into blossom. Then it is sweetest, and it never grows better, especially for cows in milk and for young stock. Cut early, and dry less, therefore, and try it for a year or two, and, my word for it, you will find it to your interest to try it longer.

1863

⌘⌘⌘

WITH the mowing machine, the hay spreader, and the horse rake, but little is left of the drudgery of haying except pitching on and off, and for the latter many a farmer is now using the horse fork, which generally works well. These facilities for turning off work leave the farmer more time for improvement, and he is untrue to himself who does not make the most of it.

1865

THE cost and trouble of finding efficient labor have led to the introduction of machinery on the farm to a greater extent than ever before. It has become a sort of necessity. The mowing machine was running everywhere at the last haying, even far up among mountain and hill farms. As a natural result, greater effort has been made to clear up rough mowing lands, and put them in order for the mower. The hay tedder was sold in large numbers last year, and those who had it found it wholly indispensable. It does the work of six or eight men in the same time, and does it better. By it the grass can be kept flying in the air and cured much faster than by the old processes. The horse rake, of course, everybody expects to have. In short, wherever there is a reasonable prospect of economizing labor, the farmer is willing to buy machinery.

1865

⌘⌘⌘

SMALL grains need looking after. The oats begin to whiten on the light stem as they hang like raindrops in the air; the rye is getting yellow, and ready for the cradle; while the wheat and the barley, with their dull green and their swelling ears, begin to nod before the breeze that sweeps over them. They must not get too ripe. Cut them while still a little green, and the grain is better and heavier. These grains ought to be cut about ten days before they are quite ripe.

1874

⌘⌘⌘

IT IS high time to cut up corn for the silo. If sown at the right time in June, it is now at its best, both as to quantity and quality, and may be cut and packed down to be fed, as the winter comes on, in the shape of ensilage.

There is still some doubt as to the economy of this mode of handling it, but those who have tried it claim that it is the true way of saving it as the food of stock, and that they can make milk at a less cost than by the old method of feeding hay alone. It gives a chance for a change of food, and some green and juicy feed in winter is just what cattle want. Fed with a little cotton seed, or Indian meal, or shorts, it seems to add to the yield of milk, and to keep up the health and condition better than hay alone.

1884

⌘⌘⌘

FARMERS are generally better at growing crops than at selling them. Taking all sorts of farm produce into account, they seldom get more than half, and often not even a third, of the retail sales price. This is particularly true of truckers. They ought, wherever practicable, to form associations and sell in co-operation rather than in competition. Fruit growers and milk producers have done so, and why not the market gardeners?

1905

⌘⌘⌘

ARE there summer hotels in your neighborhood, or people from the city occupying cottages during the summer who do not raise their own fruits and vegetables? If only you can sell to them you'll have a market right at your door. Keep your premises in first-class condition; it won't be a bad scheme to show your customers over them.

1907

⌘⌘⌘

PACK some sunshine away in your hay. The stock will find that sunshine when they nuzzle the hay in the dairy days.

1909

⌘⌘⌘

STUDY the wants of your customers. If they like to have their vegetables, eggs, fruits, or fleeces of wool packed, done up, or tied up in a certain way, try to gratify them. Many a long-time customer has been secured in that way; and a man that sticks to your products year after year deserves generous consideration, even if you do sometimes think he has notions and prejudices.

1909

A HOUSEWIFE coming in from the garden with an apron stuffed full of succulent variety is a pleasing sight. The man who has set that garden will not get sour looks if he tracks on the clean kitchen floor.

1909

⌘⌘⌘

THE WESTERN "boom" is no longer frightening the progressive Eastern farmer who has taken up "extensive intensive farming" and is getting all his acres as busy as himself. Acquaint yourself with an intelligent system of crop rotation. Use your brains on your farm as other men take far looks ahead into the business that flourishes in cities. Then when you are certain and your program is ready, dig in hard. Don't use muscle when you can use machinery that will multiply the efficiency of muscle. Intelligently capitalizing your farm is better than stowing money away in the bank. Make improvements and improvements will make you.

1910

⌘⌘⌘

MANY farmers begin haying after the Fourth of July. We know better but we do not do better. In ordinary seasons it would be money in our pockets if we could get all the upland hay into the barn before the Fourth. Let no grass stand uncut in dry weather after it has blossomed. It then contains the largest amount of soluble, digestible materials. If allowed to stand until it seeds, much of the nourishment goes into the seeds, many of which pass through the animals not only undigested but unbroken. They are then worse than wasted as they remain in the manure to germinate and plague us later as weeds in our cultivated lands. When grass stands until the seeds have ripened, the stalks become mere innutritious woody fiber and much of the food value of the hay is gone.

1918

⌘⌘⌘

LET a handful of corn run slowly through your fingers and think of the miracle of saving and life and growth. Recall, if you can, the days when the best ears of corn were saved for seed, the husks stripped back from the yellow kernels and braided with that of other ears and hung in a safe, dry place. There was a time when seed corn was the most precious material thing in the household of the pioneer.

1935

⌘⌘⌘

THERE is nothing in America which makes an American feel more nationally at home than the sight of a field of Indian corn. The plant is beautiful at all stages of its growth, coming to its best, perhaps, in the heat and fruitfulness of the American midsummer, when the green stalks meet above one's head and the dry, living rustle of the leaves grates delicately upon the listening ear. A botanical mystery still, the plant is the creation and the gift of the Indian peoples, and as long as its tassels stir in the August breeze, there will be a thought given to the old owners of the soil, to the lean hunters and fishers who covered the seed with a clamshell hoe before the first sailers came to trade their kettles and knives for furs.

1938

ASPARAGUS

ASPARAGUS is practically the first vegetable to appear in spring and it is a welcome sight to the grower because it brings him in money at a time when cash is short, and is very welcome to the consumer because it gives him a fresh vegetable and a very fine tasting one. However, there is no asparagus quite as good as the kind you get out of your own garden. Pick it and cook it within an hour and you will have all the natural flavors and sugar which this vegetable contains. If you keep it overnight, these sugars will change in the fiber and the asparagus will lose a lot of its flavor. If you want a real asparagus treat, you must grow your own asparagus, harvest it yourself, and cook it immediately after harvesting.

Asparagus is very easy to grow. Select a sunny place away from the shade of trees, dig a trench about two feet deep, fill it half-full of well-rotted manure and rich soil. Then set year-old asparagus plants in this trench, cover with about an inch of soil, and gradually fill up the trench as the asparagus grows up through. You have to wait two years before you can start cutting. At about the third season you make your first cuttings; do not cut it longer than about four or five weeks. In the fourth season you can cut it the whole season through.

1939—*J. R. Hepler*

⌘⌘⌘

WHEN the water is pouring off you in the hayfield, get the womenfolk to bring out a gallon of oatmeal water—two handfuls of oatmeal with Adam's ale from the spring. And there's nothing better to quench thirst and stay by you than a half gallon of buttermilk (just on the turn to sour) and a half gallon of water. Rum and hay don't mix.

1944

⌘⌘⌘

WOODCHUCKS, or deer, or rabbits, or all three may be taking an interest in the produce now. An empty barrel stood upright in the middle of the garden will usually frighten the woodchucks. If you enclose the whole growing area with a single-strand string fence, hung at intervals of four or five feet with tar paper, deer will seldom go through or over it. Number 7 shot is the surest way to let Peter understand you mean no trespassing.

1945

⌘⌘⌘

EPHRAIM BULL moved from Boston to Concord for his health's sake and bought a house next to Nathaniel Hawthorne's in 1838. He started improving his health by rambles about his estate, and one day found a wild grape vine—the Northern Fox. Its vigorous quality took his fancy and he gathered a number of the grapes. These he planted whole at a depth of two inches. After nursing the resultant vines for six years, he finally obtained many varieties. Only one, which he called the Concord, did he deem worthy of cultivation. On September 10, 1849, he got his first bunch of Concord grapes. Not only were they soft of skin, large, and attractive, a striking blue, but they ripened early—just right for New England that had a season shortened at both ends by late and early frosts. A few years after, he was selling thousands of seedlings at five dollars each. He guaranteed that his gold leaf would not rust nor his grapes rot or fall off the vines—and to this day the true Concord properly grown does not.

1953

Birds

Look around on the feathered tribes who have returned again to greet you with their matin songs, and of them learn cheerfulness. View their assiduity in piling up those little abodes for their young, and learn industry.

1804

⌘⌘⌘

The lark's sweet carol proclaims the break of morn! That is to say in plain lingo, it is high time for us to be stirring.

1817

⌘⌘⌘

"Who was it that killed cock robin? 'Twas the great wanton fool, who was never shipt at school, but who now deserves a good drubbing." The present practice of destroying the feathered tribe every spring is most shameful, and deserves the severest reprehension. Insects are very well known to be the favorite food of the smaller birds, and certainly the immense increase of the former in years past is undoubtedly caused by the vast destruction of the latter by inconsiderate sportsmen and cruel, shameless boys. We may try our various experiments to destroy the millions of troublesome insects, but it will be all in vain. Nothing but the birds can aid us to effect this desired purpose. They alone will be able to relieve us, for which they are formed by nature, and for which "their habits, wants, and capacities qualify them"; and it is said that the parents of one young nest of birds have been calculated to destroy many thousands of insects in a day, which may prevent the existence of as many millions. What then can be done for us? The Legislature would probably esteem it trifling and derogatory to be enacting bird laws. Yet they have passed an act for the protection of snipes and woodcocks. Where then, I would ask, is the dishonor of extending it to blackbirds, catbirds, woodpeckers, and boblincons?

1831

THE THRUSH

This little merry and pleasant songster always appears about this time. He is called by some the "New England mockbird," and certainly has a singular drollery in his note, unlike any other of the feathered race hereabouts. The boys will often give a sort of translation of it, thus: "Here I come! here I come. Charley, Charley, Charley! What, what, what? Going to plant? going to plant? Scratch 'em, scratch 'em, scratch 'em! Whew! hah, hah!" Then away he flies to some other field, and perching upon a tree top, entertains the laborers there with his innocent melodies.

1853

***

The lark no more is heard to whistle over the lawn, but the mild Indian summer, of which so many are most fond, brings us the booming note of the solitary partridge, who, in some deep glen, now struts along, back and forth, like a military dandy, upon his old fallen hemlock, beating out the thorough bass with his nervous drumsticks, to the entertainment of such musical amateurs as love to hear nature's deep tones of solemnity!

1856

⌘⌘⌘

If you will watch a bluebird, when it has a brood of young to feed, you will see the little busybody fly from the nest empty-mouthed, and then fly back with an insect in its bill, more times in the day than you will have patience to count.

1859

⌘⌘⌘

The bluebird and the robin, welcome guests, come to cheer us with their modest song, and the brooks that were bound in ice run leaping and sparkling with new life. Every living thing seems to be glad.

1879

⌘⌘⌘

All persons living in the country, and especially farmers' children, have an excellent opportunity to study nature, and should be encouraged in that direction. In some places, societies have been formed for this purpose, and particularly for the study of birds.

1902

⌘⌘⌘

The demand for first-class turkeys about this time always exceeds the supply. If you intend to raise your first turkeys the coming year, remember that the young ones need special care when molting. They should not be allowed at this stage of their growth to run at large in wet weather or while the dew is on the grass, for they seem unable to withstand such exposure; but if kept in until the dew has disappeared, for the rest of the day they may have the run of the field, and the larger the field the greater their supply of insect food.

1908

WHEN this month comes in, the great autumnal migration of birds is at its height, and our little feathered friends from the North, the warblers and thrushes, may be seen gleaning insects in the orchard and shade trees, while the sparrows are busy eating the seeds of weeds in field or garden or by the roadside. No bird is more useful as an insect and weed destroyer than the bobwhite or quail. Horace Greeley once said that it would be about as sensible to allow the gunner to shoot our cattle, hogs, or poultry as our birds. We should protect these useful birds and teach our children to care for them.

1909

⌘⌘⌘

A CHARMING old Scandinavian custom is that of putting out a Christmas tree for the birds. Why not put a shelf outside one of the house windows, or upon a post or pole supported from the ground, early in the month, mount upon it a little Christmas tree with bits of suet hanging from its branches, strew the shelf with chaff and crumbs, and invite the birds to the feast? If they do not come at first, scatter a little chaff on the ground and tie some suet to the nearby trees to entice them.

1910

⌘⌘⌘

THE wild geese are flying northward and the crows are busy in the meadow. While the solemn crow and the creaking blackbird in some ways do pronounced mischief, yet if it were not for them and the whistling lark, the merry bobolink, the happy native sparrows, and all their cheery kind, grubs, cutworms, army worms, grasshoppers, and others of that pernicious sort would soon make havoc with the grass crop. A million leaf hoppers in the pasture would hardly attract notice, but they would consume as much grass as a cow, and how could we prevent it? We cannot spray with poisons the grass that our cattle eat; but if we have birds enough, they will keep down leaf hoppers, grasshoppers, grubs, and all their evil tribe.

1911

THE weeds are ripening their seeds in our neglected cornfields and our potato fields, and here come the native sparrows on their southward journey—field sparrows, vesper sparrows, song sparrows, whitethroats, and more, too numerous to mention. They are the harvesters of the weed seeds. Each little fellow snaps a seed with his dainty beak, husks it, swallows it, and snaps up a fresh one, all done in the twinkling of an eye. The seeds disappear one after another down his little gullet, running into the thousands in the course of the day.

1911

⌘⌘⌘

THE disappearance of the good old "Bob White" from our fields is both a financial and a sentimental loss for which the substitution of the pestilent English sparrow in no way satisfies us.

1914

⌘⌘⌘

NESTING boxes for birds should not be put up in the deep woods which are the haunts of hawks, jays, squirrels, and other of their enemies. Places where there are fewer trees are better; and bird-houses on poles in the open will ensure still greater safety. Bird protection is all-important.

1917

⌘⌘⌘

THE Indians say that when the leaf of a white oak, which puts forth in the spring, is of the size of the ear of a mouse, it is time to plant corn; they observe that now the whippoorwill has arrived, and is continually hovering over them calling out his Indian name *Wekolis*, in order to remind them of the planting time.

1918

⌘⌘⌘

THE month of June is apt to raise considerable doubt in the minds of some as to the net helpfulness of birds on the farm and the garden through their services in holding insects in check. Especially will this be so in the case of the home gardener with a few cherries, currants, or berries which he had hoped to enjoy as the fruits of laborious hours, but which the birds seem intent on sharing with him. Young and old, we are all glad to see and hear the returning birds in spring. To workers out of doors the robin's cheerful note is better known than the rest, but sad to say, he is one of the worst offenders against small fruits and berries. Fortunately, development of agriculture in some sections of New England has made available a material most useful as protection from birds. This is tobacco shade cloth, which after being employed by the tobacco growers for one year is sold, largely for paper stock, at a price bringing it within reach of the home gardener. Wires stretched across a strawberry bed at intervals of about ten feet at a height of about a foot above the vines will support the cloth, and if it be kept in place for an hour or two before sundown to a few hours after sunrise, the field will be well enough protected. Cherries, too, on small trees, can be protected by the use of shade cloth.

1921

⌘⌘⌘

THE other evening we had a delightful picnic supper with the Smiths. We drove out the Post Road, turned into the woods, and in three-quarters of an hour we were among magnificent maples and oaks, under which a spring bubbled forth its cold water. There was not a sign or sound of other human occupation.

While the baskets were being unpacked, a fire-red streak darted through the trees, and alighted overhead. Never, in my sixty years, had I seen such a brilliant bird. James, eight years old, joyously proclaimed: "A scarlet tanager! The first we have seen this year! The twenty-seventh bird for my list!" He informed me that it spends the winter in South America, arrives about May, and leaves in October. A man offered him ten dollars for a red baby tanager, but he knew they were not red before their second season.

Where did he learn these facts? Two years ago his uncle had given him a bird book on his birthday. James told me many things about birds. Tomorrow afternoon I shall call on him and his mother. They promised to show me catbirds, which nest in the barberries in their garden. It may seem singular to have a child teach a grandfather, but one never becomes too old to learn.

1924

⌘⌘⌘

About this time the cherries begin to ripen; and the robins, bluejays, and squirrels become nuisances in that they destroy more fruit than they eat. Many scarecrows and devices have been used to keep them away from the trees, but with little effect.

The fruit growers in some parts of the country have tried a new method by which they keep them away quite successfully. Purchase a number of bright colored artificial snakes, made of jointed wood, and place them in natural positions on the trees, using two on each tree. When the intruders arrive, the sight of the snakes causes an early departure.

1929

Farm Animals

A WAG advertised a carriage to perform without horses, with only one wheel, and invited the curious to see it. Many of the members of the society of the arts attended, and, in the ardor of expectation, were shown—a wheelbarrow.

1797

⌘⌘⌘

ATTEND to your cattle, see that they do not faint for want of a little salt. Do not let your bees take French leave of you. Do not be in a rage to be done haying; 'tis a boyish notion. Repine not at the good of thy neighbors; nor rejoice at the misfortune of anyone. Drink little cold water.

1809

⌘⌘⌘

GALLANT and Golding are a noble pair of cattle, owned and bred by Farmer Simkins. They are straight, trim, and handsome, and will pull or back, two to one, with any other pair in the neighborhood. The farmer generally drives them himself, but sometimes another is allowed to take the whip. I say *whip*, but mind ye, my friend, here is no lashing nor thrashing, as is so much the practice with many. When Farmer Simkins has the whip, hush is the word, with *steady, my good hearts.*

"Oh, it provokes me madness," says the old gentleman, "when I see Squire Small-gains and his three boys all belaboring his poor little linebacks, hallooing and bellowing like a pack of bloodhounds."

1822

COW HOUSE

THE floor should be tight and descending a little backward, that the stale or urine may not be lost. Let it be conveyed into the cellar, if you have one, or to the sides of the dung heap. The slovenly and negligent farmer may think this is being too nice and exact; but I assure you that the urine of cattle is most valuable, containing abundance of rich salts, oils, etc. The floor over the cattle should be so tight as to prevent the falling of dust, chaff, etc., and so high that a man need not stand in fear of having his head broken by it. Many of our old-fashioned cow stalls or stables are none too high for a pigsty; and a man, when he would enter one, must squat like a goose to save his brains. Let it be of good width also that the dung may be shoveled back and not discommode the milk-maid. Let the door have a good fastening and the windows good shutters to keep out the cold and storm.

1826

⌘⌘⌘

"A HORSE, a horse, my kingdom for a horse!" said Richard. Give me a high neck, a full and bold breast, a lively and sparkling eye, a strong back, a stiff dock, full buttocks, extensive ribs, large and well-formed hoofs, and, by all means, a good gait.

Are you in search of a horse? Do you wish to purchase? Look out for Captain Bitemslily.

When a horse gets worn out, or, what is called, broken down, he is sold to some jockey. These people are always ready for trade, at some rate or other. Next some horse barber takes him in hand, and he is put into bilboes. His teeth are filed down, and his tail pricked up; and his stomach and bowels are drenched with gin, brimstone, and other antifogmatics. Bear's grease and various horsemetics are then applied to his skin, and his hair soon is made to shine, like a greasy Indian's. Now, fitted for market, he appears upon the public turf, metamorphosed into a prancing, dandy nag!

Captain Greds must now take good heed, or, ten to one, he will repurchase his old dobbin of seventeen for a dexterous young courser. Look out for jockeys everywhere and in everything. My neighbor Spinage, last season, purchased of an honest peddler a pound of wooden cucumber seeds!

1830

⌘⌘⌘

The fee for pasturing long-tailed horses is more than that for short-tailed ones. The long-tailed ones can whisk off the flies and eat at their leisure while the short-tails are running around from morning to night and not eating much.

1839

⌘⌘⌘

Would you have a mule without fault? Then keep none.

1844

⌘⌘⌘

Our New England farmers make more use of horses than they formerly did. A man may do all his labor without oxen, provided he takes good care of his horse, as he ought to do. Be merciful to this willing and valuable animal. Oh, the way that some use a horse is most abominable. Spavined, hoof-bound, wind-broken, glanders and gigs, these come by cruel usage, and the "high mettled racer," once the pride of the stall, diseased, foundered, crippled, sinks, falls, dies, and becomes food for the hounds! Shame for humanity! It was not so in the good old days of Deacon Dupy. I was but a lad, to be sure, but the deacon's pacing mare is fully in my remembrance. When Sunday came, the best saddle with the blue pillion was always put on; the deacon mounted, "smart as two sticks," and from the horse block received his better half. Gently down upon the quilted pad she sat, safe and sure, as a mountain squatter, and, holding on by the deacon's button-hole, away they bestrode, gaffer and gammer, while the younkers trudged along on foot. Any man who will abuse this noble animal deserves to ride a poor one all his days.

1847

RIDE AND TIE

THIS was a clever, economical mode of journeying in good old times, when we could boast of rigid honesty among men. It was done after this wise. If John and James, two young farmers, both wanted to go to Boston at the same time—having but one horse between them, and neither chaise nor buggy—John would first mount the saddle and ride on, while James set off on foot. Having rode a few miles, John made fast the bridle to a post or tree, and then became the pedestrian in his turn. James, coming up, took his turn to ride a bit, and in this way of *ride* and *tie* they effected their journey with ease and safety.

Dobbin stood perfectly safe and secure with the saddle bags across him, holding the cold junk and bread and cheese on one side and a stone to balance on the other. Such a thing as thieving was not thought of, any more than in the famous good moral reign of the excellent King Alfred of England. Say, my friend, how would such a project answer now, when a man must watch his coat hanging up in his own entry, to have it safe against pilferers? Alas, for the degeneracy of the times!

1855

"Tom," said a horse trader to his son, "I want you to ride this horse, and let us see his paces."

"Shall I ride him to buy or to sell?" asked the precocious lad.

1860

⌘⌘⌘

A cow is only a machine for transforming a given amount of forage into milk or beef. Stint her, and she will be revenged with double interest. Some farmers feed on poor swale hay, and think they are getting on cheaply. It is no such thing. Feed a woolen machine with shoddy, and the product is shoddy still. If you want to make money on cows, feed well. If you want to make more, feed better.

1865

⌘⌘⌘

The old time for turning the cows to pasture was the twentieth of May, but it was too late. It is best for the cows and best for the grass to get them out early, as soon as there is a fresh bite. Two or three hours a day will do at first, and keep up the feed in the barn at the same time. Make the change slowly, so that they will not lose a relish for hay. If you wait till the grass starts all over the pasture, and then turn in the cows, they reject the rank growth and it runs up to seed. They will not touch it; while if they had a nip at it when it first started, they would have kept it down.

1879

⌘⌘⌘

It seems at last as if the silo had come to stay. Those who have tried it in the best way, who have sowed their corn and have cut it up at the right time, and packed it down in the right manner, still say that it is the true way to feed a stock of cows through the winter; that it gives them a lot of sweet and juicy feed which they couldn't get in any other way; and that it is the cheapest way to make milk and put on flesh.

1886

When I was a boy the farmers used to think that it made cattle "tough" to stand out through the cold days of winter, shivering from head to foot. They did not seem to know that cold takes off a large share of animal heat which they can get only from food, and that the more they are exposed the more food will they need. Most folks know better now, or if they don't, there's a society with a very long name that stands ready to teach them.

1888

⌘⌘⌘

It was observed of a certain high-tempered man that after he was converted his oxen became remarkably gentle. A friend inquired what had so much improved the disposition of his cattle.

"Why," said he, "formerly, when my oxen were a little contrary I flew into a passion and beat them unmercifully; this made the matter worse. Now, when they do not behave well I go behind the load, sit down, and sing 'Old Hundred.' I don't know how it is, but the psalm tune has a surprising effect upon my oxen."

1889

⌘⌘⌘

If swine are to be fat enough to kill at Thanksgiving, they should gradually receive a larger proportion of Indian meal. If they have been fed on swill, take this away and feed on sweet meal and shorts; a few sweet apples will tend to make them healthy.

1902

⌘⌘⌘

Do not say, "Our bull is as gentle as a lamb," for it is just such gentle bulls that are really dangerous. Bring him up from youth to obey; lead him out only when double-held by staff and rope; give him no chance to play tricks.

1904

LET the sunlight freely into your barn, for it is nature's great germ killer. You will find that a sunbath is good for the stock and bad for microbes. In the long run window glass costs less than disease or dirt, and it is a deal more pleasant. A greenhouse is a better dwelling for cows than a basement.

1904

⌘⌘⌘

IF you are wintering a horse which is but little used, he may be kept in fair condition on a few ears of corn, a quart of carrots, a moderate ration of hay, and as much bright oat straw as he will eat. It may be well to add a few handfuls of oil meal from time to time.

1905

⌘⌘⌘

OXEN as draft animals are becoming scarce. Two generations ago ox teams were common everywhere; now a yoke of oxen in the streets of cities or populous towns will attract almost as much attention as a pair of elephants or camels. The patient ox is too slow for this hurrying age and is being supplanted by the horse. But on many of our rocky New England farms the slow but sure ox is not to be despised. He has been an important factor in the past in reclaiming these farms from the wilderness and bringing them into their present state of cultivation, and he is still very useful in operations where speed is not a consideration. For clearing fields of rocks or breaking up and plowing rocky land, he cannot be equaled.

1907

⌘⌘⌘

ALL the tackle required for a pair of cattle is a yoke and chain. Compare this with the expensive harness needed for a pair of horses. Put two bowpins in place, slip the ring on the cart tongue or hook on the chain, and your team is ready for business before one of your horses is half-harnessed. The slowness of motion lessens the chances of accident to team or plow. When the latter strikes a fast rock, the oxen do not become nervous and jump forward, breaking some of the tackle, but wait with unbounded patience until the plowman has cleared the obstacle.

1907

⌘⌘⌘

It is best to take the newborn calf away from the mother at once unless there is trouble with the cow's udder, which the presence of the calf may assist in correcting. With a little skill and considerable patience the calf may be taught to drink. Give new milk at first, gradually changing to skimmed milk thickened with flour bran or fine oatmeal. As the calves grow, they should have the run of a convenient lot, with plenty of shade, where they may also get a bite of grass, which they will soon begin to pick up.

1908

⌘⌘⌘

The day of encouraging milk flow with the flat of a barn shovel and of removing dust from bossy's coat with a milking stool instead of brush and currycomb is happily past. It is a fact that the modern, well-bred cow resents even harsh commands and loud words. An angry or frightened cow has power to control partially the sphincter muscles of her udder ducts. Don't lose the confidence of your cow or you will find the milk supply decreasing.

1910

⌘⌘⌘

It is well to investigate whether a better grade of stock may be substituted to advantage. The most successful dairymen think it good to grade up their herds to very high standards. In many cases purebred and pedigreed cows are kept in dairies producing regular market milk. The offspring from such cows, if intelligently bred and then registered, sell for much higher prices than ordinary calves. In such herds, advanced registry is also to be considered, as being frequently more valuable to the farmer than the original pedigree itself.

1914

⌘⌘⌘

THERE are still, happily, many folks who take more solid comfort in riding behind a good horse than they do in rushing through the country in an automobile. They relish the sociability that is impossible when the road ahead must be watched closely and constantly, and they like the slow pace that affords a chance to see the surroundings. But there is not much opportunity for such to take pleasure in riding over the slippery, motor-crowded main roads; they must perforce keep to the side and less frequented highways. For the benefit of these people—and they make up a considerable portion of the community despite the ubiquitous automobile—New England towns should keep their country roads in good shape. Then, too, there are some who occasionally like to motor away from the speedways. There is another excellent reason for maintaining these less frequented roads in good condition. It is a business proposition. They are the feeders over which the farmer must haul his produce. Whether he sends it to market by motor truck or by railroad, in most cases he has to cover a part of the distance on a dirt road. If the road is good, he can haul big loads and many of them; if it is bad, the loads must be light and the progress slow. Maintenance of a dirt road in good condition is comparatively inexpensive.

1919

⌘⌘⌘

THE best of our harvest is a good solid lump of security in our bins. No man owns more than we, nor feels more fully the pride of ownership. The crammed, sweet-smelling lofts, the well-filled silo, our cattle sleek in their stanchions—these are the second harvest and the fullest.

1944

OF THE MIND

OLD dog Johnnie lies at my feet, his head on his paws and one eye cocked at me. John's got more brains then I have. He goes out of doors when he asks out, sees his friends downstreet, takes care of any other interesting business that comes his way, returns, asks in, and goes to sleep. Johnnie doesn't waste his time thinking. If he does, he manages it with his eyes closed. But I don't. I sit here and think about what I've got to do till it's too late to do it—and then sit some more and think about what I should have done.

Well, now, when I've a mind to it I can plan a crop and make it; I know pretty well how I can make a dollar and how I am going to spend it or stick it away; I figure how to pay my taxes and have something left over.

But there's that cussed Planning Board meeting tonight. Town meeting just around the corner. Lord Harry, I wish I wore John's collar and not mine.

Well, Johnnie, I'll let you out to watch the yard. Look up to the stars, boy, and figure out how to give the kids higher education and find me a road up there that the town can slap in readymade. See you later, Johnnie, under the old desk. Got to think, got to worry, got to plan, got to hurry.

Legislation and Taxes

As you now have time for reading, and inquiring about public business, see that you rightly prepare yourselves for April and May meetings; that no man may impose upon you in the newspaper, or at the meetinghouse door.

1803

⌘⌘⌘

Be not overmuch troubled about government, so long as your farming goes on well; and if you have a quarrelsome neighbor, let him alone; for an old Italian proverb says, "From an ass you can get nothing but kicks and stench."

1804

⌘⌘⌘

All hands at the highways! Good roads and good taverns make good-natured travelers. See how industrious the men are under the direction of Captain Brisk, the surveyor.

A man of liberal notions will never cheat the public, standing idle all the day when he ought to be every moment engaged to improve the road. But who is he yonder, leaning upon his hoe, and gaping and growling and scowling like a surly slave at his task? Now and anon he scratches with his hoe among the dirt, and then looks up at the sun, which he angrily seems to chide for its slowness! His day's work is not worth ninepence. If his taxes are crossed out, it is all he wishes.

1822

He that preaches war is the devil's chaplain.

This old proverb is true preaching. What a pest is one of these missionaries of Beelzebub! Live at peace, farmers, with all men; and if, at any time, there happens to be a hard thought or two arising in your bosom toward your neighbor, because, forsooth, he may have diverged a bit from a straight line of intercourse, see to it that you take not the advice of a mischiefmaker. He that tells you to put in the spurs, and to lash up on such an occasion, is one that is sent out by that old thunderbolt, Mars, who never can bear the sight of a peaceful neighborhood. Cannot we drive side by side together without chafing? Cannot we hitch our horses to the same post when we go to mill? And can we not even whistle in the same key, while we are driving home from the wood lot? Poh! Let all our movements be for peace, and even our sleigh bells jingle in harmony.

1844

⌘⌘⌘

Don't forget to go to town meeting. It is the duty of every good citizen to do his part in the affairs of the town, the state, and the nation. The grand structure of our liberties is based upon the knowledge of our people, as gained and shown in the management of the town meeting. It is the primary source of our Anglo-Saxon independence and self-government. See where the great French Revolution left the people, after their freedom from tyranny had been fully gained, and compare it with the position of our fathers at the end of their revolution. Both peoples were free to establish a form of government to suit themselves. The familiarity of the one with the conduct of affairs in the primary, old-fashioned town meeting enabled it to bring order out of chaos, and to create a form of government which was little more than an expansion of the system which had been already adopted and practiced in every town in the country. The other was left to drift like a mob before the tide of circumstances, or led at will by any popular demagogue. That's just the difference; and the habit of going to town meeting, and doing the duty of an independent man and citizen, made the difference.

1863

❋❋❋

Why not have a village improvement society in your neighborhood? Such an organization will look after the roadsides and unsightly corners.

1907

❋❋❋

It is of great importance that the members of the national, state, town, and other committees of the respective political parties be men of ability and integrity. These positions have been too lightly regarded. It should be an honor to be elected or placed on them the same as to be elected or appointed to public office, as that term is generally understood. Though in a different way, a man on one of these committees may be serving his fellow men as effectively as an officer in one of the departments of the government, state or national. Thus far in the history of this nation, political parties have been a necessity. There is nothing yet in sight to take the place of them.

1917

❋❋❋

It is of course desirable that the people should know what is going on in their state legislatures and in Congress. Would it not be well to have gatherings in your neighborhood from time to time at which your state senator and representative could meet with those of their constituents living in the vicinity?

Legislating should be earnest, serious business. Laws do not always effect the objects intended by the bodies which enact them. Sometimes, on the other hand, they result in consequences never thought of. Discussion and interchange of opinion are essential prerequisites to sound legislation.

1919

THE annual duty which comes about this time of figuring up for the income tax returns is a cloud which may have a silver lining. The farmer, whether his operations tend toward the production of livestock or produce, and whether his farm be small or large, has not, in former years, been much accustomed to keeping books. What his real yearly income was, he often could not tell. Now he is obliged to figure it out, and in doing so he comes to results that are often surprising to him.

1920

⌘⌘⌘

FARMERS and gardeners should attend hearings and be prepared to speak before committees of their legislatures on matters of interest to them. They have too easily yielded the floor to those more accustomed to speaking in public. But before committees, as in life, it is character and worth which really count—though brief and forceful expression, especially if illuminated by flashes of humor and wit, is valuable. The latter are by no means rare on the farm. That farmer delivered a most effective broadside at a state legislative committee hearing who, following the protracted, wordy arguments of numerous men and women who were advocating a measure unfavorable to the farmers' interest, told a story of a man who once engaged to furnish one hundred pounds of frogs' legs to a fashionable restaurant, but found later that he could produce only one pound. Asked to account for so overestimating his stock, he said: "I judged 'em by the noise they made."

1920

BATTLE OF THE FROGS

No more stirring chapter was ever written in the history of frogdom than on the memorable and sultry night in June, 1758. Residents of the little town of Windham, Connecticut, had long since fallen into fitful slumber when suddenly out of the east there arose a cataclysmic din. From a sound like the distant rumble of thunder, to a steady chant as of human voices, it burst at last into a chorus of supernatural screams, cries, and general uproar, coming apparently from directly overhead.

Just what had happened is to this day a matter of conjecture. An act of God is the most popular theory. The frogs, it was asserted by many, finding in their migration that the usually full pond was shrunk by drought to a thin stream, had drawn themselves up in two lines of battle on the opposite sides of the trickle to fight for water rights. The world's greatest frog battle resulted.

1941

Education

EVERY good scholar is not a good schoolmaster.

1796

⌘⌘⌘

MONEY, like manure, does no good till it is spread; there is no use in riches except in distribution; the rest is all conceit. Then hire a good schoolmaster, and give your children time to learn.

1802

⌘⌘⌘

SEND your boys and girls to the common town school rather than to an academy. Fun, frolic, and filigree are too much practiced at the academies for the benefit of a farmer's boy. Let them have a solid and useful education.

1808

⌘⌘⌘

KEEP the boys at school as much as possible, and take care not to rail against the master in their presence. Some people are eternally complaining about the schoolmaster or mistress. Let the school be never so well kept, they will be dissatisfied.

1809

⌘⌘⌘

No more than this instant is thine; the next is in the womb of futurity, and no one knows what it may bring forth. 'Tis your duty to bring up your family in the ways of industry, piety, and morality. You know *"as the twig is bent, so will the tree incline."* If you let your boys ride into town too often, they will soon repay your indulgence with a large budget of bad habits; and when Tommy once gets the reins well in his hands, he will drive you with himself to death and ruin.

1810

⌘⌘⌘

THE heedless man who can just write his name and pick out a chapter or two in his Bible, and perhaps find the changes of the moon in his almanac, thinks that his children and his children's children are to go on in the same way with himself, and so is regardless of their education; but the penurious man, if it cost a cent, will see them hanged before they shall be taught to spell *Caleb.*

1813

⌘⌘⌘

"BILLY must not work," said Mrs. Juckins. "By no means. I intend him for a store." And so this smart lad is left to be a "gentleman," while his father tugs alone in the field. Instead of learning to be industrious and honest, he learns what is fashionably called "doing business"—which is to smoke cigars, snap whips, drink grog, run horses, wear a watch chain, and swear roundly. This is a great evil in the country, and it is to be hoped that the next society that shall be formed will be one for preventing the increase of upstarts.

1818

I HAVE often mentioned the importance of schooling to the rising generation. Few, if any countries, are blessed like New England with public school establishments. No stinginess about the business. See that you have an able master, and pay him well.

1820

⌘⌘⌘

DO NOT let your schoolmaster be grumbling for his pay; for the laborer is worthy of his hire. There are some, however, whom we ought not to class as workingmen in the vocation of a pedagogue. A lazy schoolmaster and a lazy clergyman are the worst of all drones. I like to have my teacher engaged in his work. The schoolmaster has much farming to do in cultivating and managing the various intellectual soils that he has in charge, and making them bring forth fruits to the best advantage. The clergyman's duties are but a little different from these. He has a more numerous and more various flock, but they demand all his care, all his attention.

1833

⌘⌘⌘

As I was saying—boys have too much an inclination, in these most singular times, not only to go ahead, but also to be at the head of affairs. We farmers must not allow this tail-foremost proceeding. It is very well that a boy be smart and active; but then, as we sometimes say of our nags, it is bad to have them feel their oats too much. The reins should be kept in the hands of the parent or master; otherwise Tommy may be apt to think himself a man, even before the beard begins to sprout upon his upper lip. Look out, farmers, how you manage these twigs; for on this more may depend than you are aware of. The sure treasure of your freehold, your comfort here, and your welfare hereafter, come into the reckoning. Treat boys, then, as *boys*, till nature brings them into adult age and years of discretion.

1842

PARENTS who wish to train up their children in the way they should go, must go in the way in which they would train up their children.

1847

❋❋❋

EDUCATION is a better safeguard of liberty than a standing army. If we retrench the wages of the schoolmaster, we must raise those of the recruiting sergeant.

1847—*Edward Everett*

PROSPERITY LETS GO THE BRIDLE

OH, yes, so it verily does. When one gets up somewhat in the world, handles a little cash, and thinks he can afford to have two coats for Sunday, what strange pranks he will play.

"Let her rip!" cried Bill Crackit, when he overturned his father's buggy going to a cattle show. This young prig was not brought up exactly in the way he should go, which was not found out till too late. His father was prosperous and became indulgent. He did not keep the reins in his own hands long enough; but, thinking his son was "a sprightly boy," gave him up the bridle. Bill gave it to the horse, and the horse to the wind. "Dash on, boy! never mind consequences; Father pays the bills!"

Now, I ask, has not the community a claim upon us all, whether rich or poor, to bring up our children to some good and useful employment? Shall we let them go without restraint, "like a wild ass's colt," because we may feel that we are well enough as to the good things of this world, and it is no one's business what course we take in our own affairs? Fie on't, fie! Ye men of thought, look to it. This notion about prosperity's giving independence is all wrong.

1849

GIVE me the girl that knows how to do up the dough and the doughnuts, the pudding and the pot luck. Our grandmothers were up to all these things. They never scowled at having something to do, but, keeping good temper on their side, carried on, with steady hands, the whole process of boiling and baking, turning the spinning wheel and rocking the cradle, in one forenoon.

1850

⌘⌘⌘

"WHAT is wanting," said Napoleon one day to Madame Campan, "in order that the youth of France may be well educated?"

"Good mothers," was her reply.

1853

⌘⌘⌘

A TEACHER who loves his occupation—and no other ought to be employed—and has a turn and tact for instructing, may realize much aid from parents, by their frequently visiting the school, to give it countenance. But men, especially, are too apt to think it is none of their concern, and so leave it to the women, who, to their praise, are not so backward in a good cause. There are some people who wish to have a *cheap* master—one that will keep his hours out—and this would seem to be all they cared for. Their children may go to school or not, as they please. But our sons and daughters should not neglect their schools.

1853

⌘⌘⌘

SOME teamsters keep up an everlasting whipping and bawling; and some schoolmasters know no other way but to fret and scold, and use the cowskin or ferule. They neither have a tact nor a love for teaching. The master contends against the scholars, and they, in turn, against the master. Hatred and malice will follow, more or less; and then how much does your instruction come to?

1854

NEVER teach false morality. How exquisitely absurd to tell girls that beauty is of no value, dress of no use! Beauty is of value; her whole prospects and happiness in life may often depend upon a new gown or a becoming bonnet; and if she has five grains of common sense she will find this out. The great thing is to teach her their just value, and that there must be something better under the bonnet than a pretty face for real happiness. But never sacrifice truth.

1886—*Sydney Smith*

⌘⌘⌘

EVERY farmer's boy should have a little garden of his own, and he should be encouraged to cultivate it in such a manner that when the agricultural fair is held he will be able to select vegetables which he will be proud to exhibit; and the girls should be encouraged to try their hand at breadmaking that they, too, may be able to contribute to the fair and carry off a first prize. The winning of a few prizes will not only make the young people interested in the annual fair, but it will encourage them to strive to stand at the head of their profession. The whole family should not only contribute meritorious articles for exhibition, but they should all attend the annual fair and carefully look over the show, comparing their own contributions with others, and thus learn how they stand. If not up to the front ranks, then go home and resolve to do better next year.

1890

⌘⌘⌘

ENCOURAGE the larger boys to train the young colts, and the smaller boys the steers; and if you would keep them on the farm, let them own the animals when trained. The farm is a dull place for boys if they are kept at work sixteen hours a day, and given only their food and clothing for their labor; but it is a very happy place if they can have a few animals for their own, and a chance to grow a few fruits and vegetables to sell and get a little pocket change.

1893

⌘⌘⌘

THE farmer who expects to keep up with the times must be a member of the Grange or the Farmer's Club, and must take an active part in the meetings; he should also encourage his boys to attend and take an active part, thus giving them opportunities not only to learn advanced principles in farming, but to stand before the public with confidence.

1894

⌘⌘⌘

STUDY your boys to see what they may be fitted for. Don't think either John or Charles must go to college, and become a doctor, a lawyer, or a minister; the world is too full of them now, and he may be better adapted to planting potatoes. If so, give him a good agricultural education. There are chances now to obtain a good one with comparatively little expense. On the other hand, if he has an unmistakable talent in some other direction, don't think he must stay on the farm.

1897

⌘⌘⌘

THE agricultural colleges are now in session. Is your boy there? You can hardly make a better investment for him than to give him a practical training along the lines of his life work. Even the short courses are very helpful and do great good to those whose time for schooling is limited.

1905

⌘⌘⌘

GIVE the boys some recreation occasionally; make their occupation interesting by teaching them the reasons for what is done; give them a chance to read and study about the secrets of plant life, and the wonders of nature's processes and products; let them experiment for themselves. There is nothing more interesting or instructive than original investigation. If, after all, the boy wants to leave it and try a city life, the probabilities are that he was never intended for a farmer.

1906

⌘⌘⌘

WHILE nature's laws have long been the subject of study and investigation, it is only comparatively recently that botany, zoology, chemistry, physics, and some others of the sciences have been taught with a view to the application of their principles to the practice of agriculture. The knowledge of the fundamental principles of these sciences will not only be of advantage to you in carrying on your farm, but it is of itself a good scientific education.

1910

⌘⌘⌘

IF you are in doubt as to the best way of effecting some improvements you are contemplating on the farm, call on your agricultural college or experiment station for suggestions. Are you on the mailing list of the station? If not, send in your name. Your college will offer short courses in agriculture and horticulture. Cannot you or your son or daughter plan to take some of these courses?

1911

⌘⌘⌘

IT is time that New England farmers should begin to form co-operative societies for business purposes. There are large numbers of such associations in Great Britain and Ireland, and in France, Denmark, and some other countries of continental Europe. Where the farmer buys at retail and sells at wholesale prices, the prospects of making much money are not brilliant. Such a society could buy your agricultural implements, fertilizers, and seeds; your insurance; and, perhaps, store and help market your products, thus saving you time, labor, and money.

1911

THE late Professor Stockbridge used to advise the young men in his classes who should engage in farming occasionally to climb a tree and look over into their neighbors' farms. This is sage advice. It pays to look up and to look around; new ideas are pretty sure to be acquired, and, at least, it will furnish change and variety to daily routine.

1912

⌘⌘⌘

THE work of the boys' and girls' clubs in matters agricultural gives promise of highly beneficial results. Gardening can be made a recreation after the necessarily enforced quiet of the schoolroom; while without intense mental effort the children are getting a comprehensive understanding of the workings of nature.

1917

⌘⌘⌘

THERE are three main reasons why every farm boy should go to college. The first is that the boy gets a special training for his life work. This is a day of specialization, when to be successful one must know how to do at least *one thing well.* Competition is very keen today in all lines of industry, and the farmer who is making the most success is the one who has had the best training and who knows how to put brains into his work.

The second reason is that a college training will broaden him out. It will enable him to get a proper perspective of ideas and situations—to see things around the corner as it were—just as our soldiers in the trenches see their enemies by means of a periscope. While a young man may be successful without a college training, who knows how much more successful he might have been with it?

The third reason is that it pays financially. In other words, a college training increases one's earning capacity and is a good investment. A recent investigation conducted by the United States Department of Agriculture shows that the labor income of farmers having a college education is $495 per year greater than that of farmers having only a common school education.

1923

⌘⌘⌘

Everyone interested in schoolwork and play should consider the possibilities of 4-H Club activities. When young people are taught to pledge their hearts to loyalty, their heads to greater thinking, their hands to greater service, and their health to better living, for their club, their community, and their country, they will become desirably keen rather than dull Jacks.

1929

⌘⌘⌘

The rural youngster can make his skis and his snowshoes in the farm shop; he can make use of them economically on occasion to go to school, to gather sap, or to visit the back wood lot.

1937

⌘⌘⌘

In 1889, I went with my mother to call on Dr. Oliver Wendell Holmes; it was his eightieth birthday; she was ten years younger. The doctor received us in his study, a wide, sunny room, full of books and globes and great atlases laid open on stands. He kissed my mother, which touched her deeply; I had a cordial handshake and greeting, but was not really in the picture. The two were together with their time and their memories.

"Ah, Mrs. Howe," said the old autocrat, "at seventy you have much to learn. I, at eighty, find new vistas opening around me in every direction."

Ten years later, when my mother was smothered in the roses of her own eightieth birthday, I reminded her of this.

"It is perfectly true!" she said.

Now I, well on in my eighties, echo the words heartily, grateful to the good poet and friend who gave me this message of cheer.

1941—*Laura E. Richards*

Farm Plans

Look to your barns and see that your cattle are well served. See that your fattening cattle have not too much given to them. Cut timber, if you wish to have it last long, it being the best time [January] in the year. Improve sledding and get your supply of wood for the summer, for it is a chance if you have a better time this winter. Visit your corn barns and granaries; see that the rats and mice don't destroy your grain. Remember your bees, and if weak, feed them with cakes made of malt flour, mixed up with sweetwort; or give them brown sugar; and once in a while salt and water, to keep them from scouring. Feed your doves, and spread ashes among their dung. Burn or sweep your chimneys.

1793

⌘⌘⌘

If you neglected cutting timber last month, be sure to cut it now [February]. Continue to sled fencing stuff where it is difficult coming at with a cart.

Get your tools in order for spring work; such as carts, plows, plowshares, harrows, etc. Have an eye to your bees. It will be a good plan now to sled out your winter dung, when you are obliged to carry it any considerable distance, as you can carry much more on a sled than you can on a cart in April, and with less damage to your ground. See to your doves. Begin to get out your hemp and flax as the days begin to moderate. Now early lambs begin to drop; give them a warm bed at night, and put them in the sun by day. Prune your fruit and other trees.

1793

⌘⌘⌘

SEE that your cellars are well stored with good cider, that wholesome and cheering liquor which is the product of your own farms; a man is to be pitied that cannot enjoy himself or his friend over a pot of good cider, the product of his own country, and perhaps of his own farm, which suits best his constitution and his pocket, much better than West Indian spirit.

1793

⌘⌘⌘

OVERSEE your workmen. No man will work for his brother as for himself. If they be boys, separate them; for it is true: one boy is a boy; two boys are a half of a boy; but three boys are no boy at all.

1804

⌘⌘⌘

Now attend to building walls. A stone machine, invented by Major Lazell of Bridgwater, Massachusetts, is a very excellent thing for this purpose, where large rocks are to raised and transported. A man and boy can raise a stone of from one to five tons' weight, and after it is drawn to the place one man alone can command it, as it hangs suspended by a swiveled chain under the machine.

1806

⌘⌘⌘

CAREFULLY house your tools. Every farmer should have a place on purpose for this business. If you have borrowed a tool of your neighbor make haste to carry it home, lest it cause a hue and cry next spring to find it.

1807

DIG stone that you may sled them in the winter. Pay your taxes. Plant and set fruit trees. Thresh out grain. Rack off cider, and put it into clean barrels. Put up cattle. Listen not to tattlers. Employ no quacks. Drink no drams in the morning.

Keep aloof from all quarrels; be neither witness nor party.

1807

❈❈❈

I KNOW many men, who are called farmers, that deserve not the name any more than a cobbler does that of a shoemaker. They are such as have inherited from their ancestors large tracts of land called farms, to which they have never added the least kind of improvement, but go on with the same routine of plowing and sowing, reaping and mowing, every year, as their fathers did before them. Their meadow is made of bulrushes and their upland of brambles. The fences are poor; the barns are shabby; the cattle are lean; the hogs are starved; the houses want new ceiling; and to complete the whole, in many places the master loves new rum, and the mistress is a slut!

1807

❈❈❈

VAST improvement is made by the introduction of Merino sheep. The business at present is expensive, but perhaps a few neighbors might join and purchase a pair of those most valuable animals. In a few years they would abundantly repay the expense and trouble.

1810

❈❈❈

HERE comes the grand secret at last, and the main requisite in farming. You may have good land, good implements, manure enough, and all things handy, yet, without you are industrious, and ever on the lookout, it will all amount to but a trifle; nothing important will be accomplished. If you have hired help, you must be with them. If you have crops growing, you must examine them personally. If you have cattle in your stalls, you must see to their tending. Watch your hay, your grain, your vegetables, your everything. *Economy*, too, is to be practiced. Without this, all your efforts to get along will be fruitless. *Order* and *system* also are required. It will not do to go on confusedly in your business; for, in this way, you will effect but little.

1831

⌘⌘⌘

"Oh, the dogs take it!" cried Uncle Jonas. "Must I be patient under all this? Six good sheep in one night taken off by these rascally varmints! I would not give the skin of a mosquito for all the yelpers in Christendom; and yet neighbor Hardhack keeps five, Jowler, Towler, Gouge, Nipper, and Fleetfoot, and they ramble, night and day, throughout the bailiwick."

This is, indeed, most vexatious and harassing, and, were it my case, I would have it settled by true dog law, i.e., *nux vomica*. As for the necessity of a dog upon a farm, it is about the same as for a cat in a buttery. It is said that a dog will keep bread from molding; so will hens, chickens, and other poultry do the same. As for Hardhack, he is a sportsman, and let him take heed to his pack. He would ransack creation, with hounds and horn, for the sake of one poor woodcock. And then there is the digging for woodchucks, and the trailing and tramping of fishermen up and down the meadow, and the smashing of fences, and a thousand vexations for the farmer to endure.

1851

⌘⌘⌘

There was once a large farmer, who had three sons. When the first was married he gave him a quarter part of his farm. He thought he got as much from what he had left as he did before. When the second wanted to settle down, he gave him as much more, and so to the third. To his surprise, he found he could raise as much, and with less work, from his own part as he did with four times as much land. He cultivated higher, and got more. Better let some of that old pasture run up to wood.

1861

⌘⌘⌘

A GREAT many little things add to the value of a farm. It is very handy to have water brought into the house and the barn. It saves a world of work and worry, and there is nothing like having a-plenty of it. Can't you tap some spring on the hill, and lead the water down in pipes both to the house and barn? Be sure and lay the pipes deep enough.

1873

⌘⌘⌘

A SPUR in the head is worth two in the heels. Head work is what we want on the farm. It is brain power that makes things move in this world, and keeps them on the track. Make and lay out the plans for the year. Map out the fields so as to know just where and when to put in the work. The great secret of luck on the farm is to do things at the right time and in the right way. A notebook in the pocket is a handy thing. Strict farm accounts, with each lot under its own head, tell a plain and true story. Jot down a new thought on the spot; it saves a heap of time.

Hire farm hands early. The best are sure to be snatched up first, and the best are the cheapest in the end, even if they cost a little more by the month.

1877

⌘⌘⌘

MIGHT as well lend money to a spendthrift, with no security, as to buy tools for use on the farm and not take care of them. 'Twon't do to let them lie 'round and rust. Now is a good time to mend them up, give them a coat of paint where they need it, and get ready for spring's work.

1883

THERE was a time when each man had to make his own shoes, weave his own cloth, shoe his own horse, and hew out the frame of his own house. That time has passed, and it is well that it has; for we can get better work from those who give their whole time and thought to one thing. A mixed farming is the rule here in the East, and it is all well enough, and gives us the means of living; but it doesn't prove that it isn't a good plan to work up some one line of culture, and look to that as the money crop of the farm. It matters little what it may be, if it is the very thing that one can do best. It may be bees or poultry, milk or butter, small fruits or garden vegetables of some kind; or it may be hay, grass, or the raising of stock. Only let it be a product suited to the place, as well as the man.

1884

⌘⌘⌘

THE cranberry bog must not be forgotten when the cool nights set in; keep the ditches full of water, and when a frost is expected raise the water to the surface, but not so high as to cover the fruit, unless it be very cold, and then only long enough to prevent the fruit from freezing. To leave the cranberry in water more than twelve hours is a risk to its keeping qualities. Better pick a little earlier than to have to cover the fruit with water. On most bogs cranberries should be picked before the end of the month. Pull the weeds in the garden before the seeds are ripe, and put them in the compost heap for manure.

1891

⌘⌘⌘

DO NOT forget to build at least a few rods of farm road every year, and keep what has already been built in good repair. No improvement on the farm pays better than this.

1898

⌘⌘⌘

THE farm separator is rapidly replacing all other creaming devices, because of its greater efficiency and economy. When you are ready to buy, choose wisely. Have the machine put in on a month's trial, test the thoroughness of its skimming, and study its strong and weak points, its ease of running and of cleaning, its durability, and the like. A centrifugal thus chosen will coin dollars which heretofore have been lost.

1905

⌘⌘⌘

Not only is a telephone serviceable in everyday affairs, but it may be used to help you sell your produce. You can let the dealers in nearby or distant places know what you offer for sale from day to day. You can thus keep in touch with the market quickly and effectively.

1905

⌘⌘⌘

It is unwise to depend upon a well or spring which fails in times of severe drought. If you dig deep enough to strike a strong flow of water in such a season, you may feel that you are safe at any time. After making sure of the sufficiency and quality of the supply, the next step is to provide for conveying it to the house and farm buildings. The means to be used will depend upon the situation in each case. If the source is higher than the buildings, the problem is simple, merely to provide the pipes and allow the water to run by gravity. If the source is lower, there are various ways of raising the water. Windmills are most commonly used. For large consumers steam may be the most economical power. Then again the gasoline or alcohol engine or the hydraulic ram may be the cheapest and best. Whatever the method, remember to guard against Jack Frost, who is always looking for a chance to upset your plans.

1907

⌘⌘⌘

It is important to get rid of any pools or areas of stagnant water which may be upon the estate. Not only is this advisable on general principles, but these waters, especially such as are protected from the wind, are the breeding places of mosquitoes. Mosquitoes are also liable to breed in rainwater barrels and in the water which may be in old tin cans or broken bottles.

1908

✻✻✻

How about your ladder equipment? These hot days and tindery roofs should remind you that you ought to have ladders at hand in case of a fire call. And keep them where you can quickly get at them, for you'll need those ladders in a desperate hurry if you do need 'em.

1909

✻✻✻

It is as true of the farm as of the factory that scarcity of labor and high wages can be counteracted by the employment of machinery. The farmer, therefore, may profitably study the steps other industries are taking. One of these is motor equipment—car, truck, and tractor.

The farmer with a car, for instance, makes his trips to the town in a fraction of the time taken by the horse. With the motor truck he not only is able to make more market trips in a day than with the horse, but his selling opportunity extends over a much greater area. With his truck the farmer can promptly take advantage of the best market within fifty miles or more and can sometimes get better than wholesale prices.

The small farm tractor that does the work of draft animals in the field and wood lot is coming into use rapidly. It is not an expensive machine and supplies a mobile power plant, not alone for plowing, harrowing, and hauling of all sorts, but for wood sawing, silo filling, grinding, and pumping. The tractor is coming into notice as a community proposition.

1919

WOODCHUCKS burrow deeply and the farmer should early seek to rid himself of delvers of this class, for it is well known that they reap where they sow not and trample down yet more. By August the young "chucks" have left the parent hole to set up housekeeping for themselves and they are particularly vulnerable and more easily destroyed at this time.

Find the holes, which are relatively simple and small at first, and be sure that "backdoor" entrances are closed tight by earth trodden or tramped in; then saturate a mass of cotton rags with bisulphide of carbon and push it down into the main entrance as far as convenient and quickly close the opening by treading in earth. With care to do this work when the youngster is at home, he will never come out; and the only special direction needed is to avoid handling carbon bisulphide when smoking or near fire or blaze of any kind.

1920

⌘⌘⌘

MANY of our large manufacturing establishments are placing on the market important and profitable by-products. For example, sulphate of ammonia from the manufacture of illuminating gas, and bran and middlings from the making of flour.

With the farmer, what we may call "side lines" are analogous to the by-products of the manufacturer. In the main, the farmer grows three classes of products. First, those which he and his family consume at home. Second, those which he feeds to animals and sells indirectly. Third, those which he sells for cash. In addition to these, the thrifty, wide-awake farmer will have a list of side lines which of course will vary with his location and type of farming. Such a list would include maple syrup, blueberries, wild blackberries, fruit of various kinds, eggs and poultry, honey cider (now sweet), buttermilk and cottage cheese, sweet corn, and many other things. Many of these side-line products can be sold at a small, attractive roadside booth right at the farmer's door where his marketing costs are low. The advantage to the consumer is fresh goods at a moderate price, and to the farmer an income from products which might otherwise go to waste. Farming conditions are changing and the farmer must meet them.

1924

⌘⌘⌘

For many years certain individuals have claimed to be able to locate underground veins of water by means of a divining rod or with a forked twig of a peach, bitter elm, or swamp willow tree. With the operator holding the twig with thumbs down and the fork resting on his chest, he claims that when he crosses a vein of water the fork will cave forward to the ground. By extending the fork out over the vein it will begin to vibrate and the number of full downward strokes will indicate the number of feet to the vein.

It is a well-known fact that the course of underground water veins is very irregular, and there is no assurance that a well sunk thirty feet or even less from a good existing well will not be a failure. If there is any reliable means that might be used in locating strong veins of water, thousands of dollars which are now expended annually in drilling dry holes could be saved. That there is any power which reaches from 25, 50, or 100 feet in the ground to the surface, and causes a twig from a peach or other tree to turn in one's hand when a supposed vein of water is approached, seems highly improbable.

1925

⌘⌘⌘

The use of artificial lights in the houses of laying hens during the winter months has become a common practice on many poultry farms. The use of artificial lights increases the number of eggs laid during the fall and winter months to a greater extent than the total for the year. The advantage of this is that the larger proportion of the annual production is obtained when egg prices are relatively the highest. The lights are used from about the first of November to the latter part of March.

1929

It might be well at this time to consider some of the many things that cause the well-meaning farmer to fail in his efforts.

Perhaps he grows only one crop, keeps no livestock, and considers chickens and gardens as nuisances.

Possibly he takes everything from the soil and returns nothing, or doesn't stop the gullies but lets the topsoil wash away, until he has "bottom land."

He should take time to do some hard thinking and planning about his farm work and not trust to luck.

1929

⁂

If you have any old buildings or cellar holes on your place, now is a good time, with the days growing longer, to look for hand-wrought iron. Nails and spikes in good shape bring from two to fifty cents. Folks fixing up old houses are wild for them. They pay well for spear-point hinges, pot hooks, and every other kind of hook, almost. Latches are best liked of anything. Be sure to get all of a latch from both sides of the door and the hook on the door frame, too. Parts of latches bring a little, but not much.

If you find stuff you don't know about or pieces from farm tools or wagons, keep it. Somebody may want it for something different than what it was made for. Put it all in a big box and let folks choose what they want to buy. A little extra money comes in handy.

1941—*Asa C. Jerome*

WAYSIDE VEGETABLE STANDS

In running a small roadside vegetable stand try to see things from the customers' viewpoint. Arrange the stand so everything is easy to see from a car. Instead of flashy paint and signs, use the vegetables for color and attractiveness. Pick them at least four times a day; and scrub, sprinkle, or set in neat containers of water to keep everything crisp and fresh looking. Be sure they get shade all day. Green grass and shrubs help set off a stand. The neater they are, the better they set it off. Rake over the grass and gravel several times daily if necessary. Round up your berry boxes (berries shrink) and cover with cellophane. Charge the market price for goods of like quality, but give extra good measure. A handful of string beans or a small tomato extra is the difference between a delighted customer and an indifferent one. If a customer wants something special, go and pick it willingly. Never lean on cars or gossip about other customers. Have plenty of change at all times. Never smoke, eat, or chew gum while attending a customer; it looks ignorant and easygoing. When people leave say, "Thank you," but not "Come again," for if they want to, they will. It's up to you to make them want to.

1941—*Silas Farnham*

⌘⌘⌘

WHEN the first farmer cleared his first fields, erected his stone wall, and went on to fell more and more trees and make more and more fields, he was upsetting the balanced ways of the primitive wildlife. But with the passing of the years and the centuries there can be no question that wildlife has found a way of adjusting itself to man, and especially the farmer—of finding a new balance. Hedgerows, brush-covered walls, brushy corners at the edge of mowing and grain fields are literally refuges for pheasants, and quail, as well as rabbits. The ways of all wildlife, the countryman knows, whether it be deer, woodchuck, porcupine, fox, or what you will, take their pattern from his way of life. In great part they live off him, naïvely or boldly steal from him, unconsciously work for him, often purposely seek his protection when he is least aware of it. He is their meal ticket, and though he hunts them, their guardian.

1947

THE chains of winter are shaken off at last and nature goes to its business of breeding, borning, growing. That the swallows shall return at the same time to the same place year after year to begin their nesting, that the dens of the foxes and rabbits and woodchucks have been widened, cleaned, and made snug for the litters already there—these are wonderful and orderly procedures that the farmer has little time or patience to consider.

But the farmer's way and the way of birds and all wildlife about him follow each the pattern of spring. With this difference, it is the farmer's knowledge to plan and plant his fields, to grow and fatten his flocks, to sell and make subsistence and cash for the future for more breeding and growing, while it is the instinct of the birds and the beasts to multiply their own according to their natural calendar—as demanding and as exact as the calendar on the farmer's kitchen wall.

When the farmer takes his feet out of the oven along the latter part of March, he comes by what energy he may from a sense of urgency. His fields are hungry for his plow—hungry for the sowing. There is for him a duty and a clarion call of crops he must make.

1952

Reading

Now comes on the long and social winter evenings, when the farmer may enjoy himself, and instruct and entertain his family by reading some useful books, of which he will do well in preparing a select number. The following I should recommend as books worthy of perusal by every American: Ramsay's *History of the American Revolution*; Morse's *Geography*; and Belknap's *History of New Hampshire*.

1793

THE *Life of Dr. Franklin*, I would recommend for the amusement of winter evenings, also the *Life of Baron Trenck.*

1794

⌘⌘⌘

THE best liberty is to serve God and mind your business. Read newspapers, but consider before you believe; for common report is often a great liar.

1802

⌘⌘⌘

BELIEVE not half you *hear;* and how to believe of what you *read in the newspaper* is not in my power to tell or imagine, in these wild party times. But if you read at all, I advise you to read both sides.

1806

⌘⌘⌘

YOU now have all your matters adjusted, and all your affairs in good order. Well then, do not go lounging at the grogshop, but rather take a book and improve your mind in useful reading. I would recommend to read the history of our own country, and of our revolution.

1808

⌘⌘⌘

"WHAT a strange mass of nonsense this almanac maker sends out every year," cried an old codger the other day. "And now I affirm, I believe our Suzy could write as nice as he does; and, now you, I thought he was rather too tight upon Mr. Captain Bluster." I told the good old man that, in the Farmer's Calendar, no particular person was ever meant to be satirized by anything there written.

1810

It is one thing to be stiff and another to be steady in an opinion. The steady man changes when reason requires it, but the stiff-necked is at war with all reason.

1812

⌘⌘⌘

When the ass and the mule unite in the person of one of your neighbors, you must surely have a most disagreeable associate. You can have no pleasure from passing your winter evenings with him. You had better take the life of Washington and read it to your family, or some other work which shall be equally useful.

1812

⌘⌘⌘

Parents! when you buy suitable books and place them in your houses, you procure for your children good company. Company which is always near and ready, and which may keep them from that which is low, ignorant, foolish, expensive, or vicious. Give your children good schooling and good books, and encourage them in reading.

Above all, let the Bible, the Sabbath, and the pulpit be respected as the best means of intellectual and moral improvement and of present and future happiness.

1812

⌘⌘⌘

The men who are farmers by book are no farmers for me. They make much talk and parade about their compost and all that, but give me the man who prefers his hands to books and with a little will fetch a great deal to pass. Let those who follow husbandry for amusement, try experiments. Poh, nonsense! Why, my wife, the other day, silly woman, undertook to bake a pudding by the book. And she book'd it and book't it, and after all never cook't it.

"Zounds," said I, "Sarah, this never will do for working farmers; if we undertake to make puddings and sow turnips by the book, we shall get to the last page of our business before we are half ready.

Let learned men attend to cases, genders, moods, and tenses, you and I will see to our dairies, flocks and fields and fences."

1819

⌘⌘⌘

"It is a good horse that never stumbles."

Yes, my friends, and it is a good almanac maker that has no errors in his calculations and no blunders nor mistakes nor slips in any of his work. There is no one without his weak side. I hope you will extend your charity to me for all my imperfections; for certainly my errors are of the head and not the heart.

1821

⌘⌘⌘

The stage has come, and the mail is opened! The farmer stops his team in the furrow! The carpenter lays aside his broad ax! The shoemaker lets fall his lapstone! The blacksmith leaves his iron in the fire! The doctor forgets his sick patient! The lawyer drops his quill, and the parson shuts his Bible! Away, away they all hasten, greedy for the news! Like hungry hounds around the shambles, longing for the first snap at the offals, they stand, and with feverish impatience wait the unbundling! Even old age and decrepitude have essayed to reach the place! Business is stopped and all other pleasures and cares are laid aside until the perusal is finished. Then the farmer and the mechanic and the doctor and the lawyer and the priest and the rest of them, all retire to their different employments, no more satisfied and no more wise than they were before, but filled with an increased longing for the next arrival of the mail!

1826

⌘⌘⌘

Novel reading vitiates and palls any appetite for literary food.

1832

SETTING DOWN IN WRITING IS A LASTING MEMORY

"I LOVE roast goose," said Attorney General Sullivan, when addressing a jury. "Yes, gentlemen, roast goose is a most profitable meal for Thanksgiving Day, or any other day; for it puts us in mind of an important duty. Gentlemen, while I am picking the wing of a goose, I think of the quills that once grew out of that wing, and then comes up the thought of pen and ink, and then, perchance, a recollection that I have neglected to put down in my daybook some little item that should not go uncharged. Why, gentlemen, give me a goose, and away with your turkey or sirloin, coot or canvasback, turtle or titbit; for a goose, simple and silly as he may be, will open the eyes of a man, and bring him to a sense of his duty, as a neighbor and as a friend."

How many hard thoughts, how many contentions, how many expensive and ruinous lawsuits might be prevented, if we were more particular and familiar with the quill! Yet some there are who keep none of these records, except a few chalks upon the buttery door. Can this be a "lasting memory"? By no means, for a little brush of the hand may obliterate the whole in a moment. Let no farmer then depend on such loose and uncertain scrawls as regular memorandums of business and charges between neighbor and neighbor.

1843

⌘⌘⌘

WHAT! A newspaper? That's all right. Every family should be supplied with more or less of them. It is of no little importance that a farmer should know what is going on in the world beyond his own territories, or his own neighborhood. A newspaper will afford you this; but see to it that you do not read yourself into a flaming politician, and so become noisy at town meetings, with, perhaps, more sail than ballast.

1846

THE word "newspaper" is derived not from the word new, but from

N
W E
S

which it was usual in old times to put at the head of a periodical publication, indicating that the information was derived from the four quarters of the globe.

1847

HUME OF THE BOX

THIS old chap, it is said, dwelt in the lowlands of Scotland, and was famous for telling false stories, a sort of Munchausenite. He took delight in making people wonder, and keeping up the agitation for the fun of it. Whether he was a farmer, or what he was by profession, no account is given. No doubt, however, he was a loafer and busybody in other people's concerns; about as contemptible a biped as we have among us nowadays. From "Hume of the Box" comes "Humbug," very naturally. Humbugs are so common that they need no description. We must all look out against false pretenses in these times of trap and device. If you "buy a pig in a poke," you know now what will be the end of the bargain. It may turn out a sell.

1855

⌘⌘⌘

BOOKS are masters who instruct us without rods or ferules, without words or anger, without bread or money. If you approach them, they are not asleep; if you seek them, they do not hide; if you blunder, they do not scold; if you are ignorant, they do not laugh at you.

1857

SHOW me a thrifty, practical farmer, and I will show you a man who reads works on farming, and takes and reads an agricultural paper.

1858

⌘⌘⌘

BY THE way, smoking that pipe over the kitchen fire is not going to make you either wiser or richer; and had you not better knock out the ashes, and the pipe, too, and be reading some book that will give you information about your business, or looking to your tools, and getting them ready for spring work?

1858

⌘⌘⌘

A NEWSPAPER is a window through which men look out on all that is going on in the world. Without a newspaper a man is shut up in a small room, and knows little or nothing of what is happening outside of himself. In our day newspapers keep pace with history and record it.

A good newspaper will keep a sensible man in sympathy with the world's current history. It is an ever-unfolding encyclopedia; an unbound book forever issuing, and never finished.

1870

⌘⌘⌘

A GOOD free library is a great boon to any town. It makes every farm worth more, and puts it in the power of every citizen to grow better and more intelligent. But it is of no use to have it unless you're going to use it, and now is just the time.

1880

⌘⌘⌘

A WARM tool house is handy just now [December], and there is always something to mend. A few hours' work will save many a bill at the blacksmith's. The plows, the carts, the shovels and hoes, the rakes and other tools, ought to be looked over and put to rights. But the days are short now, and we must make the most of them, so as to have some time left for reading and study. Good books ought to be the farmer's choice companions. Through them he can talk with the greatest minds that ever lived, and seek inspiration from the grandest of human sources. There is no lack of mental food nowadays with a free library in almost every town.

1885

⌘⌘⌘

SPEND some of these long winter evenings looking into the possibilities of forestry. Consider whether it would not be worth while setting out that back pasture to white pine, spruce, or locust—quick-growing, marketable material. Wood is being used up faster than it is made. A good wood lot is a valuable farm asset today, and will be more so thirty years hence.

1906

⌘⌘⌘

SEE that the sitting-room table is well supplied. The agricultural and scientific press of today is of inestimable value. Encourage the boys to read it.

1906

⌘⌘⌘

IT MAY be a question for what purposes and to what extent foreign languages should be taught in our public schools; but no effort should be spared to bring it to pass that every permanent inhabitant of this land shall speak the English language. That is the language of a free people who believe in a "government of laws and not of men." In order to know what the laws are, the people must be able to read them. All those intending to live among us who do not speak our language should be made to feel that they are expected to learn it. In order to think alike, people must speak alike. Ignorance of the common language on the part of any of the members of a community to an extent impairs the efficiency of that community in the exercise of its functions. Such impairment is especially deplorable in time of war.

The English language has shown its adequacy in poetry, in the affairs of state, and in great enterprises, world-wide in their extent. It is the language of the Constitution of the nation, and of the constitutions of the several states. These constitutions are the heritage of every citizen, whatever the tongue in the use of which he was reared. But along with these benefits he assumes certain obligations and duties, which he is bound to understand, observe, and perform.

1919

APPROPRIATE PROXIMITY

THE perfect hostess will see to it that the works of male and female authors be properly separated on her book shelves. Their proximity, unless they happen to be married, should not be tolerated.

1946—*Godey's Lady Book, c. 1853*

⌘⌘⌘

"GO WEST, young man." Attributed to Horace Greeley.

The famous editor used this admonition in a New York *Tribune* editorial after reading it in the Terre Haute (Indiana) *Express* in 1851. When it became popular, Greeley tried to give credit to the originator, John Babson Lane Soule, but it was too late.

"Everybody talks about the weather but nobody does anything about it." attributed to Mark Twain.

Charles Dudley Warner, editor of the Hartford *Courant,* is now believed to have coined this epigram. Mark Twain did say, "If you don't like the weather in New England, just wait a few minutes."

"They shall not pass!" Attributed to Marshal Pétain.

Instead of Pétain, the man who uttered this historic challenge was his successor in command at Verdun in World War I, General Robert Georges Nivelle.

"Lafayette, we are here." Attributed to General Pershing.

Not the commander of the AEF but Colonel C. E. Stanton of his staff said that.

"The forgotten man." Attributed to the late President Roosevelt.

The forgotten man in this case seems to be the author of the expression, Professor William Graham Sumner of Yale.

"Praise the Lord and pass the ammunition." Attributed to Captain William Maguire of the United States Navy.

Another Navy chaplain, Lieutenant Howell Forgy, gave this battle cry which inspired a popular song.

1948—*Dow Richardson*

Entertainment

SUFFER not your horses to be too frequently harnessed in a pleasure sleigh; and be careful, when they are, not to suffer them to be driven by young and inexperienced drivers.

1800

As SOCIABILITY is the life of a good neighborhood, let no one consider a little cheer as waste of butter, beef, and beer.

1802

⌘⌘⌘

A full purse, a full table,
A full mow, a full stable,

and a pleasant wife makes winter pass cheerily with the farmer. In cold stormy evening, himself and possessions secure from the tempest, he enjoys more real happiness over his cider mug and checkerboard than any nobleman of Europe or nabob of India amid pomp and grandeur.

1804

⌘⌘⌘

SLEIGH riding is pleasant; let your girls and boys have enough of it; but do not keep Dobbin continually in the harness. I have derived very great advantage therefrom.

1806

⌘⌘⌘

BOWLING greens have become of late mightily in fashion, to the ruin of many unfortunate young men. Scarcely a day passes without the rattle of the pins in front of landlord Toddy Stick's house. Every boy is distracted to get away from his work in order to take his game. At sun two hours' high, the day is finished, and away go men and boys to the bowling alley. Haying, hoeing, plowing, sewing, all must give way to sport and toddy. Now this is no way for a farmer. It will do for the city lads to sport and relax in this way, and so there are proper times and seasons for farmers to take pleasure of this sort; for I agree that all work and no play makes Jack a dull boy.

1815

COME, neighbor Juckins, let's you and I take a game of checkers for love and good will. No betting, sir: but here, Betty, bring a mug of old orchard and a bowl of nuts. Let each crack for himself and come on, boy, here's beat ye, three out of five. There is no sledding until the storm is over.

1819

⌘⌘⌘

THIS is the month for cattle shows and other agricultural exhibitions. Premiums are offered by various societies for the greatest crops, the best stock, and the best domestic manufactures; and thousands are pulling away for the prize with all their might. Huzza, huzza for the premiums! Here's to the girl that can best darn a stocking, and to the lad that shall raise the biggest pumpkin!

1824

⌘⌘⌘

"COME, wife, let us make a husking," said Uncle Pettyworth.

"No, no," replied the prudent woman, "you and the boys will be able to husk out our little heap without the trouble, the waste, and the expense of a husking frolic. The girls and I will lend a hand, and all together will make it but a short job."

Now, had the foolish man took the advice of his provident wife, how much better would it have turned out for him! But the boys sat in, and the girls sat in, and his own inclinations sat in, and all besetting him at once he was persuaded into the unnecessary measure, and a husking was determined upon. Then one of the boys was soon mounted upon the colt with a jog on each side, pacing off to Squire Hookem's store for four gallons of whisky. The others were sent to give the invitations. The mother, being obliged to yield, with her daughters went about preparing the supper. Great was the gathering at night round the little corn stack. Captain Husky, old Busky, Tom Bluenose, and about twenty good-for-nothing boys began the operations. Red ears and smutty, new rum and clack-jaw, were the business of the evening.

1828

It seems to be the fashion to drive a horse at his fullest speed, without discretion and without mercy. Young dashers now will be altogether for sleigh riding. Crack away, Jack! and be sure to work out your eight cents a mile. Hurrah, we go! This is a cruel piece of business, and he that is a prudent man, taking good care of what Providence has trusted to his charge, will never suffer his beast to be thus tormented by heedless, inexperienced drivers.

1833

CATTLE SHOW

This grand annual jollification is good for all concerned. Although it is called a "cattle show," it is not altogether an exhibition of the beasts of the field. The "bulls of Bashan," fat beeves, and stanch workies, Ayrshire and Durham, Devon, Hereford, and Teeswater milkers, bellowing calves, and grunting porkers—these make a part of the outdoor show. The plowing match—here is the scene of attraction for the husbandman who prides himself on his talent at educating cattle for the draft. All is engagement! And order is observed most strenuously. Twenty teams stand waiting for the signal, which being given, they shoot ahead, and every eye of the thousand spectators is fixed steadily upon them!

Now into the hall for butter and cheese, and fruits and manufactures. See the elegant carpets, rugs, counterpanes, blankets, and tablecloths; the beautiful bonnets, baskets, ottomans, crickets, mats, mantles, collars, workbags, etc. But what seems most pleasant is the throng of ladies.

1848

⌘⌘⌘

"What harm is there in playing a game of checkers?" says Tom Trifler. None at all, if you will only be temperate about it. But yet, it is poor business for a man that is able to bring something to account, besides whiffing an offensive cigar, and moving blue beans from place to place.

1848

⌘⌘⌘

DID you ever know a man who did not "lose his luck," if he fished, gunned, gadded, or loafed, instead of attending promptly to his business?

1849

⌘⌘⌘

YES, boys, we still have something to do, other than to play football, pitch quoits, or loiter at the village.

1851

⌘⌘⌘

THROW off your wet garments, and seat yourself in this, my "old armchair," which has passed down from generation to generation, an heirloom, year after year, and has had many a new leg, round, back, and bottom, but remains *the same old chair yet*, like the boy's jackknife. There is a real pleasure in having our friends call upon us in this way; and it is also a profit, as I am disposed to think, thus, occasionally, to hold a tête-à-tête together on the various ways and means of doing business. Professional gentlemen have their meetings for consultation, and why not farmers? Meet together socially, friends, and talk over farming matters.

1856

⌘⌘⌘

THE merchants, the mechanics, and most of the professional men are having a vacation, while the farmer is busy at work in the hot midsummer sun, and his wife may be sweating over a hot fire cooking for her fortunate cousins, who sit in the veranda breathing the pure country air.

Is it not about time for the farmer to have a summer vacation that he may take his family to the seashore for a few days to enjoy the invigorating sea breezes? With the present numerous improved farm implements, the intelligent farmer can do his work so rapidly that he can at times take a short vacation without injury to his crops, leaving behind enough help to do the daily chores. This is no more than the merchant is obliged to do.

1895

⌘⌘⌘

THE long winter evening should be utilized by those who have children by giving such entertainments as are adapted to the ages of the children, and of a character which will tend to make them wiser and better, as well as happier and more closely attached to their homes. When farmers' sons find their homes less attractive than the corner grocery or the neighboring saloon, it would be well to find out why this is so; and advisable for farmers to endeavor to brighten up their homes, and if possible make them so attractive that the boys will have no desire to leave them.

1900

⌘⌘⌘

TO BE on good terms with one's neighbors and to meet them often is not only pleasant, but is essential to good citizenship. But don't let your sociability be limited to conversations at the cross-roads and the grocery.

1902

⌘⌘⌘

THE rural free mail delivery, the home telephone, and the Grange are three destroyers of farm isolation. They mean much—more than menfolk think—to the women. They make for happiness, wide-awakeness, and profit. If your community lacks them, interest your neighbors in having these wants supplied.

1906

THE winter is ahead. Begin the going habit. Get gregarious. Don't hibernate after the manner of bears. A merry gathering, a good laugh, a frost-bitten ear, and spring will be with us again.

1909

⌘⌘⌘

AS THE weather grows colder without, hearts should grow warmer within. Work should not be so pressing as to prevent a day's fishing through the ice.

1910

⌘⌘⌘

THIS month [July] is the first of the two in which most vacations are taken. The practice of taking them by automobile is steadily increasing, and for the past two or three years a new problem has arisen for the owners of farms and country lands. This is caused by the ever-growing number of tourists who, either for reasons of economy or from a genuine love of out-of-doors, put up for the night, not in hotels, but on the roadside. The litter they leave, the cutting of small trees, and the constant menace of fire during the dry period are both an annoyance and a peril to owners of land along the more frequented roads.

Some cities and towns have provided public camping places, but many of the tourists are not satisfied with these, and seek out their own camp sites notwithstanding. Prohibiting signs do not always avail, and the landowner's vigilance of many months may be brought to naught by one fire.

One partial solution of the difficulty has been for owners of likely spots to grant camping permits, either for a small sum or in some cases without charge. This involves the giving of the camper's name and address, which somehow serves to create in him a greater sense of responsibility, both as regards his littering and otherwise damaging the land itself, and in his care not to start a fire.

1922

This is one of the months when we enjoy changes of scenery. The city dweller escapes to the country at every opportunity. Those of us who are so fortunate as to live in the country are equally susceptible to wanderlust. Mother Nature invites us to bring our food. She provides dining rooms de luxe: the soft green orchard sod, fruit trees a-bloom, and a chorus of singing bees; brown needle rugs under pine trees, melodious winds overhead; a large rock on the river's edge, with the music of the waters below. However fastidious our tastes may be, they can be satisfied, and without cover charges.

1928

⌘⌘⌘

His neighbors say that things are coming to a pretty pass. They honestly believe Farmer Brown enjoys the radio more than he does the party telephone.

1935

⌘⌘⌘

Country dances are just mere names now, along with the old-time tin peddler, red-flannel ankle-lengths, and dried apples in the attic. However, in a few isolated "islands" dotted over the country, the dances have been actually fanned back into life. And in the remoter hillbilly sections the dances are probably still being done to the tune of a sawing fiddle or two for want of anything more available. In still other places is found a merging of town and country, young and old, modern and antique—examples of true democracy. For over the thresholds of these town halls you are always the equal of you. For instance, old Mrs. Velvet Bustle of New York City and Palm Beach trips lightly with Ben Bumpkin and loves it. Old man Hayseed never fails to date with Deborah Deb from the city in a lithesome basket quadrille. Of course, when imported people first began to sprinkle the sets with their untutored selves, there was resentment. But as old-timers realized that the jigs were changing to fall in with more speedy times, they opened up their attitudes and thankfully realized the country dance

ANT FLY
PALMER
GREEN DRAKE
GREAT DUN
DUN CUT
HAWTHORN

was being carried along by coming generations—and not being hurtled to an undeserving grave.

1941—*Beth Tolman and Ralph Page*

⌘⌘⌘

You may have a chance to take in some auctions this month. A good opportunity for you to pick up that horse rake and logging chain you've been looking for. Take the family along and make a day of it. You'll need Ma to put the brakes on you.

1945

⌘⌘⌘

You owe it to the boy and yourself to give the old fishing hole a try now and then. This time of year the trout will usually be found in the big pools where the water is deep and cool. But there's nothing better than a string of horn pout from the pond or river after dark—if you can stand the bugs.

1945

⌘⌘⌘

Now, before the real snows have come and the weather holds cold and still, we have our best skating. Nothing is more exhilarating on a brisk December day than to follow the frozen track of one of our winding rivers. The skates sing and cut, and the rushing cold reddens our cheeks and waters our eyes. Familiar landmarks flash past: the rotting wharf where we fish for horn pout on summer nights, the gaunt pine with the remains of the eagle's nest still in it, the expressionless backs of the village houses as they flank the river. Then we are under the covered bridge, and stopped at last by the old dam and broken mill, we note as we pause for a "breather" that the mountain seems suddenly very near and clear, and there is a golden mist of clouds, wispy and faraway along the southwestern horizon. Tomorrow the big snow will come and we may hang up our skates for this year.

1947

THERE'S still the old swimming hole under the same twisted alder where Dad flung his pants and shirt as a kid, and where Dad's boy flings his of a hot afternoon. Come Sundays, now and then, the "old boys" join their young fry down there and splash and dive. Then after a bit they lie back on the bank and smoke, remembering the days when they stuffed sweet fern and dried raspberry leaves and alfalfa into homemade pipes, and tied knots in the shorts of the last fellow out.

1947

⌘⌘⌘

Now the kids have cut poles and in the riled waters catch the silly shiners and little trout. Strange that in this thrashed pool they bite at their best. Dad says there were really big trout here in his day, and recalls the years when the beaver dam made the pool twice this size. He recalls a fifteen-inch whopper he caught in those days. Old Dan snorts, "Pshaw! It warn't but ten—and I caught it." And that starts a kids' wrangle of words from the oldsters with a heap of unreliable and dimly recollected evidence, till young Dan lets out an Injun whoop and all hands are on their feet. A wild scramble and grabbing in the ferns till he holds up the fish, flopping and wriggling. "Gosh! Gosh!"— and old Dan takes the trout and lays it in the palm of his hand—and turns to Dad—a twinkle in eye. "Gosh, feller, I guess this tops ours, sure." And the sun goes down.

1947

⌘⌘⌘

I HAVEN'T seen a real old-time tramp for many a spring, but he and his brethren used to be a sign of spring in our town.

And the gypsies, harbingers of spring as well, where are they? The last band I saw were in an enormous Pierce-Arrow and an equally enormous Locomobile that had once been a hearse. The gypsies in the hearse were making a merry home of it with the back doors flung wide-open and all the interior bright with their colors.

Then there were the Italian women who used to come waddling over our lawns and fields to get dandelion greens. Well I remember them—bandannas on head, stomachs enormous within tightly tied aprons—ungainly silhouettes that could, however, with astonishing ease and rapidity, bob up and down as they filled their aprons.

And, of course, there was the Italian with his monkey and hurdy-gurdy. We still see him now and then, and, when we hear the rusty strains of *La Traviata* and *Il Trovatore* cranked out once more, it is April in our hearts.

1953

⌘⌘⌘

OUR own old farmhouse is set high upon a hill with a view over valley and river, straight to the great blue mountain. It is ours every day of our lives, a threshold to the sky, one with shadows and storm and clouds. I am glad that we can always look to it, but I am not sure that I should not be just as glad if we could not.

This has been a thought I have pondered ever since we visited for a few days with a good friend. She had built her house to suit her needs and placed it where she would.

The house is in a corner of her land that places it between the houses and the friendly picket fences of two neighbors. Her front door and garden and its picket fence are met by the meadow and elm trees with a pattern of leaves against patches of sky. That is her view. Had she chosen she might have built beyond the elms or under them and looked forever over blue mountains and the sea.

I asked her why she had not done so. "I very nearly did," she replied. "I had planned my house beneath the elms. But then I found myself always, as I walked to the spot through the meadow, with feeling of wonderful expectation, as if I were sure to find something I had never seen before. And so, I built my house here. I didn't want to spoil the view. And I haven't, since I must walk to find it."

1957

Finances

ADJUST your accounts; see that your expenditures do not exceed your income.

1793

⌘⌘⌘

SETTLE with, and pay off, your mechanics, laborers, and servants; for though the sums due to them be but small, they may be of more consequence to them than you may imagine.

Call upon your debtors for settlement before the new year opens.

1794

⌘⌘⌘

DO BUSINESS but be not a slave to it.

1796

⌘⌘⌘

ALL complain for want of money, but none for want of judgment.

1796

⌘⌘⌘

SINS and debts are always more than we think they are.

1797

⌘⌘⌘

He who spends more than he should,
Shall not have to spend when he would.

1799

⌘⌘⌘

WHEN the borrower of a dollar, whom the lender did not expect to repay it, did so promptly, and then in a few days tried to borrow a much larger sum, his intended victim said, "No, you have deceived me once, and I am resolved you shall not do it a second time."

1803

Cut your coat according to your cloth; that is, balance accounts between your expenses and your income; and again, plant no more ground than you have dung for; and again, relate no more stories than you can support by good vouchers.

1807

⌘⌘⌘

"THEY don't calculate," said neighbor Tom, when he saw Bob Holdfast, the sheriff, carrying a man to prison for the small sum of three dollars. "Let's examine this case," said Tom; "first, the man runs in debt for a dollar, is sued, and the cost makes it three dollars, and now he is going to gaol in the midst of spring work, and must pay his board, or the town will have to, and there is turning the key, and swearing out bill, etc. If he was at home, and would mind his business, and pay attention, he could have a dollar per day for his labor. Again, the creditor must pay the officer and the lawyer, court and all, and lose his debt into the bargain. Oh fie on't, I see neither debtor nor creditor has calculated here, but the lawyer, the sheriff, etc., have made the whole calculation."

1808

⌘⌘⌘

THE rich man may have the more meat, but the laboring poor man the better stomach.

1816

⌘⌘⌘

"BOOK it, John," said Farmer Simkins, when his son told him that Squire Slouch had used the cart and oxen half a day. "Book it, Father?" replied John. "It is so trifling that I can remember it." "I say, John, book it; for we must take care of the pence, and the pounds will take care of themselves."

Farmer Simkins can tell to a snow flea's value the whole extent of expense he has incurred in the various operations of agriculture for the last year; and where all the profit and where the loss comes from. Let us all endeavor to imitate this industrious, this worthy, this liberal, this valuable citizen. And like him remember, too, that "an honest man's the noblest work of God."

1820

⌘⌘⌘

"Train up a child in the way he should go,
and when he is old he will not depart from it."

"Peter, my son," said Captain Cheatem, "do you know one Zackery Dokes over in Scrambletown, or does he know you?"

"I guess neither, Father."

"Well, Peter, he takes a fancy to our linebacks and wants to swap oxen. He thinks the linebacks have no fault, and so let it be, Peter. Now we don't agree exactly as to the boot; he offers fifteen dollars and I do suppose, to be honest, that is enough, for the cattle, though they look finely, yet they are darn'd deceitful lubbers. But we must say *thirty*, Peter, mind that, say *thirty* dollars!"

"Aye, Father."

So, giving Peter his lesson, Old Cheatem sat off for the bargain. He found poor Dokes at home, and after a little parley, agreed to leave the amount of boot to the first man who should come along; and pretty soon, at a signal given by the old sharper, Peter was seen trudging along and soon came up. They stated their case, and he, acting out the stranger, heard both pleas, and after examination of both pairs of oxen, he fixed the boot at *thirty* dollars! There was not a word to be said. Each paid the stranger twenty-five cents and he went his way.

1827

⌘⌘⌘

Why thus alone at your plowing, Mr. Thrifty? "Oh, sir, my boys have all left me and turned shoe peggers. I was in hopes to keep at least one of them to help carry on the farm; but they have all five gone into the leather line—Bill, Jo, Nathan, Tom, and Jonas. And then there was old Patrick M'Coulter, he had lived with us for years, you know; I never thought of losing him. He was one of the best at the plow; he could swing a scythe as easy as my lady waves her fan in dog days; and then, with a cradle in the grain field, there was no one up to him; it was mere walking, *walking*, sir, for amusement! But Pat, too, a foolish booby, has turned cobbler! If this is the way things are going on, our farms must soon run up to bushes. There is scarcely any help to be found hereabouts, unless we pay treble the amount of former times. I expect that, ere long, lawyer, doctor, and parson will *awl*, at *last*, as the saying is, become knights of the *brogue;* for, you see, the making of a pair of shoes brings twenty-five cents, and twelve pairs a day is no great affair. So, sir, money, much money, comes of shoe pegging. Yankees love money, and will leave farm and all to obtain it."

1837

⌘⌘⌘

He who loves gold is a fool; he who fears it, a slave; he who adores it, an idolater; he who hoards it up, a dunce; he who uses it, is the wise man.

1840

⌘⌘⌘

How many prosperous, honest yeomen have been ruined for having only just left their plow, stepped into the house, and put their signatures to a bit of paper to oblige a friend! It is indeed right that we here throw in a caution, and say, farmers, beware! It is well to do a neighborly kindness; but it is wrong not to take heed, lest, by doing this act, you may bring ruin upon yourself and family; lest, by doing this act, the grappling tongs of a mortgagee get hold of your premises, and then, where are you?

1841

⌘⌘⌘

Well, farmers, a little capital is not very inconvenient in our line of business. We have sometimes an inclination to spend a few dollars in the purchase of manure, which is the custom of some. However, it is better to make all the manure you can on your farm, and do without the rest, than to hire cash to purchase it with.

Dig gold out of the ground—be your own miner—you must not go beyond the depth of the soil to find it. The coin thus procured will abide with you better than that which is obtained by mortgaging your farm.

If you do not look pretty sharply into your own affairs, your creditors will.

1850

⌘⌘⌘

In jogging quietly along for the past half century, I have made up my mind what is the sure way to have a light heart and a heavy purse. It is, "*Pay as you go.*" Do this, and "*Do not buy what you do not need,*" and, as Franklin directs in his "Way to Make Money Plenty in Every Man's Pocket," "*Spend each day less than you earn,*" and, as far as money is concerned, you may snap your fingers at "the times," if they are ever hard.

1859

⌘⌘⌘

If a man must be all the time in debt, let it lie together, due to one or two, and not scattered all over town. A lot of little bills that hang along not paid, keep a man in hot water all the time. The best way is to pay as you go; but if you can't do that, square up the odds and ends, and see just how they stand. Short credits make long friendships, and prompt pay makes good neighborhood.

1874

⌘⌘⌘

Live within your income, but do not be so miserly as to refuse to buy John a sled, or Jane a doll, even if you have to cut short your rations of tobacco to do it.

1891

LET the boys have a few rods of land that they may grow a few strawberries for market and thus earn a little pocket money.

1891

⌘⌘⌘

TEACH the boys the importance of rejecting for market all vegetables that are not of good quality, and also impress upon them the importance of having the inside of the package just as good as the outside.

Neighbor Cheathim is very careful to put all the best peas on the top of the box, and the small stalks of asparagus in the center of the bunch, and then wonders why he does not get as good customers and as high prices as his neighbor, who picks only good peas, and rejects all vegetables that are so poor that even the ungenerous man wants to hide them. If you expect your boys to be successful in any business, teach them to be generous as well as honest in all their business transactions. A good set of customers can never be secured by the miserly or ungenerous man.

1898

⌘⌘⌘

THE prudent farmer rarely gives notes on time, and has not to worry about collecting outstanding bills to meet them; and as a rule, he has produce enough on hand to carry him through the winter, so if hard times come, he can live on corn bread and butter, pork and beans, potatoes and salt beef, ham and eggs, and baked Indian pudding; and if he has a sugar orchard, he can have apple and squash pies, and many other luxuries which the farmer's wife knows so well how to make; and thus, however hard the times, he will come out in the spring in good condition for the farmwork.

1899

WHEN the farmer asked for a $1,000 loan, the banker told him, "It's all right, George, you can have the money but on unsecured loans we have a rule that requires the note to be endorsed. Suppose you get your neighbor, Henry, to endorse your note."

That sounded okay to George, so he propositioned his neighbor, a respectable and solid farmer. "Aw, shucks, George," the neighbor replied, with a twinkle in his eye. "Let's keep this business among us farmers. You go tell that banker that if he'll endorse your note, I'll lend you the money myself."

1901—*The Furrow*

⌘⌘⌘

ECONOMY is a virtue; but there is a true and a false economy. To let the stock run down for want of a proper ration of grain or other foodstuffs, to get along with worn-out or insufficient tools or teams too light for their work, is no economy at all. A judicious expenditure for first-class tools, improved stock, machines, and good help, even though costing more, may be a saving in the end.

1907

⌘⌘⌘

IF you have no bank account, would it not be well to consider the expediency of opening one? The time has gone by for keeping any large amounts of money in the house, whether in bureau drawers, under mattresses, or hid away in old stockings.

1918

⌘⌘⌘

ECONOMY is a way of spending money without getting any fun out of it.

1927

⌘⌘⌘

IF a farmer has a horse or a cow or some other animal of which he does not take reasonable care, the "Society with the Long Name" will soon get after him. Nobody, however, enters a complaint when the farm tools are not properly cared for. Neglect of both animals and tools on many farms is the source of some mighty big leaks in the farmer's profit.

1933

⌘⌘⌘

A COUNTRY merchant advertised in *The Old Farmer's Almanac* in 1804 various commodities for sale and gave notice that he would take in payment all kinds of country produce except promises.

1935

⌘⌘⌘

BUY good tools; they are worth what they cost. They will last forever if you take decent care of them, but cheap tools won't. Their handles split or come off; their edges are ephemeral things; they get out of condition and because of them your work will become more difficult and far less finished.

1937

⌘⌘⌘

"So far as I can see, most of the people living in New York have come here from the farm to try to make enough money to go back to the farm," said Don Marquis, that great philosopher and friend of The Old Soak.

1940

⌘⌘⌘

A RECESSION is a period in which you tighten up your belt. A depression is a time in which you have no belt to tighten. When you have no pants to hold up, it's a panic.

1942

⌘⌘⌘

ON Groundhog Day, February 2, half the wood and half the hay should be left—compared with what you had at winter's start.

1943

⌘⌘⌘

NOTHING nicer than a little bit of store credit, come April.

1948

5.

ANECDOTES & PLEASANTRIES

THE serious business done with, most almanac editors wind up at the end each year with a page or two of humor. In this respect, Robert B. Thomas was no exception. Much of what follows, to be most enjoyed, must be read in the light of the time in which it appeared. But possibly you will be amused at how some of it lives on. Recently we were at a social gathering where we heard one of the guests telling "Bad Luck by Degrees" (see page 217) almost verbatim, just as if it were a brand-new story, never told before.

⌘⌘⌘

A COUNTRY farmer, not long since, having married a second wife, complained much of the rheumatism in his hips. He asked his wife one day what was the matter with her goose, that she did not hatch; she answered shrewdly that she supposed the gander had the rheumatism in his hips.

1796

⌘⌘⌘

Two very honest gentlemen, who sold brooms, meeting one day in the street, one asked the other how the devil he could afford to undersell him everywhere as he did, when he stole the stuff, and made the brooms himself. "Why, you silly dog," answered the other, *"I steal them ready-made."*

1796

⌘⌘⌘

A DRUNKEN fellow carrying his wife's Bible to pawn for a pint of gin to the alehouse, the man of the house refused to take it. "What a pox," said the fellow, "will neither my own word *nor the word of God pass with you?"*

1796

⌘⌘⌘

A BUTCHER who lay on his deathbed, said to his wife, "My dear, I am not a man for this world, therefore I advise you to marry our man John, he is a lusty, strong fellow, fit for your business." "Oh, dear husband," said she, "if that is all, never let it trouble you, *for John and I have agreed upon that matter already."*

1796

OF THE SENSE OF SMELLING

AT Antwerp, a countryman coming into a perfumer's shop fell immediately into a swoon and could not be brought to himself but by applying horse dung to his nose.

1796

ADVICE TO COUNTRY POLITICIANS

Go weed your corns, and plow your land
And by Columbia's interest stand
Call prejudice away
To able heads leave state affairs
Give raling o'er and say your prayers
For stores of corn and hay

With politics ne'er break your sleep
But ring your hogs and shear your sheep
And rear your lambs and calves
And Washington will take due care
That Briton never more shall dare
Attempt to make you slaves.

1797

EPITAPH—ON A VIOLENT SCOLD

Beneath this stone, a lump of clay,
  Lies ARABELLA YOUNG,
Who, on the twenty-fourth of May,
  Began to hold her tongue.

1801

EXTRAORDINARY ANECDOTE

Two soldiers being condemned to death, in Flanders, the general was prevailed on to spare one of them; but not having a preference, wishing only that the execution of the other might be held up as an example to his army, he ordered the unfortunate soldiers to cast lots for their lives, with dice, on a drumhead. The first, throwing two sixes, fell to rubbing his hands, with the mingled sensation of gladness and sorrow; but was surprised when his companion threw two sixes also. The officer appointed to see the execution ordered them to throw again. They did so, and each of them threw two fives; at which the soldiers that stood round shouted, and said, neither of them was to die. Hereupon the officer acquainted the council of war, who ordered them to throw again. They did, and up came two fours. The general, being informed of the circumstances, sent for the men and pardoned them, saying, "I love, in such extraordinary cases, to listen to the voice of Providence."

1801

⌘⌘⌘

When Pat shot at a hawk on the top limb of a tree and it fell to the ground with a thud, Mike said, "Pat, you might have saved your powder and shot, for the fall would have killed it."

1803

⌘⌘⌘

An Irishman, upon being asked why he ran away in time of battle, said, "My heart was as bold as a lion, but my legs were cowardly and would run in spite of me."

1803

⌘⌘⌘

A married couple determined on being divorced; but not being able to agree with respect to the disposal of the children, they referred the dispute to an aunt to settle. "We have three children," said the husband. "I insist on keeping two, the third shall be left to the care of its mother." "But I," said the mother, "have right to two; the care of one will be more than sufficient for him." "There is no way of settling this dispute," said the aunt in a tone of the utmost gravity, "but by setting about to make immediately a fourth child."

This decision produced a laugh; and restored good humor. The contending parties embraced, and the idea of a divorce was forgotten.

1804

LETTER TO THE EDITOR WRITTEN IN 1947 BY A NATICK, MASSACHUSETTS, NEWSDEALER

Dear Sir:

Some of my people went to the Sportsman's Show where you had a booth for the sale of *Almanacs*. And you told them that the issue for 1834 was the rarest one. That for 1806 is more so as it contains "Jonathan's Courtship." As this is torn out of most copies for 1806, look out when you buy one that it is in it. I have been sixty years in the R.B.T. business, bought duplicates from William Ware for two cents each and the year 1793 for one dollar and sold for ten dollars. William Ware lived at the Hotel Touraine and had no office downtown.

Yours Respy,
Edwin Batcheller
Natick, Massachusetts.

The poem to which Mr. Batcheller refers, taken from the 1806 *Old Farmer's Almanac*, reads as follows:

JONATHAN'S COURTSHIP

A merry tale I will rehearse,
  As ever you did hear, sir;
How Jonathan sat out so fierce,
  To see his dearest dear, sir.

His father gave him a new suit,
  And money, sir, in plenty;
Besides a prancing nag to boot,
  When he was one and twenty.

And more than that I'd have you know,
That he had got some knowledge,
Enough for common use, or so,
But had not been to college.

A hundred he could count, 'tis said,
And in the Bible read, sir;
And by good Christian parents bred,
Could almost say the Creed, sir.

One day his mother said to him,
"Come here, my son, come here,
Come fix you up so neat and trim,
And go a-courting, dear,"

"Why, what a plague does Mother want;
I swigs! I dare not go;
I shall get shun'd—and then plague on't
Folks will laugh at me so."

"Poh! Poh! fix up—for you shall go
And see the Deacon's Sarah;
She has a great estate, you know,
Besides, she wants to marry."

Then Jonathan, in best array,
Did mount his sorrel nag,
But trembled sadly all the way
Lest he should get the bag.

When he came there, as people say,
'Twas nearly eight o'clock,
And Moll hollo'd, "Come in, I say,"
As soon as he did knock.

He made of bows 'twixt two and three,
Just as his mother taught him,
All which were droll enough to see;
You'd think the cramp had caught him.

Now this was all the manners he
From home with him had brought,
Namely of bows 'twixt two and three,
The rest he had forgot.

At length come in the Deacon's Sal,
From milking at the barn,
And that she was as good a girl,
As ever twisted yarn.

The ladies all, as I should guess,
And many a lady's man,
Would wish to know about her dress;
I'll tell them all I can.

Her tire of gray was not so bad,
Her skirt not over new—
One stocking on one foot she had,
On t'other one a shoe.

Now Jonathan did scratch his head,
When first he saw his dear,
Got up, sat down, but nothing said,
Because he felt so queer.

When all the folks went off to bed;
It seem'd they took the hint,
But Jonathan was some afraid—
Sal thought the deuce was in't.

At length says Sal, "They're gone, you see,
And left us here together."
Says Jonathan, "I think they be—
'Tis very pleasant weather."

Sal cast a sheep's eye at the dunce,
And sat toward the fire,
He muster'd courage all at once,
And hitch'd a little nigher.

Ye young men all, and lads to smart,
Who chance to read these verses,
His next address you'll learn by heart,
To whisper to the ladies.

"Why, Sal, I's going to say as how
You'll stay with me tonight;
I kind o' love you, Sal, I vow—
And Mother said I might! ! !"

"Well done," says Sal, "you've broke the ice.
With very little pother.
Now, Jonathan, take my advice
And always mind your mother."

"Well, Sal, I'll tell you what," says he,
"If you will have me now,
We will be marry'd, then, you see,
You'll have our brindle cow!

And Father's got a great bull calf,
Which you shall have, I vum—"
"Tell him," says Sal, "He'd best by half
Keep his bull calves at home."

Now Jonathan felt rather bad,
He thought she meant to joke him,
And tho' he was a spunky lad,
His courage quite forsook him.

Sal asked him if his heart was whole.
His chin began to quiver,
He did not know he felt so droll,
He guessed he'd lost his liver.

Now Sal was scar'd out of her wits
To see his trepidation;
She hawl'd, "He's going into fits!"
And scamper'd like the nation.

A pail of water she did throw
Upon her tremb'ling lover,
Which wet the lad from top to toe;
Like a drown'd rat all over.

Then Jonathan he hurried home,
And since I've heard him brag,
That tho' the jade had wet him some,
He didn't get the bag.

1806

⌘⌘⌘

A Scotchman, thinking he was about to die, had his worst enemy brought to him.

"I want your forgiveness," he said. "Give me your hand." As the man was leaving, the sick man called him back. "But," he added, "if I should not die, things are to be just as they were before."

1807

A MITTEN SAVES A LIFE

SMALL things are sometimes the means of saving a man's life. Uncle Hiram used to say to me, "Never go duck hunting alone," and then he would tell me this story.

"One morning I started with my gun for a day's shooting on Pixie Ledge. I pulled my boat upon the rocks and went across the top to wait for the birds to begin to fly. In a very short time a flock came into range and before they flew away I had shot five of them. As I did not take my old dog with me I had to go out after them with the boat. So laying my gun down, I went back to where I had left my dory.

"She was gone!

"A heavy swell had taken her off the rocks, for I had neglected to take out her anchor! I could see her about twenty-five feet off the ledge, dancing up and down on the waves. There I was, on rocks that, when the tide came in, would be many feet underwater. It was very cold and I knew that if I swam out to her I would freeze. I had to think fast and I did.

"I took off one of my heavy, homemade mittens which were knit of yarn by Aunt Mary and spun from the wool of our own sheep. I unraveled the mitten in a hurry and tying a small stone onto the end of the red yarn I threw it out toward the drifting boat.

The first time I did not make it and the stone fell into the water and I had to use much care in drawing it back to me. I threw it a second time, offering a silent prayer. It dropped into the boat, caught, and I pulled the dory slowly and carefully onto the ledge. Then, picking up my birds, I went home having had enough shooting for one day, vowing that I never would go out alone again; for where one person might make this mistake of neglecting to secure the boat, two would not be likely to fail to do such a necessary thing."

And I have always remembered what Uncle Hiram told me.

1941—*As told to Doris Saltus*

THE BURNING BOY

STILL unexplained is the greatest curiosity of the nineteenth century—little Jerry Hibbert of New Orleans who was seen to be on fire by a reporter from the *New Orleans Times Democrat*. Sitting there in the back gallery of his house, with his legs crossed and in a perfect state of nudity, chubby Jerry was enveloped in a flame red with heat. Just about this time his nurse came in, screaming the boy was on fire. Water was thrown over him but to no purpose. Then they wrapped him in a blanket but it was useless. Jerry continued to burn right along. The incident created quite a commotion in the house and baffled the ingenuity of the inmates. Just then, however, the door swung open, and gusts of wind came in, and Jerry went out.

After a while it got around among the neighbors that this curious burning boy was nearby. In fact, many children and nurses at times saw the boy but no credence was given to their stories. Thus those who had seen and believed became used to the phenomena and, among themselves, occasionally you would hear them say—"Little Jerry is afire again," and that would be an end to the talk. It was not until the *Times Democrat* reporter overheard this remark one morning and went to see for himself that the public began to take real notice.

1948

BAD LUCK BY DEGREES

Sir James Hall and his servant Peter

SCENE—Parlor

SIR JAMES: Well, Peter, what news?
PETER: Nothing particular, Massa, 'scept Bob's lame.
SIR J: Bob lame! What's the matter with Bob?
PET: He hurt himself trying to stop de horses, Massa.
SIR J: Horses! What horses, pray?

PET: Old Massa's horses run de way wid de carriage.

SIR J: Horses run away with the carriage! What started them?

PET: Cannon, Massa.

SIR J: What was the cannon firing for?

PET: To alarm de folks, Massa, and make 'em come and help put de fire!

SIR J: Fire! What fire?

PET: Your big new house burnt all down, Massa!

SIR J: My new house burnt down!

PET: He catch fire while we all gone de funeral, Massa.

SIR J: Funeral! Who's dead?

PET: Your father dead, Massa; 'cause he hear the bad news.

SIR J: Bad news, what bad news?

PET: De bank fail, Massa, and he lose all de money.

SIR J: You rascal, you, why didn't you tell me this bad news at once?

PET: Cause, Massa, I afraid it too much for you all at once, so I tell you little to time.

1823

⌘⌘⌘

A SELF-CONCEITED coxcomb was introducing to a large company an acquaintance, whose physiognomy was not very prepossessing. Thinking to be extremely witty, he thus addressed the company, who rose at his entrance, "I have the honor to introduce Mr.—, who is not so great a fool as he looks to be." The young man immediately added, "Therein consists the difference between my friend and me."

1824

REMARKABLE COINCIDENCES

THERE are many surprising coincidences in regard to the lives and deaths of Mr. Adams and Mr. Jefferson. They commenced their political lives together, both rose gradually, both became foreign ministers of the highest grade, and both were subsequently elected to the highest stations in the nation. They were the only two who signed the Declaration of Independence on the fourth of July, 1776, who were alive on the same day in 1826. Both were on the committee which drafted that document. One of them was the writer, and the other the seconder of the motion for adopting it. Political events subsequently made them rivals, and bitter enemies of each other. Both were the leaders of opposite and powerful political parties. Both the most prominent objects of the bitterest invectives of their foes, and the most boisterous praise of their friends. Both, after retiring from the high stations, the contention for which had estranged them, found themselves in the same political ranks, became friends, and both died on the same day, on the fiftieth anniversary of the important event in which they were engaged together. Mr. Jefferson died the same hour in the day during which the Declaration was adopted, and Mr. Adams on the same hour in which it was promulgated to the people. And both were native of the only states which have ever furnished the Union with a President. A further remarkable coincidence is the fact that of our ex-Presidents, John Adams was eight years older than Thomas Jefferson; Thomas Jefferson eight years older than James Madison; James Madison eight years older than James Monroe; and James Monroe eight years older than John Quincy Adams. Mr. Adams was the only President who has been succeeded in the highest office by his son, and he was the only President who had a son to succeed him. And the son has been elected to the high trust by the same party which elected the father. This is the most wonderful chapter of coincidence that we ever knew.

1827—*N. Y. Com. Adv.*

THIRTY DAYS

Thirty days hath September,
April, June, and November.
February hath twenty-eight alone,
And all the rest have thirty-one,
Except in Leap Year, at which time
February's days are twenty-nine.

1828

DO YOUR WORST

A CLERGYMAN was called out of his bed on a cold winter's morning to marry a couple, who were then waiting for him. The parson hurried up, and went shivering to his room where, seeing nobody there but an old man of seventy and a woman about the same age, he asked in a pet what they wanted of him. The old man replied they came to be married. The parson looked sternly at them, "Marry'd!" "Yes, married," said the old man hastily, "better to marry than do worse." "Go, be gone, you silly old fools," said he, "get you home and do your worst."

1828

GOING TO CHURCH

Some go to church just for a walk;
Some go there to laugh and talk;
Some go there for speculation;
Some go there for observation;
Some go as it their charms displays;
Some go upon those charms to gaze;
Some go there to meet a friend;
Some go there the time to spend;
Some go to learn the parson's name;
Some go there to wound his fame;
Some go there to doze and nod;
But very few to worship God.

1830

DIAMOND CUT DIAMOND

A SIX-FOOT Vermonter lately entered a store, on one of our principal wharves, in search of employment. He could do any kind of chore, he said, and boasted of his strength. "Stout as you are," said the clerk, "I'll bet ten dollars you cannot carry that bag of salt [pointing to one] twice across the store and never lay it down." The Yankee stood for a moment, scratching his head, and gazing at a rope, with a hook at its end, which hung through a scuttle, and then accepted the wager. He shouldered the bag with utmost ease, carried it twice backward and forward, and then hung it upon the aforesaid hook. "Mister," said he, "I guess I'll trouble you for that are ten. I didn't lay it down—I hung it up." The clerk, much to his dissatisfaction, handed over the money; the Vermonter left the store, saying, "Catch a weasel asleep! Not so bad a day's work. Better than chopping logs!"

1834—*B. Gal.*

REASONABLE FEAR

"I AM afraid of the lightning," murmured a pretty woman during a thunderstorm. "Well you may be," sighed a despairing adorer, "when your heart is steel."

1834

⌘⌘⌘

AT a dinner table, on board a steamboat, a gentleman, who carved, perceiving one lady who had not been served, inquired if she would be helped to some pig. She replied in the affirmative, and he, accordingly, handed her the plate which he had reserved for himself. Her ladyship, feeling somewhat offended at so bountiful a service, observed, with protruded lips, loud enough to be heard all round, "I don't want a cartload!" The gentleman, at her remark, became the object of attention of all near him, and, determining to retort upon her exceeding civility, watched her motions, and observed that she had dispatched the contents of the plate with little ceremony. When this was accomplished, he cried out, "Madam, if you'll back your cart up this way, I'll give you another load!"

1834

⌘⌘⌘

IN a work printed in 1628, being a popular miscellany of those times, a story is told as a good joke.

A sea captain on a voyage with thirty passengers, being overtaken by a violent storm, found it necessary, to save the ship, to throw one half of the crew overboard, in order to lighten the vessel. Fifteen of the passengers were Christians, and the other fifteen were Jews; but in this exigency they unanimously agreed in the captain's opinion, that he should place the whole thirty in a circle, and throw every ninth man over, till only fifteen were left.

The captain being determined to save the Christians, in what order is he to place his thirty passengers to effect his purpose?

1835

Answer to the Query

Mr. Thomas, sir—Perhaps some of your numerous readers may expect an answer to your query. I therefore send you the following answer.

B. D.

First, 4 Christian; 2nd, 5 Jews; 3d, 2 Ch.; 4th, 1 Jew; 5th, 3 Ch.; 6th, 1 Jew; 7th, 1 Ch.; 8th, 2 Jews; 9th, 2 Ch.; 10th, 3 Jews; 11th, 1 Ch.; 12th, 2 Jews; 13th, 2 Ch; 14th, 1 Jew;—in all, 15 Christians and 15 Jews. Or:

CCCCJJJJJCCJCCCJCJJCCJJJCJJCCJ

1836

AULD LANG SYNE

Should auld acquaintance be forgot
And never brought to min'?
Should auld acquaintance be forgot
And days of o' lang syne?

So here's a hand, my trusty friend,
And gie's a hand o' thine:
We'll take a right guid-willie shake
For auld lang syne!

1837

CHANGE OF FORTUNE

A plain statement of facts

SOME SIXTY-FIVE or seventy years ago, a vessel from Boston arrived at a wharf in London. Among the hands on board was one named Tudor, a steady, well-looking, young man, who acted as a sailor. Very early one morning, a young, beautiful, and decently dressed female came tripping down, and enquired of Tudor for the captain. She was told he was not risen, but she insisted on seeing him without delay. Tudor called him up; she addressed him with:

"Good morning, Captain, I have called to see if you will marry me."

"Marry you?" Believing her to be a suspicious character—"Leave my vessel, instantly, if you know what is for your good." She next went to the mate, and received a similar answer, she then went up to Tudor, who was engaged in handling ship tacks, and put the same question to him. "With all my heart," answered Tudor, in a jocular manner. "Then," said she, "come along with me." Tudor left his work and followed her. By the time the principal shops were opened, the lady entered a barber's, followed by Tudor. She ordered the knight of the razor to take off his beard and hair, both he stood in need of. She faced the bills, and entered a hat store. She requested the best of beavers in the store, and told Tudor to select one, the price was paid by the lady. Tudor threw his old tarpaulin aside. They next visited a shoe store, and selected a pair of boots, the lady paying for them. Tudor, by this time, was puzzled to divine the object the lady had in view. He solicited an explanation, but she told him to be silent. She led the way into a clothing store. Here Tudor was told to select the best suit of clothes in the store. His tar-bedaubed pants and checkered shirt were in a few minutes metamorphosed into as fine a gentleman as walks the streets. The bill, as before, paid by the lady. Tudor's amazement was now complete. He now again earnestly insisted on an explanation, the only answer he received was, "Follow me, and be not alarmed—all will be explained to your satisfaction"; he therefore resolved to ask no more questions. Next she conducted him into a magistrate's office, and politely requested the minister of the law to unite her and her companion in matrimony; this was rather a damper to Tudor, but he yielded; the ceremony over, the couple were pronounced man and wife. Without uttering a word, or exchanging a kiss, Tudor and his wife left the office, not, however, until she paid the magistrate his fee. The couple walked along in silence—Tudor hardly knowing what he was doing or what he had done. Turning the corner, Tudor saw a splendid house, toward which the wife seemed to direct her steps, and into the front door they entered: the room was furnished in a style of magnificence. She sat him down, telling him to make himself contented, while she passed into another room. The first one who addressed her was her uncle, calling her, demanded how she had escaped from her room, and where she had been. Her only answer was, "Thou fiend in human shape, I allow you just one hour to remove your effects from this house. You have long deprived me of my property, and meant to through life, but you are frustrated. I am mistress of my own house, I am married, and my husband is in the front room."

I must leave the newly married couple for the purpose of giving the history of Mrs. Tudor. She was the only child of a wealthy gentleman, Mr. A.—his daughter's name was Eliza. He had been at great expense in her education, being the only object of his care; his wife died when she was quite young. A short time before his death he made a will, by which his brother was to have possession of all his property till his daughter was married, when it was to be given up to her husband. On condition if Eliza died without marrying, the property was to go to her uncle and his family. After the death of Mr. A., his brother removed into his house; Eliza boarded in his family. Eliza soon discovered that her uncle did not intend she should ever marry. He shut her up in one of the center rooms in the third story and refused her associates, by telling them when they called she had gone on a journey. Three years was the unfortunate girl thus shut out from the world. Her scanty breakfast happened one morning to be carried her by her old servant Juan; Eliza, seeing the face of her old friend and servant, burst into tears. Juan well understood the meaning, "Hush, Eliza, some of your old servants have long been planning means for your escape." "What!" said Eliza, "is it possible that I am to be delivered from this vile place?" It is unnecessary to detail all the minutiae of her escape. Suffice it to say that on the evening of the fourth day after the interview, she made her escape. This was about daylight. She immediately bent her steps to the wharf where the Boston vessel lay. The amazement of Tudor, and transports of his wife, at the sudden change of fortune, may possibly be conceived, but cannot be expressed. One pleasant morning, some days after the marriage, the crew of the Boston vessel's attention was drawn by a splendid carriage approaching the wharf—the driver let down the steps, and a gentleman and lady, gorgeously dressed, alighted; the gentleman asked the captain what port he was from, and many other questions (all the while avoiding the scrutiny of the captain), at last turning to, "Captain — [calling him by name], before leaving your vessel, permit me to make you acquainted with Mrs. Tudor!" The captain and those about him had not recognized him to be their old friend and shipmate, Tudor! They supposed some fatal accident had befallen him. You may judge of the congratulation that followed.

1840

A PLEASANT OCCURRENCE

Mrs. W., consort and helpmate of Mr. W., merchant of New York, was a very economical woman, and, if the eulogist was not mistaken, had a very strong apron. The circumstances, as narrated by the friend of Mrs. W., were as follows: Mr. W. was a merchant in affluent circumstances, did a heavy business, and conducted all his affairs with the utmost regularity. Every department of business was completely systematized; every family expenditure was restricted to regular daily appropriation; and no surer is the sailing master of a ship to make his observation, work his traverse, and ascertain his exact latitude and longitude every noon, than was Mr. W. to have his accounts nicely balanced, and ascertain his exact whereabouts in business every night. But wise, prudent, and punctilious as he was, he could not withstand the temptation to overtrading during one of the great paper expansions; and when the revulsion came, he found himself embarrassed beyond all his efforts to extricate himself. He had stood firm as a rock while many of the most reputable houses tumbled to ruins around him; but he could not collect money due him from his best customers, and there was one remaining note of ten thousand dollars that would fall due in a few days, and he could devise no way to meet it. The notice came from the bank; but three days remained, and every resource failed. The first of these three days was spent in fruitless attempts to borrow. The second was as fruitlessly spent in trying to force a sale of goods. Nobody had any money to purchase goods at any price. Failure presented itself before him with all its frightfulness.

The day of grace arrived, and horror was depicted in his countenance. Mrs. W. knew nothing of his troubles, and on perceiving him evidently in great distress of mind, she insisted on knowing what was the cause of his trouble. It was folly to conceal his ruin from her, and he condescended to make her acquainted with the cause of his misery. "How much," she inquired, "will save you from failure?" "Ten thousand dollars," he replied, "will pay my last note in the bank; but for want of this I must suffer the disgrace of having my note protested, assign my property for the benefit of my creditors, and suffer my name to go to the world as a bankrupt." "Is this all?" said she. "Why, bless me, my dear Mr. W., I can supply you with that sum without going out of the house." Not waiting to hear the question he was prepared to ask, she tripped upstairs, and in a few minutes returned with twelve thousand dollars in change and small bills in her apron, which she had saved within a few years from her daily allowance of market money, of which her husband had been very liberal.

All who heard the recital of this circumstance by the friends of Mrs. W. were highly delighted with it, save one sharp-nosed, slab-sided Yankee, who observed that she must have "tarnal strong apron strings."

1842—*Saturday Courier*

AN OLD GUN

Zadock Thompson, Esq., of Halifax, Plymouth County, Massachusetts, has now, or lately had, in his possession an old gun, which has descended to him from his ancestors, who came from Plymouth, in the third embarkation from England, in the month of May, 1622. The gun was brought to this country at that time. It is of the following description: The whole length of the stock and barrel, seven feet, four and a half inches; the length of the barrel, six feet, one inch and a half; the size of the caliber will carry twelve balls to the pound; the length of the face of the lock, ten inches; the whole weight of the gun, twenty pounds and twelve ounces. At the commencement of Phillip's war, the Indians became so morose, the people, in the month of June, fled for the safety of the fort, which was built near what was called the Four Corners, in Middleboro'. The Indians would daily appear on the south-easterly side of the river, and ascend what is called the "hand rock," because there was the impression of a man's hand indented on it. There they would be in fair sight of the fort. Here, according to an antiquarian author, the Indians would show themselves to the people in the fort, and make their insulting gestures. The people became tired of daily insults. Lieutenant Thompson, the commander in chief, ordered Isaac Howland, a distinguished marksman, to take his gun and shoot the Indian while he was insulting them. This he did, and gave the Indian a mortal wound. Filled with revenge for their wounded companion, the Indians took to the woods, running down the hill to the mill just below the fort, where the miller was at work; he discovered them, and seized his coat and fled. Placing his coat and hat on the end of a stock, as he ran through the brush to the fort, and holding his coat over his head, the coat was perforated by several balls. The Indians dragged their wounded companion two miles and three-quarters to the deserted house of William Nelson, on the farm now occupied by Major Thomas Bennett. The Indian died that night and was buried with the accustomed ceremonies, and the house was burnt. In the year 1821, nearly one hundred and fifty years after the Indian had been buried, Major Bennett, in plowing the land, disinterred some of his bones, a pipe, a stone jug, and a knife, all much decayed by the slow but all-destroying hand of time. Major B., a few years since, measured the distance from the fort to the rock where the Indian was, and made the astonishing distance of 155 rods—nearly half a mile.

1844—*Bar Gazette*

A STUFFED CAT

An old chiffonnier (or ragpicker) died in Paris in a state of abject poverty. His only relation was a niece, who lived as a servant with a greengrocer. The girl always assisted her uncle as far as her means would permit. When she learned of her uncle's death, which took place suddenly, she was on the point of marriage with a journeyman baker, to whom she had been long attached. The nuptial day was fixed, but Susan had not yet bought her wedding clothes. She hastened to tell her lover that the wedding must be deferred—she wanted the money for her bridal suit to lay her uncle decently in the grave. Her mistress ridiculed the idea, and exhorted her to leave him to be buried by charity. Susan refused. The consequence was a quarrel, by which the young woman lost her place and her lover, who sided with her mistress. She hastened to the miserable garret where her uncle had expired, and, by the the sacrifice not only of her wedding attire, but nearly all her slender wardrobe, her pious task was fulfilled. She then sat herself down alone in her uncle's room, weeping bitterly, when the master of her faithless lover, a good-looking young man, entered.

"So, Susan, I find you have lost your place," said he. "I came to offer you one for life. Will you marry me?"

"I, sir! You are joking!"

"No, in fact, I want a wife, and I can't find a better one."

"But everybody will laugh at you for marrying a poor girl like me."

"Oh! if that is your only objection, we shall soon get over it. Come, come along; my mother is prepared to receive you."

Susan hesitated no longer; but she wished to take with her a memorial of her deceased uncle. It was a cat he had had for many years. The old man was so fond of the animal that he determined that even death should not separate them, for he had her skin stuffed, and placed it at the foot of his bed.

As Susan took down Puss, she uttered an exclamation of surprise at finding her so heavy. The lover hastened to open the animal, when out fell a goodly quantity of gold coins, which had been concealed in the body of the cat; and the money, which the old miser had starved himself to amass, became the just reward of the worthy girl and her disinterested lover.

1845

THE YOUNG IDEA OF HARPOONING

An exchange paper tells the following very good story of a young whaler in Nantucket:

"Passing through Nantucket last summer, we stopped at an out-of-the-way house for a glass of water. As we approached the half-open door, we beheld the following scene, which excited our risibility at the time to a considerable extent: An urchin, some six years old, had fastened a fork to the end of a ball of yarn which his mother was holding, which he very dexterously aimed at an old black cat, quietly dozing in a corner. Puss no sooner felt the sharp pick of the fork than she darted off in a jiffy, while the experimenter sung out in high glee, 'Pay out, Mother, pay out; there she goes, through the window!' "

1849

GOOD ADVICE TO EVERYBODY

If wisdom's ways you wisely seek,
  Five things observe with care:
Of whom you speak, to whom you speak,
  And how and when, and where.

1851

AMERICAN NEWSPAPERS

The British *Banner* pays a high compliment to the newspapers of America, when it attributes to them the enlightenment of the people. The *Banner* says: "It is agreed on all hands that the United States is the most enlightened portion of the globe; and no marvel, for public papers are cheap beyond all cheapness, and every house has its one or more weekly, and a large portion of them, daily papers." Editors cannot estimate the dignity and responsibility of their position too highly, nor can they estimate the lasting wrong that may be done by a paper which, instead of maintaining an elevated tone, ministers to low and corrupt tastes, and envious or malicious feelings.

1852

THE farmer whose pigs were so lean that it took two of them to make a shadow has been beat by another who had several so thin that they crawled out through the cracks in their pen. He finally stopped that fun by *tying knots in their tails!*

1853

⌘⌘⌘

"WHICH is the way to the next village?" asked a traveler.

"There's two roads," said the native.

"Well, which is the best?"

"Take which you will, before you get halfway, you'll wish you'd tuck t'other."

1854

THE PROBLEM OF THE STOICS

WHEN a man says, "I lie," does he lie, or does he speak the truth? If he lies, he speaks the truth; if he speaks the truth, he lies.

1865

⌘⌘⌘

A LADY was once declaring that she could not understand how gentlemen could smoke. "It certainly shortens their lives," said she.

"I don't know that," exclaimed a gentleman; "there's my father smokes every day, and he is now seventy year old."

"Well," was the reply, "if he had never smoked he might have been eighty by this time."

1865

⌘⌘⌘

SHERIDAN was once staying at the house of an elderly maiden lady in the country who wanted more of his company than he was willing to give. Proposing, one day, to take a stroll with him, he excused himself on account of the badness of the weather. Shortly afterwards she met him sneaking out alone.

"So, Mr. Sheridan," said she, "it has cleared up."

"Just a little, ma'am," said he, "enough for one, but not enough for two."

1872

⌘⌘⌘

"The sound of a dinner horn," said Josh Billings, "travels half a mile in a second; while an invitation to get up in the morning, I have known to be three-quarters of an hour going two pairs of stairs, and then not have strength enough left to be heard."

1875

HOW TO BUY TENDER GEESE

It was Platt Evans of Cincinnati who taught his friends how to buy tender geese. One morning he saw a lot, and inquired of the farmer how many there were.

"About a dozen," was the reply.

"W-w-well," said Platt, "I k-k-keep a b-b-boardinghouse, and my b-b-boarders are the darndest e-eaters you ever s-s-saw. P-p-pick out n-n-nine of the t-t-toughest you've g-g-got."

The farmer complied, and laid aside the other three tender ones.

Platt picked them up carefully, and putting them in his basket, said, "I b-b-believe I'll t-t-take these three."

1876

⌘⌘⌘

A windy orator in the legislature, after a lengthy effort, stopped for a drink of water. "I rise," said Bloss, "to a point of order." Everybody stared, wondering what the point of order was.

"What is it?" asked the speaker.

"I think, sir," said Bloss, "it is out of order for a windmill to go by water!"

1877

⌘⌘⌘

A QUAINT old gentleman had a man at work in his garden who was quite poky.

"Jones," said he, "did you ever see a snail?"

"Certainly," said Jones.

"Then," said the old boy, "you must have met him, for you never could overtake him."

1877

MODERATION IN DIET

IF YOU wish for anything like happiness in the fifth act of life, eat and drink about one half what you could eat and drink. Did I ever tell you my calculation about eating and drinking? Having ascertained the weight of what I could live upon, so as to preserve health and strength, and what I did live upon, I found that, between ten and seventy years of age, I had eaten and drunk forty-four horse wagonloads of meat and drink more than would have preserved me in life and health! The value of this mass of nourishment I considered to be seven thousand pounds sterling.

1882

⌘⌘⌘

A POLITICIAN making a stump speech in the country said: "My friends, I am proud to see around me tonight the hardy yeomanry of the land, for I love the agricultural interests. And well I may love them, fellow citizens, for I was born a farmer. The happiest days of my youth were spent in the peaceful avocations of a son of the soil. If I may be allowed to use a figurative expression, my good friends, I may say I was raised between two rows of corn."

"Gosh! a punkin!" shouted a rude boy, just in front of the speaker.

1886

⌘⌘⌘

INVALID (*just arrived*): Is this a restful place, boatman?
BOATMAN: It used to be sir, afore folks came 'ere to rest.

1900—*Philadelphia Ledger*

⌘⌘⌘

RESORTS are where people go for a change and a rest and where the waiters get all the change and the landlord gets the rest.

1900

⌘⌘⌘

"WHY, Uncle 'Rastus, you don't expect to loaf all the time, do you?"

"Oh no, not all de time; get to sleep some o' de time."

1903

AT DADDY DAN'S

I heard the wind this morning when the brahma rooster crew;
It whistled at the window with a sigh and soft "Wher-ew-w-w!"
It whistled till it woke me, and it seemed to me to say,
"Oh, Daddy Dan, get up, my man! The folks are on the way!"

A golden wedding for Daddy Dan!
Yes, gold in the life of a common man.
Gold fresh-coined from the Bank of Bliss,
With the pat of a hand or a smile or kiss
Making their mint marks day by day;
And somehow the years have slipped away,

While wife and I have bought success
With the coin of the realm of happiness.
Is it legal tender for pomp and pride?
No, but it's gold full-weight and tried.
And all that an honest life can hold
Can be purchased, friends, by that kind of gold.

Whatever our fortunes at Daddy Dan's,
Joyful triumphs or shattered plans,
Plenty of poverty, smiles or tears,
We have trudged together adown the years!
And if two good comrades, hand in hand,
Grope through the shadows and safely stand
In the light at last, yes, somehow we
Find matters about as they ought to be.
We'll strike the average, eh, good wife?
After all, 'tis a worth-while life!

Come. Stand here at the window, Mother! Rest a little while.
It's time the boys were coming. Why, that's a most girlish smile!
Let me put my arm about you in our good, old, loving way.
Hold up your face! Thank God's good grace for our golden wedding day.

1914—*Holman Day*

⌘⌘⌘

Put down your age, multiply it by 2, add 5, multiply by 50, add the change in your pocket, subtract the number of days in the year (365), add 116 for good measure.

Now the two left-hand figures should show your age and the two right-hand figures the amount of change in your pocket.

1937

When a man is rebellious, he is red; when afraid, yellow; when "straight," white; when loyal, true blue; when inexperienced, green; and when uninteresting, colorless.

1945

GOOD SENSE, YANKEE FASHION

The city fellow was discussing the general wild state of spending and nobody paying with a resident of a small Cape Cod town. The old man listened, agreed, and then opined, "Nossir, I don't hold with all these new ideas. I've allus made it a point to never wash more'n I can hang out!"

1946

BOTH GOOD MEN

Joel Stevens and Deacon Epharium Tenney were the backbone of their little New England town. But they didn't always get along. The deacon was hot-tempered, known to be a sharp trader, and inclined to stretch the truth. Joel wasn't one to get "haired up" over anything.

At one selectmen's meeting an argument came up and Epharium made a statement grossly unfair and untrue, which Joel convincingly refuted. Epharium, instead of recognizing that anyone could be right except himself, demanded, "Joel, do you mean to call me a liar?" To which Joel replied in his slow drawl, "No, Deacon, I don't. But ain't ye?"

1946

SO THE ROOF FELL THROUGH

It was just after a terrific downpour and we were driving down a lonely road "north of Boston," when we came upon an old fellow surveying the ruins of his home. We asked him what had happened. He explained that the roof had fallen in. We could see that, but why?

"Well," was the answer, "that roof has leaked so long, she's just rotted through."

Why in the world hadn't he fixed it long ago?

"It just seemed I couldn't get at it. When it was fair, there warn't no need of it, and when it rained it was too derned wet."

1947

MR. LINCOLN SAID IT

When Mr. Lincoln was a young lawyer practicing in the courts of Illinois, he was once engaged in a case in which the lawyer on the other side made a speech to the jury full of wild statements.

Lincoln opened his reply by saying, "My friend who has just spoken to you would be all right if it weren't for one thing, and I don't know that you ought to blame him for that, for he can't help it. What I refer to is his reckless disregard for the truth. You have seen instances of this in his speech to you. Now the reason of this lies in the constitution of his mind. The moment he begins to talk all his mental operations cease, and he is not responsible. He is, in fact, much like a little steamboat that I saw on the Sangamon River when I was engaged in boating there. This little steamer had a five-foot boiler and a seven-foot stop whistle, and every time it whistled the engine stopped."

1947

NEW ENGLAND WEATHER

In a long-time-since-famous address at a dinner of the New England Society of New York, someone told of the visitor to New England who figured out that conditions for the next day would be "something about like this: probably northeast to southwest winds, varying to the southward and westward and eastward and points, between high and low temperatures, swapping around from place to place; probable areas of rain, snow, hail, and drought, succeeded or preceded by earthquakes, with thunder and lightning. . . . You fix up for the drought; you leave your umbrella in the house and sally out and two to one you get drowned."

1948

THE RULE

A MAN who had climbed up a chestnut tree had by carelessness missed his hold of one of the boughs, and fell to the ground with such violence as to break one of his ribs. A neighbor coming to his assistance remarked to him dryly that "had he followed the rule in such cases, he would have avoided this accident."

"What rule do you mean?" asked the other.

"This," replied the philosopher, "never to come down a place faster than you can go up."

1950

HOW LONG, O LORD?

A YOUNG businessman, a deacon in his local church, was going to New York on business, and while there was to purchase a new sign to be hung in front of the church.

He copied the motto and dimensions, but when he got to New York discovered he had left the paper behind. Whereupon he wired his wife: "Send motto and dimensions."

An hour later a message came over the wire and the new lady clerk, who just came from lunch and who knew nothing of the previous message, read it and fainted.

The message said: "Unto us a child is born. 6 feet long and 2 feet wide."

1951

BELIEVE in signs?

There's the sign that read: "Ladies Ready to Wear Clothes." Below it someone had written: "It's about time." and the sign over the little Japanese dressmaking store in Honolulu: "Ladies Have Fits Upstairs."

A large New England hennery proudly proclaims: "All Our Hens Lay Fresh Eggs." And on a real estate development this arresting sign: "If You Lived Here, You'd Be Home Now." Outside a riding academy: "The Best Thing for the Inside of a Man is the Outside of a Horse."

1952

TOO LATE

A MAN boarded the train in New York late one evening and said to the Pullman porter, as he prepared to retire, "I have an important engagement in Syracuse in the morning and must get off there. I am a very hard man to awaken but I am going to give you this five-dollar bill. You see that I get off the train in Syracuse."

Some time later the man awakened and discovered that the sun was shining. He called the porter and asked, "Where are we now?"

The porter replied, "We'll be getting into Buffalo in a short time."

The traveler burst out in an angry protest to the porter, using words that do not ordinarily appear in print.

The Pullman conductor overheard the conversation and called the porter. He said, "You are expected to be courteous to people on the train, but you don't have to stand for conversation of that kind."

The porter replied, "If you think that is bad, you should have heard the man I put off in Syracuse."

1954

WISHED HE HAD

I HAD stopped my old car before Dick's house and blown the horn. We were going fishing. Dick was our local Rip Van Winkle, a dear fellow who was always going out the back of the house when there was work to be done in front. But now he came out the front door—in a hurry—with his wife right behind him, shrilling her opinions of "good-for-nothing-go-fishing bums," and I guess that included me as well as Dick.

When we pulled away, leaving the tempest behind, Dick got out his pipe, packed it slowly, and sighed.

"You know," he said, "when I met Gertie nigh onto thirty years ago, she was so derned sweet and purty, I could have up and et her."

He paused to light his pipe, then added, "And now, by gosh, I wished I'd done it."

1955

REDHEADED SCHOOLTEACHER

THE blizzard was raging. It was really hypering down. The young traveling salesman's car finally just couldn't get through the next snowdrift and stuck. But he could see in the whirling whiteness a faint light ahead. It was a farmhouse, the friendliest he had ever seen. With numbed hands he beat on the door.

After a spell it opened, and there was the farmer, lamp in hand, nightshirt flapping, shanks a-shivering. "Come in, Bub," he said. And the salesman gratefully accepted, saying that he was storm-bound and just had to have some kind of shelter.

The farmer ruminated. "We got the house pretty nigh filled with all you fellers stuck in the snow, but, come to think of it, you could share the front-parlor sofa with the redheaded school-teacher."

Despite his weariness and chill, the young fellow flushed to the roots of his hair. "I'd have you know, sir," he managed with great dignity, "that I am a gentleman."

"Why, sure," said the farmer, "so's the redheaded schoolteacher."

1955—*B. M. Rice*

THE GOOD SCRATCH

A FRIEND of mine, a well-known minister, was having his yearly physical examination. All seemed well until the doctor noticed a small eczema-like patch below the minister's right hip. "Well," he said brightly, "we can give you a little salve for that and it will disappear in no time."

"No, you don't," said my friend. "I've been working on that place for a long time and I've got it to be a real good itch. It just happens that when I am up there in the pulpit it seems as though I always had to be scratching—my nose, the back of my neck, the top of my head. As my wife said, I always had to go after some place that everyone could see. Now all I've got to do is scratch away down here at this itch where *no one* can see. Don't meddle with it."

1956

6.

USEFUL AND ENTERTAINING MATTER

IN EACH edition of *The Old Farmer's Almanac* one finds several special features. Those presented here were chosen either because they seemed amusing or because they suggested the wide range of general subjects which *Almanac* readers have found among its pages.

FROZEN DEATH

THE EVENTS described herewith took place within twenty miles of Montpelier, Vermont. They were first found recorded in a local diary which the author verified with an old man who vouched for their truth—and said his father was among those operated on. The practice is not commonly carried on today.

"January 7. I went on the mountain today and witnessed what to me was a horrible sight. It seems that the dwellers there who are unable either from age or other reasons to contribute to the support of their families are disposed of in the winter months.

"I will describe what I saw. Six persons, four men and two women, one man a cripple about thirty years old, the other five past the age of usefulness, lay on the earthy floor of the cabin drugged into insensibility, while members of the families were gathered about them in apparent indifference. In a short time the unconscious bodies were inspected by one man who said: 'They are ready.'

"They were stripped of all their clothing except a single garment. The bodies were carried outside and laid on logs exposed to the bitter-cold mountain air, the operation having been delayed several days for suitable weather.

"Soon the noses, ears, and fingers began to turn white, then the limbs and faces assumed a tallowy look. I could stand the cold no longer and went inside, where I found the friends in cheerful conversation. In about an hour I went out and looked at the bodies. They were fast freezing.

"Again I went inside where the men were smoking their clay pipes but silence had fallen on them. Perhaps they were thinking that the time would come when they would be carried out in the same way.

"I could not shut out the sight of the freezing bodies outside, neither could I bear to be in darkness, but I piled on the wood in the cavernous fireplace and, seated on a single block, passed the dreary night, terror-stricken by the horrible sights I had witnessed.

"January 8. Day came at length but did not dissipate the terror that filled me. The frozen bodies became visibly white on the snow that lay in huge drifts about them. The women gathered about the fire and soon began to prepare breakfast. The men awoke, and affairs assumed a more cheerful aspect.

"After breakfast the men lighted their pipes and some of them took a yoke of oxen and went off into the forest, while others proceeded to nail together boards making a box about ten feet long and half as high and wide. When this was completed they placed about two feet of straw in the bottom. They then laid three frozen bodies in the straw. Then the faces and upper part of the bodies were covered with a cloth; more straw was put in the box and the other three bodies placed on top, and covered the same as the first ones, with cloth and straw.

"Boards were then firmly nailed on top to protect the bodies from being injured by carnivorous animals that made their home on these mountains. By this time the men who had gone off with the ox team returned with a huge load of spruce and hemlock boughs which they unloaded at the foot of a steep ledge, came to the house and loaded the box containing the bodies on the sled and drew it near the load of boughs.

"These were soon piled on and around the box and it was left to be covered with snow which I was told would lie in drifts twenty feet deep over this rude tomb. 'We shall want our men to plant our corn next spring,' said the wife of one of the frozen men, 'and if you want to see them resuscitated, you come here about the tenth of next May.'

"With this agreement I left the mountaineers, living and frozen, to their fate and returned to my home in Boston where it was weeks before I was fairly myself."

Turning the leaves of the diary, I came to the following entry:

"May 10. I arrived here at 10 A.M. after riding about four hours over muddy, unsettled roads. The weather here is warm and pleasant, most of the snow is gone except where there are drifts in the fence corners and hollows. But nature is not yet dressed in green.

"I found the same parties here I left last January. They were ready to disinter the bodies, but I had no expectations of finding life there. A feeling that I could not resist, however, impelled me to come and see.

"We repaired at once to the well-remembered spot at the ledge. The snow had melted from the top of the brush, but still lay deep around the bottom of the pile. The men commenced work at once, some shoveling, and others tearing away the brush. Soon the box was visible. The cover was taken off, the layers of straw removed and the bodies, frozen and apparently lifeless, lifted out and laid on the snow.

"Large troughs made out of hemlock logs were placed nearby, filled with tepid water, into which the bodies were placed separately with the head slightly raised. Boiling water was then poured into the trough from kettles hung on poles nearby until the water was as hot as I could hold my hand in. Hemlock boughs had been put in the boiling water in such quantities that they had given the water the color of wine.

"After lying in the bath about an hour, color began to return to the bodies, when all hands began rubbing and chafing them. This continued about an hour when a slight twitching of the muscles, followed by audible gasps, showed that vitality was returning.

"Spirits were then given in small quantities and allowed to trickle down their throats. Soon they could swallow and more was given them when their eyes opened. They began to talk, and finally sat up in their bathtubs.

"They were taken out and assisted to the house where after a hearty meal they seemed as well as ever and in no wise injured, but rather refreshed by their long sleep of four months."

1942—*Robert Wilson*

PROGRESS OF A HUNDRED YEARS

THIS NUMBER of *The Old Farmer's Almanac* completes its record of one hundred years. During this century great changes have taken place, many wonderful discoveries and inventions have been made.

At the time of the first census, in 1790, the population of the United States was determined to be 3,172,006 whites and 757,208 blacks. The census of 1890 gives a total population of 62,622,250, of which the colored people in the South with Kansas and Missouri are 6,996,166.

At the time of the first issue of this *Almanac,* the national domain was bounded on the west by the Mississippi, and comprised 827,844 square miles; today, its western limit is the Pacific, and, exclusive of the vast region of Alaska, it comprises 3,025,600 square miles.

In 1790, there were but six cities or towns which contained 8,000 or more inhabitants: Philadelphia, 42,520; New York, 33,131; Boston, 18,038; Charleston, 16,359; Baltimore, 13,503; and Salem (in round numbers), 8,000—an aggregate of 131,472. In 1890, there were 443 cities and towns, with a population of 8,000 or more, or an aggregate urban population of 18,235,670.

In 1790, the number of post offices in the United States was 75, the aggregate length of the post roads 1,875 miles, and the postal revenue $37,935. In 1890, the number of post offices was 62,401, the length of the post routes (in round numbers) 428,000, and the postal revenue nearly $61,000,000.

The second year of the *Almanac* (1794) was marked by the invention of so important a labor-saving machine that it should not be overpassed—the cotton gin, which removes the seeds from the fiber.

A century ago there were no railroads, no steamboats, no electric telegraphs. Articles of domestic use which have now become necessities were unknown: there were no friction matches, no India-rubber shoes or overcoats, no waterproof clothing, no gaslight, no electric light, no coal oil or kerosene.

Photography, lithography, chromo-lithography, photo-lithography, stereotyping, electrotyping, and electroplating have all come into use during the last hundred years. The power press, or printing machine, driven by steam, now enables a single newspaper establishment to print hundreds of thousands of copies for daily circulation.

The threshing machine has superseded the flail; the mowing machine has, to a great extent, taken the place of the scythe; the reaping machine, of the sickle and the cradle; the horse rake, of the hand rake; the power loom, of the handloom, common in farmhouses a century ago. The sewing machine has cheapened wearing apparel. The Bessemer process has made steel attainable at a cheap rate. Our iron mines, mainly unworked a hundred years ago, now give an annual production of more than 14,000,000 tons of ore. Our coal mines, then practically unknown, now have an output of more than 130,000,000 tons each year.

Huge iron steamers have supplanted sailing vessels; and powerful steamships of war, clad with steel plates, the old wooden frigates. We span wide rivers by iron and wire bridges; we bore tunnels for miles through mountains of rock.

Some of the most wonderful discoveries are but of yesterday: the use of electric power and electric lighting; the telephone, which instantaneously reproduces the exact tones of the human voice spoken hundreds of miles away; and the phonograph, by which the speech and music of today may be preserved to future generations.

Even in the briefest sketch we must not omit to mention the use of anesthetics, that inestimable boon to humanity, by which surgical operations are made painless.

We have destroyed slavery; we have established asylums for the care of the blind, the deaf and dumb, the idiotic and the insane; our common schools and higher institutions of learning bring the means of a good education within the reach of all the children of the Republic.

All these are but a part of the achievements which add so immeasurably to our power and comfort—all made since the birth of *The Old Farmer's Almanac.*

1893

COLONIAL FARMERS

As THE FIRST CENTURY of the history of our country is so soon to draw to a close, we naturally recur to the early days of the fathers by whose struggles and sacrifices, by whose heroic endurance and triumphs, was founded a free government, which we claim to be the highest type of civil polity which the world has ever seen.

Few of us, indeed, of the present generation can realize the hardships and privations which the early farmers had to endure. They were strangers to the climate as well as to the country. They could have had no experience of pioneer life. They knew little or nothing of the natural productions of the soil at the time of their arrival. All these they had first to learn the value of, and then to learn how to grow them, to meet their pressing necessities.

One of the chief obstacles they had to encounter, to add to the hardship of their lot in the cultivation of the soil, was the difficulty of procuring suitable implements. A few, no doubt, were brought with them; but it is not likely that all could procure them in this way; while the only metal they had was made of bog ore, and that was so brittle as to break easily, and put a stop to a day's work. Most of their tools were made of wood, rude enough in construction, heavy of necessity, and little fitted for the purposes for which they were made. The process of casting steel, it is to be borne in mind, was not discovered till the middle of the last century, and then it was kept a secret in Sheffield, England, for several years; nor were there any means of casting iron even, in this country, for many years after the settlement.

The few rude farming tools the colonists had were for the most part of home manufacture, or made by the neighboring blacksmith as a part of his multifarious business, there being little idea of the division of labor, and no machinery by which any particular implement could be exactly duplicated. Under these circumstances, it is wonderful that they got on so well as they did.

We are to consider, moreover, that no attention was paid to the culture of the grasses for the winter feeding of stock, even in England, in the early part of the seventeenth century, and but slight indeed till far along in the eighteenth, while but very few of the roots now cultivated and used as food for stock had been introduced there. The introduction of red clover into England did not take place till 1633; that of yellow clover, not till 1659; that of white clover, not till 1700.

Of the natural grasses now well known, timothy is supposed to have been first brought into cultivation in this country, and there is no evidence that it was ever cultivated in England till the year 1760, while the culture of orchard grass was first introduced there from Virginia in 1764. In fact, there is no evidence of any systematic or artificial cultivation of the grasses in the mother country till the introduction of perennial rye grass in 1677, and no other variety of grass seed appears to have been sown there for many years. The *Edinburgh Quarterly Journal of Agriculture*, the highest authority in such matters, says the practice of sowing grass seed was never known in Scotland previous to the year 1792. Such being the case in a climate so severe as that of Scotland, it is not at all surprising that the custom of seeding down land to grass in this country dates back only little more than a hundred years. If anyone can imagine the whole system of grass culture to be stricken out of existence, and every farmer compelled to rely upon the natural production of our swamps and the salt marshes along the seashore for the support of his stock, he can form some idea of the position in which the early colonial farmer was placed.

To this is to be added that no systematic improvement in stock was undertaken, in England, till long after the settlement of this country. The cattle of those days were poor of their kind, as compared with the stock of the present day; while it is not probable that the colonists took any pains to procure even the best specimens then known. The difference in animals, what may be called the best points, were nowhere studied, appreciated, or understood, two centuries ago. The cattle of the settlers, like their owners, had to browse for themselves, and death from starvation and exposure was by no means uncommon. Farming, therefore, in the early days, was a hard struggle for existence.

1875

A Few RECEIPTS in COOKERY from

THE COMPLETE WOMAN COOK

Inserted to oblige some particular female friends

TO ROAST A PIECE OF BEEF

If it be a sirloin or chump, butter a piece of writing paper and fasten on the back part of your meat with small skewers, and put it down to a soaking fire at a proper distance. As soon as your meat is warm, dust on some fine flour and baste it with butter; then sprinkle some salt, and at times baste it with what comes from it. About a quarter of an hour before you take it up, remove the paper, dust on a little flour, and baste it with a piece of butter, that it may go to the table with a good froth. Garnish your dish with scraped horseradish, and serve it up with potatoes, onion sauce, &c.

TO MAKE ONION SAUCE

Boil some large onions in a good deal of water till they are very tender; put them into a colander, and when drained, pass them through it with a spoon; put them into a clean saucepan with a good piece of butter, a little salt, and a gill of sweet cream; stir them over the fire till they are of a good thickness.

TO ROAST A TURKEY, GOOSE, DUCK, FOWL, ETC.

When you roast a turkey, goose, fowl, or chicken, singe them clean with white paper. Put them down to a good fire; baste them with butter, and dust on some flour. As to time, a large turkey will take an hour and twenty minutes; a middling one, a full hour; a full-grown goose, if young, an hour; a large fowl, three-quarters of an hour; a middling one, half an hour; and a small chicken, twenty minutes; but this depends entirely on the goodness of your fire.

When your fowls are thoroughly plump, and the steam draws from the breast to the fire, you may be sure that they are very near done. Then baste them with butter, dust in a very little flour, and as soon as they have a good froth, serve them up.

Geese and ducks are commonly seasoned with onions, sage, and a little pepper and salt. A turkey is generally stuffed in the craw with forced meat or the following stuffing: Take a pound of veal or beef fresh, as much grated bread, half a pound of suet, cut and beat very small, a little parsley, with a small matter of thyme or savory, two cloves, half a nutmeg, grated, a teaspoon of shredded lemon peel, a little pepper and salt, and the yolks of two eggs. Sauces in general.

TO ROAST PORK

Pork requires more doing than any other meat; and it is best to sprinkle it with a little salt the night before you use it (except on the rind, which must never be salted) and hang it up; by that means it will take off the faint, sickly taste.

When you roast a chine of pork, put it down to a good fire and at a proper distance, that it may be well soaked.

A sparerib is to be roasted with a fire that is not too strong, but clear; when you put it down, dust on some flour, and baste it with butter. A quarter of an hour before you take it up, shred some sage small; baste your pork, stew on your sage, dust on a little flour, and sprinkle a little salt before you take it up.

1800

THE SHAKER FAVORITE COOKING RECEIPTS

Ann Lee, founder of the Shakers in the United States, settled near Albany, New York, shortly before 1782. By 1882, there were about eighteen "families" of Shakers of about one hundred each. Celibates, they did not marry; and vowed to perform some sort of honest labor each day, and to owe no man. Extremely cleanly, everyone was struck with the excellence of what they produced.

CLAM CHOWDER

Put in a pot a layer of sliced pork, chopped potatoes, chopped clams, salt, pepper and lumps of butter, and broken crackers soaked in milk, cover with the clam juice and water, stew slowly for three hours, thicken with a little flour. It may be seasoned with spices if preferred.

BOILED LEG OF LAMB

Time: one hour and a quarter after the water simmers. Select a fine fresh leg of lamb, weighing about five pounds; soak it in warm water for rather more than two hours, then wrap it in a cloth and boil it slowly for an hour and a quarter. When done, dish it up and garnish with a border of carrots, turnips, or cauliflower around it. Wind a cut paper around the shank bone, and serve it with plain parsley, and butter sauce poured over it.

CABBAGE SALAD

One small head of cabbage, one-half bunch of celery, one-quarter cup of vinegar, one tablespoonful of mustard, one egg well beaten, one tablespoonful of sugar, pepper and salt. Take a little of the vinegar to wet the mustard, put the rest over the fire; when boiling, stir in the ingredients and cook until it becomes thick; pour it over the cabbage while hot, and mix it well. When cold, it is ready for the table. The same sauce, when cold, will do for lettuce.

YANKEE PLUM PUDDING

Take a tin pudding boiler that shuts all over tight with a cover. Butter it well. Put at the bottom some stoned raisins, and then a layer of baker's bread cut in slices, with a little butter or suet, alternately, until you nearly fill the tin. Take milk enough to fill your boiler (as they vary in size), and to every quart add three or four eggs, some nutmeg and salt, and sweeten with half sugar and half molasses. Drop it into boiling water, and let it boil three or four hours, and it can be eaten with a comparatively clear conscience.

TOMATO SOUP

Three pounds of beef, one quart canned tomatoes, one gallon water. Let the meat and water boil for two hours, or until the liquid is reduced to a little more than two quarts. Then stir in the tomatoes, and stew all slowly for three-quarters of an hour longer. Season to taste, strain and serve.

DELIGHTFUL PUDDING

Butter a dish, sprinkle the bottom with finely minced candied peel, and a very little shredded suet, then a thin layer of light bread, and so on until the dish is full. For a pint dish make a liquid custard of one egg and one pint of milk, sweeten, pour over the pudding, and bake as slowly as possible for two hours.

CORN OYSTERS

One pint grated green corn, one cup flour, one spoonful of salt, one teaspoonful of pepper, one egg. Drop by the spoonful in hot lard, and fry.

1942

FARM PROVERBS

Let everyone mind his own business, and the cows will be well tended.

To wash an ass's head is but loss of time and soap.

Two sparrows on the same ear of corn are not long friends.

A muffled cat never caught a mouse.

The sheep on the mountain is higher than the bull on the plain.

Muddy water won't do for a mirror.

The sun passes over filth and is not defiled.

He who has a straw tail is always afraid of its catching fire.

One eye of the master sees more than four eyes of his servants.

Many a good cow has a bad calf.

Mules make a great fuss about their ancestors having been horses.

Of what use is it for a cow to give plenty of milk if she upsets the pail?

Eagles don't breed doves.

Better on the heath with an old cart than at sea in a new ship.

The master's eye and foot are the best manure for the field.

Roses fall, but the thorns remain.

Who undertakes too much succeeds but little.

Painted flowers have no odor.

There's no making a donkey drink against his will.

Everything has an end, except a sausage, which has two.

Bread is better than the song of birds.

1881

RAILROADS TO THE PACIFIC

When this article meets the eye of our readers the Pacific Railroad will have become an old story, and to cross the continent of America in seven days will be a thing so common as to be little thought of. Yet the opening of this road in May, 1869, was an event of great moment. Other roads will follow, and the great interior of the continent, with its vast mineral and agricultural resources, will be thrown open to the thronging hosts of Europe, Asia, and America, and the wilderness will become a garden. Our public lands still unsold are of vast extent. The building of these roads will bring millions of acres of them into the market, stimulating immigration from Europe, and thus building up great states, which will help pay interest and principal of the public debt.

Three great trunk roads are planned, and have been chartered and endowed with lands by Congress. These are the Northern, the Central, and the Southern. But one is as yet built. This, as our readers well know, is the Central road, running near the 41st parallel, and owned by two great corporations. The Union Pacific runs 1,084 miles from Omaha, on the Missouri river, to Promontory in Utah, near the Great Salt Lake; and the Central Pacific owns from there to Sacramento, 690 miles. Sacramento is on a navigable river, and communicates, both by steamers alone and by a railroad and steamers, with San Francisco. The highest point of the road is at the summit of the Black Hills, 8,240 feet above the sea, 800 miles from Omaha. About 150 miles farther, at Bridger's Pass, the road goes through the Rocky Mountains, 7,534 feet above the sea. In California it crosses the Sierra Nevada at the height of 7,042 feet, 105 miles this side of Sacramento. The distance by this route from Boston to San Francisco is as follows: Boston to Chicago, 1,017 miles; Chicago to Omaha, 493 miles; Omaha to San Francisco, 1,900 miles; in all, 3,410 miles—which is passed over in 7⅓ days.

Some four hundred miles north of the Central road, near the 46th parallel, is to run the Northern road, chartered by Congress in 1864. This road will strike across from Lake Superior to Puget Sound, Washington Territory, with a branch to Portland, in Oregon. When built, it will give access to upper Minnesota, Dakota, Montana, Idaho, Washington, and Oregon, thus opening a great mining and agricultural region to the settler.

1870

PREVENTING DOGS FROM KILLING SHEEP

If an inveterate antipathy to the sight of a sheep can be produced in a dog, our harmless flocks would certainly be at all times safe from their depredations. This aversion can certainly be produced in the following manner. When the dog is about six or eight months old, tie him to one of the strongest sheep in the flock, leaving a space of about five or six feet between them; when let loose, the sheep will run and drag and choke the dog until his strength is exhausted; it will then turn upon him and butt him severely. Take care to have the dog well flogged with a switch while the sheep is dragging him. If he is a dog of high temper and spirit, and is not sufficiently humbled by the first lesson, give him a second, tied to a fresh sheep. It sometimes happens that he will snap at his antagonist; this may be remedied by muzzling him, or tying a string over or around his mouth above his long teeth. Take care to have the whole flock of sheep in a small enclosure with the coupled one and the dog; it often happens that several in the flock will join in inflicting heavy blows upon him. By this time the dog has taken such an aversion to the company and presence of sheep that he never forgets or outgrows it.

The above remedy I have never known to fail in a single instance, and am encouraged to recommend it by long experience, having raised dogs of different descriptions—hounds, spaniels, curs, and pointers—at different times; all of which, without a single exception, that I now recollect, have undergone the above discipline, and not one instance has occurred when there was the smallest disposition shown for mischief. I at this time have a very high-spirited pointer, as much so as can be, which when he unluckily falls in with sheep, while hunting in the field, always cowers, and sneaks off another way.

1826—*American Farmer*

TOO GOOD NOT TO TELL

THREE AMERICANS had gone to Europe together in 1883: Dr. McVicar of Philadelphia, Phillips Brooks, and Mr. Richardson, the builder of Boston's Trinity Church. Richardson stood 6 feet 2 inches in his stockings; Dr. McVicar measured 6 feet 4 inches; and Brooks exceeded 6 feet in height. Richardson was sensitive about his length, and suggested in order to avoid comment the three tall men avoid being seen together. Arriving in England, they went direct to Leeds, where they learned that a lecturer would address the working classes on "America and Americans." Anxious to hear what Englishmen thought of the Great Republic, they went to the hall. They entered separately, and took seats apart. The lecturer, after some uninteresting remarks, said that Americans were, as a rule, short, and seldom if ever rose to the height of five feet ten inches. He did not know to what cause he could attribute this fact, but he wished he could present examples to the audience.

Phillips Brooks rose to his feet and said: "I am an American, and, as you see, about six feet in height, and sincerely hope that if there is any other representative of my country present he will rise."

After a moment's interval Mr. Richardson rose and said: "I am from America, in which country my height—six feet two—is the subject of no remark. If there be any other American here, I hope that he will rise."

The house was in a jolly humor. Waiting until the excitement could abate in some degree, and the lecturer regain control over his shattered nerves, Dr. McVicar slowly drew his majestic form to its full height and exclaimed: "I am an—." But he got no further. The audience roared, and the lecturer said no more on that subject.

1902

HOW TO RECOGNIZE THE TREES IN WINTER

Leaves, flowers, and fruit are our guides to the study of trees in the summer. The leafless tree bears equally infallible tokens, which, once known, renders it impossible to mistake its identity. There are: (1) winter buds, (2) leaf scars, (3) general character of the yearling twig, (4) color and shape of pith. It is necessary only to examine branchlets from a few well-known trees at any time during the winter in order to be convinced that these characters are very apparent and always constant to the species.

Winter buds are quite conspicuous objects on the branchlets during the winter. They first appear with the developing leaves in the preceding spring, as small excrescences, just above the spot where the leaf stem joins the twig. They increase in size during the summer and attain their characteristic winter color and appearance by the time the leaves fall. They consist of a few or many papery or leathery scales that fold over and protect a group of tiny leaves and sometimes flowers also which are to develop into the branch of the coming season. One needs only to compare the large, sticky, brown buds of the horse chestnut; the very small, dry buds of the elm; the long, slender, spindle-shaped buds of the beech; the velvety, gray buds of the butternut; and the buds of the various species of maple to see how very diverse they are in appearance and how easy it is to recognize each one a second time. The buds of the common locust and the honey locust are not however to be seen, as they are concealed beneath the bark, through which they push in the warm days of late spring. Flower buds are usually rounder and stouter than those which contain only leaves.

Leaf scars are to be found below each winter bud; they mark the place whence the leaf fell and correspond in shape to the base of the leaf stem. On them are raised dots, the broken ends of woody fibers. Nature gradually prepares for the fall of the leaf, heals the tissues even while it is breaking off and makes a clean scar, whereas if a leaf is torn off violently before its time an ugly wound results. Leaf scars are as characteristic as the winter buds. Note the large, concave, depressed scars of the horse chestnut; the elevated scars of the ash, the minute scars of the elm and birch; the three-lobed scars of hickories; and the tufts of down above the leaf scars of the butternut.

Twigs of a year's growth show peculiarities in shape and size, in the color, texture, and markings of their bark, and sometimes also in taste and odor. Especially noticeable are the rough, irregular twigs of the ash, pinched in between the pairs of leaf scars; the glossy green twigs of the ash-leaved maple; the spotted twigs of birches; and the aromatic taste and odor of yellow and black birch and sassafras.

Pith, as seen by cutting across twigs of horse chestnut, sumac, alder, and oak, varies from round to star-shaped, and in color ranges from white through many shades of green, yellow, and brown; in the butternut it is in interrupted plates, looking, when cut lengthwise, like the rungs of a ladder.

There is hardly a branch of botany more full of interest than this winter study of trees. It leads one to see much beauty heretofore perhaps unnoticed; it is of special importance to the student of forestry; moreover, the characters, though varying with every species, are exceedingly simple and with few exceptions may be noted without the aid of a magnifying glass.

1902

GUIDEBOARDS ON COUNTRY ROADS

EVERY MAN who has had occasion to travel over our country roads has been amazed at the culpable neglect of very many towns to comply with the law in regard to the erection and maintenance of proper guideboards. The selectmen of many a town are open to indictment and fine for neglect and especially for cruelty to animals, for in a vast number of cases, to our certain knowledge and experience, strangers and travelers have been led miles out of their way either from the total want of guideboards where they ought to have been or from guideboards misplaced and pointing so as to mislead. Here is the law (Mass. Public Statutes, Chapter 53) about guideposts:

SECTION 1. Every town shall erect and maintain guideposts on the highways and other ways within the town at such places as are necessary or convenient for the direction of travelers.

SECTION 2. The selectmen or road commissioners of each town shall submit to the inhabitants, at every annual meeting, a report of all the places in which guideposts are erected and maintained within the town, and of all places at which, in their opinion, they ought to be erected and maintained. For each neglect or refusal to make such report, they shall severally forfeit the sum of ten dollars.

SECTION 3. Upon the report of the selectmen or road commissioners, the town shall determine the several places at which guideposts shall be erected and maintained, which shall be recorded in the town records. A town which neglects or refuses to determine such places and to cause a record thereof to be made *shall forfeit the sum of five dollars for every month* during which it refuses so to do.

SECTION 4. Every town which neglects or refuses to erect and maintain such guideposts, or some suitable substitutes therefor, shall forfeit annually the sum of five dollars for every guidepost which it so neglects or refuses to maintain.

It is very apparent that there is law enough, and it would be a very easy matter to convict the selectmen of many towns for willful and careless neglect, and to subject such towns to very heavy penalties. No doubt they ought to be indicted, and it is perhaps the duty of individuals who suffer loss of time and inconvenience to enter complaints; but travelers are long suffering and patient, and so it clearly becomes the duty of the Society for the Prevention of Cruelty to Animals to see that the selectmen of every town comply with the law. If there is any case of cruelty to animals concerning which there can be no question, it is to mislead or to fail to guide a traveler and to compel his horse to go five or ten miles out of his way at the end, perhaps, of a long journey on a hot summer's day. This is not a supposed case. We could mention numerous instances, and it is a common complaint.

1887

THE FIRST SUNDAY

AS WOULD BE EXPECTED, the origin of Sunday as an official day of rest has roots that go far into the past. It seems to be the Babylonians who divided the week into days and named them after the planets. The Jews while in captivity in Babylon very naturally took over this planetary week in connection with their own life but they gave the seventh day of this week a special religious significance, following the fourth commandment. As the Roman Caesars began to exert their sway over the then-known Mediterranean world, they naturally adopted this planetary week. But no day was as yet recognized officially as a day of rest. The only thing that approached it was that one day a month was called the Emperor's Day, when the empire made merry in honor of the head of the state. Meanwhile, a little group within the empire was observing the day after the Jewish Sabbath in a special way. They were known as Christians, and because of Christ's resurrection on that day, it became a day hallowed with sacred associations. To them it was the Lord's Day. It was therefore observed as a day of worship with the eucharist (thanksgiving) as the primary rite of worship. But of course these early Christians were also in the fold of Judaism. That meant that they specially observed two days: the Jewish Sabbath, the end of the week, and the Lord's Day, the beginning of the week. As the Christians increased in numbers among the Gentiles—those who had no connection with Judaism—it was these who put more emphasis on the Lord's Day and ignored the Jewish Sabbath.

Although the pagans very early began a systematic persecution of the Christians, they did observe how these Christians regarded their Lord's Day as one of joy and festive spirit: a weekly holiday, whereas the non-Christians in the empire had only the Emperor's Day to which to look forward.

When Constantine became emperor, he effected an immense change. He was a Christian—the first Roman emperor who was Christian. In 316 A.D., he proclaimed his famous Edict of Milan. By this, persecutions of the Christians were not only banned (they were given the civil rights of any citizens of the empire) but Christianity became the official religion of the empire. Five years later (321 A.D.), he set aside the Lord's Day or Sunday as a feast and forbade certain labors and duties on that day.

1939—*Rev. Richard R. Beasley*

ROOTS AT SECONDHAND

One of the greatest drawbacks to our national life, with its history of constant progress and change, is that not enough people live and die in the house in which they were born. For many city dwellers, each spring means moving from one house or one apartment to another, which may be essentially no different, which has only the charm of novelty. It is usual rather than otherwise for a young married couple to begin housekeeping in an apartment, and as their fortunes progress to rent perhaps a small house, and then one somewhat larger, and eventually to build a home of their own; but even that may, if an opportunity for profit comes along, be sold.

This is unfortunate. There is no single element in the foundations of character as important as the feeling of belonging to a certain definite spot, the feeling of having your roots in the ground. This lack is perhaps necessary and inevitable in our national life; but this particular deficiency is one of the many which the state of Maine sometimes helps to fill.

There is about an old Maine farmhouse an atmosphere of permanency, and at the same time of hospitality, which teaches people who live in one for only a short period not only to feel at home there, but to feel in vague, intangible ways that they have always been at home there. All over the state this process of acquiring roots at secondhand has been going on, not only since 1929, but for thirty years.

Old houses are being reclaimed, remodeled, and made serviceable. It is true that they are usually only summer homes; but even so, they quickly lay a sort of spell upon the dwellers there, and this is a charm which is felt as much by young people as by older ones. I remember the second year we went to the shore of Penobscot Bay to spend the summer. We drove from Boston, our children with us. Our youngest son was at that time four or five years old. He had spent the previous summer in the same cottage. When, at the end of the long day's drive, we turned down the road that led to the shore, he exclaimed delightedly, triumphantly:

"Now we are home!"

1936—*Ben Ames Williams*

CAPTURE OF THE REVENUE CUTTER *CALEB CUSHING* IN PORTLAND HARBOR

ON THE MORNING OF June 26, 1863, two fishermen, Albert T. Bibber and Elbridge Titcomb, were hauling in their trawls from the dory of their fishing sloop, *Village*, about eight miles to the south of Damariscove Island, off the coast of Maine, about forty miles from Portland. While busy with their trawls, the fishermen were hailed, "Boat ahoy! Come alongside," and were taken aboard a fishing schooner called the *Archer* where they found the captain in blue frock coat and trousers, and eight roughly dressed men. They were told that they were the prize of a Confederate privateer. They thought at first this was a joke, but they soon found their mistake.

They were directed to take the vessel to Portland. That evening they anchored near Pomeroy's Rock off Fish Point in Portland Harbor. They were ordered below and fastened in, and told to make no noise. They were prisoners of the cruiser *Florida* of the Confederate navy, under command of Lieutenant C. W. Reed. Reed had been ordered by the Confederate government to proceed to the coast of New England and burn all the ships and destroy all the property he could along the shores of New England.

On the evening in question, June 26, his plan was to capture the sailing cutter, *Caleb Cushing*, and after getting out from under the forts, to return to Portland and fire such part of the city as he was able to. At 1:30 he boarded the cutter and captured her without noise or resistance, many of the crew being ashore and leaving Lieutenant Davenport on the cutter with about twenty men, who were seized by Reed and put in irons.

At daybreak the next morning, Reed liberated the captured fishermen and compelled them to pilot the vessel out by way of Hussey's Sound, where the cutter had an open seaway, and kept on out to sea as far as Green Islands. There was little air and he could make no headway.

In the meantime the cutter's capture was discovered about half-past seven in the morning from the Observatory, and the news soon spread, carrying consternation to the town. Under the lead of Captain "Jake" McLellan, Mayor, and Jedediah Jewett, Collector, both able and resolute men, prompt action was soon taken. The steamer, *Forest City*, was fitted out with guns and armament, and a detachment of men from Fort Preble, under the command of Lieutenant Merriman. The troops were under the command of Captain Andrews at Fort Preble.

The *Forest City* was a 700-ton side-wheel steamer of the Boston line. It was but a few minutes after the capture was discovered that the *Forest City*, another steamer, the *Chesapeake*, and a steam tug were put in commission, with bales of cotton to protect their sides and engines. They were manned and put in chase of the cutter.

When out beyond the Green Islands it became evident that there was some lively work to be done. Shots were exchanged between the cutter and the steamers. Soon a small boat was seen to leave the cutter, four men rowing toward the steamers. At first it was thought to be the intention of the rebels to attack the steamers and board them, but soon a white flag was seen, and the rebels were taken aboard, accompanied by their prisoners: the crew of the cutter and the fishermen who had left their boat and fishing gear. The cutter had been fired by the rebels, and was soon ablaze and sank. Lieutenant Davenport, the captain of the cutter, had refused to tell the rebels where the ammunition was. If he had told them, there might have been bloody work that day.

Captain Reed with his men were made prisoners. He is described as little more than a boy, bright-faced, alert, about twenty-three years of age. In his report to the Confederate Department he describes in a dramatic way the details of his capture and his imprisonment.

1934—*Written for* THE OLD FARMER'S ALMANAC *by Clarence Hale, Judge of the United States District Court and former President of the Maine Historical Society.*

THE FAMOUS SPECTER OF BATH, MAINE

IN 1800 AT BATH, Maine, there appeared, according to sworn testimonies, unto more than fifty men and women a particular, spectacular specter. It sang praises of the Lord, it foretold the future, it walked abroad in the day and in the night. It held sessions with guests it had invited to the cellar of one Mr. and Mrs. Blaisdel. The name of this departed spirit had been in life Miss N. Hooper, until its marriage, when it became the first Mrs. Captain George Butler.

Characteristically, its clothing was a flowing white robe, visible in the dark when nothing else was white. To many of the witnesses, in the very many times it made itself known, the first view of it would present a body of small stature, perhaps a foot or two high. It would then soon expand to the height and breadth of the Mrs. Butler it had been on earth and take on the approximate earthly physiognomy as well as deathbed voice of Mrs. Butler. The latter is best described at this late date as a hoarse croak. This specter invited handling and indeed its earthly husband testified to not only its appearance but also to the passing of his hands through its bosom without feeling anything. As proof, sufficient to at least two of its married-couple observers, of its one-time earthly residence, the specter quoted intimate family conversations known only to the participants therein. One Abraham Cummings, after twenty-six years of research, investigation, and study of the phenomena of the appearance of this specter, published a book about it in which he affirmed, by its example, the proof of immortality.*

This specter most frequently introduced itself by knocking.

"Do not be afraid," were its actual words, "I have not come to hurt you. You need not be afraid at all."

One of its earliest manifestations was in a field. There, elevated a foot or so from the ground, it walked with two people a distance of some two miles. When the news of this event spread around Bath, it caused consternation, disbelief, and criticism.

"Go," then said the specter to one of these with whom it had walked, "collect all those in the neighborhood who give the best evidence of piety and veracity. Let them hear and see: for they will tell the truth."

This man complied and gathered fifty people for an interview which lasted several hours. The most significant result of this early gathering was the specter's communication with the then Miss Blaisdel, first with the verses 2-9, Chapter 10 from Mark, later with direct advice she must marry Captain George Butler's son, and within one year, bear a child and die. Despite the extreme objections of Miss Blaisdel, her father, Captain Butler, as well as the specter's own father, the marriage, childbirth, and death apparently took place.

Once, when conversing with Mr. Blaisdel, this victim's father, and a small group of others, the former asked the specter if it knew anything about his ailing father—then two hundred miles away at York. It answered him: "Your father is in Heaven, praising God with the angels." Mr. Blaisdel learned to his dismay two weeks later the specter had been telling the truth.

**Immortality Proved . . . by the Testimony of Sense*. Printed by J. G. Torrey, Bath, 1826.

Depositions on which the foregoing is based were taken from Paul Simpson, Mrs. Sarah Simpson, Thomas Uran, Captain George Butler, Hannah Gatcomb, Paul Simpson, Jr., Sally Martin, Captain James Millar, Mrs. Mary Gordon, Mrs. Sally Wentworth, Jeremiah Bunker, Abner Blaisdel, Mary Card, Margaret Miller, Captain Paul Simson, Samuel Ingalls, James Springer, John Simson, Richard Downing, Captain Samuel Simson, Sarah Simson, Mrs. Abigail Abbott, Dorcas Abbott, Joseph Blaisdel, Captain Paul Blaisdel, David Hooper and Mrs. Joanne Hooper (the specter's earthly parents), Mrs. Eunice Scammons, Mrs. Mary Bragdon, Mrs. Dorcas Johnson.

To the last it quoted the lines of Dr. Watts:

> This is the day when Christ arose
> So early from the dead.
> Why should I keep my eyelids closed
> And waste my hours in bed?

1956

THE BIRTH OF TALLEYRAND

In the early days of 1730, a group of French fishermen—about thirty families in all—lived along the shores of Frenchman's Bay, at Piney Point (now called Lamoine Point). In the Philadelphia archives is an affidavit to this effect, made by one Captain Pote, in 1754.

Among these fisher families was an old couple who had a beautiful granddaughter. French warships frequently called at this little colony, and were hauled out onto the beach to be scraped and cleaned. It often took a stay of six weeks to complete this task. During the stay of one of these French war vessels, the captain became interested in the granddaughter of the aged couple. When the ship sailed, he promised he would return and marry the girl, but she waited in vain. A little boy was born to her. The two lived with the aged grandparents until the boy was twelve years of age.

There appeared, one day, during the boy's twelfth year, another French warship. The captain came ashore, and immediately hunted up the old couple. The girl had pined away, and died. The captain's story was that his brother was the father of the boy, and that his brother had fully intended to return, but he had died. He wanted to take the boy with him back to France. This he arranged to do through the payment of a sum of gold to the old couple. It was this little boy who was destined to be the great Talleyrand.

Talleyrand never told the story of his birth, nor did he want the facts known in France. He had the records of the church at St. Ophelia changed, when he became a man of influence in the Church. He even pointed out to the French people the house, on a certain street, in which he said he was born. It was some time after his death that his will was read—in 1871. Even his private papers were not touched. But when in that year his papers were opened, all records of his life in America and of his trip to the American shore, in 1796, were gone.

To confirm the foregoing story, I have the story from William DesIsles (in 1886) which he got from his father Louis Dupré DesIsles, in 1796. According to this story, Talleyrand appeared one day at O'Brian's in Machias. He was looking for the remains of an earlier French colony. O'Brian took him to Captain Cobb at Gouldsboro. Captain Cobb informed him of the old settlement at Piney Point, and offered to take Talleyrand across the bay to this place where there had been a settlement until 1762. Accordingly they got in Captain Cobb's sloop and sailed for Trenton Point.

Louis went to the window and looked out after Mary his wife had called his attention to a sloop crossing the bay. Louis hurried to the shore. After the sloop had landed Captain Cobb says, "How do you do, Mr. DesIsles, here is someone to talk French to you." They spoke and fell into each other's arms, kissed, and Louis Dupré invited him and Captain Cobb up to the house, but on account of the tide and the fact that they had a head wind Captain Cobb went back home. Even before they had had their dinners, Talleyrand said that the surroundings looked familiar to him.

As they walked along the shore, Talleyrand remembered the scenes of his early childhood. He pointed out to Louis Dupré Des-Isles that spot where stood his humble home. He took Mr. Des-Isles to the very spot where the pot of tar was overturned on his leg, and had crippled him for life. The people had a reception in his honor. People came from all around the countryside. Mrs. Jane Grindle, a woman in her nineties, told the writer of this, saying that her mother had often told her about the silks and satins that they wore at the reception.

1934—*J. Sherman Douglas*

Editor's Note: The above story will be most interesting to every lover of Maine. It was written by a well-known student of history for *The Old Farmer's Almanac.*

THE GREAT BLACK BLIZZARD

Anyone who experienced the Great Black Blizzard, March 31, 1955, knows that this disaster was a far greater threat to national security than the measure of the damage it did in ten of our southwestern states may indicate. Here was a huge churning mass of some 500,000 square miles of black dust, sand, rain, snow, and hail traveling for some thirty-six hours at speeds ranging from forty to seventy-five miles per hour. We hung a washed-out shirt to dry on the doorknob of a motel room in Albuquerque, New Mexico. In less than twenty minutes, dust seeped through cracks which even light could not pass in the door. It streaked that shirt with prison bars of black and our lungs with a coating of umber. Out of doors, from the Santa Fe Railroad's *Chief* next day (all day) through Colorado, and Oklahoma and Kansas, we watched, in the intervals in which we could see at all, bluebirds flying for their lives scarcely inches from the ground; trains standing on sidetracks cleaned of their paint and left with ominous grooves and gouges seered into their metal sides. Nothing living walked abroad in an atmosphere in which only the arch fiends of destruction laid their wands of destruction upon the face of our land.

This and other storms in the months of January, February, and March, 1955, damaged 10.6 million acres of Great Plains crop and range land. In April alone, another 4.4 million acres was added. This made the four-month total some fifteen millions of acres or 653 billion, four hundred thousand square feet valued, when it was still useful to man, at some sixty millions of dollars. In addition, some 18,546,000 acres, rendered useless by storms of the past, remained ready as of May 1, 1955, to blow.

The dust bowls of this ten-state region—Colorado, Kansas, New Mexico, Oklahoma, Texas in the South; Montana, Nebraska, North Dakota, South Dakota, and Wyoming in the North—ravaged by man as well as drought are by now veritable cancers in the economic and physical body of our country. Yet Uncle Sam, as recklessly and inhumanly as any storybook profligate drunkard would, unconcernedly continues to add to the malignancy of the cancers with his occasional firecracking A-bomb explosions of radiant dust.

Malignant cancer spreads. In the human body, the medical profession operates—if possible, removes it. Not so, Uncle Sam. His appropriations (some $15,000,000) against this growing threat to our national security have not amounted to even one-fourth of the damage from one great storm—and his fuel from the A-bomb probably adds as much, in each of its explosions, to the potential of the threat from the area as his total annual contributions to prevention and cure.

April 14, 1934, is considered the birthday of the old "dust bowl." That is the day that the first "black roller" roared down from western Kansas across the Oklahoma and Texas Panhandles. Then, as a forecast of worse things to come, another dust storm—that of May 10, 1934—made history. It picked up the topsoil of almost every bare field from New Mexico to Montana and deposited it 24 to 48 hours later as a blanket over Washington, D. C., New York City, even on ships at sea in the North Atlantic Ocean.

The storm of May 10, 1934, was called a "major disaster." Yet the dust bowl from which it drew its ammunition amounted to an area of only one-twentieth the size of the one today.

In this *Almanac* a year ago we voiced the opinion that an H-bomb explosion was of sufficient size and potency to affect weather all over the world. Since that time we have had solemn assurances from officialdom that the A-bomb explosions had caused only local weather upsets. The answer, as we thought it would be, now twelve months later, on the H-bomb effects is still, "We don't know."

Well, we aren't running for any office—but we know that the weather since the H-bomb explosion has been, with three hurricanes in one year and other disastrous storms, completely in defiance of the averages, unusual. We cannot prove the H-bombs caused these disasters. All we can point out is that it *could have,* just as these A-bomb explosions can be contributing to the dangerous situation right now in our Great Plains states.

Broadly speaking, any explosion, or storm, or eruption which tosses fine dust into the upper air currents has undetermined in advance effects on the climate of our earth, the health and well-being of people, and the violence of our storms. Scientists express themselves in various terms about these matters. This dust in the upper air may "occlude" rays of the sun; may act as "nuclei" for drops of rain or snow; may cause unusual temperature changes; may be a carrier of epidemics; may bring about drought or flood. Dust is as vital, apparently, to atmospheric activity as kindling wood is to a fire.

In the consideration then of the Great Plains Dust Bowl, when some 500,000 square miles of dust is allowed to churn and ogle its way into the atmosphere of this nation—and the world—it is comparable to our allowing every year the bursting of one or more of our great water or flood dams—and just as unthinkable.

We probably can't do anything at all about the upper atmosphere once the dust arrives in it . . . or even very much down here about preventing world scientists from continuing with their A-, H-, and C-bomb experiments—and these consequent man-made contributions of dangerous radiant dust to the heavens above. But we can, and this will probably be aided by nature itself in the next four or five years, come very close to eliminating the Dust Bowl Danger.

In the first place, we made it ourselves. We plowed and planted —and still are—for monetary gain—wheat and cotton on acreage which never should have been plowed up at all. We overgrazed range lands until, when the great droughts came, they could no longer sustain man or beast. We handed out millions upon millions of crop-support funds to farmers on lands unsuitable for planting.

These acres, if they are not plowed up, again—now that the droughts are apparently over for a few years—can be reclaimed by a long-range program of proper land use, good conservation, and ranching methods. An important meeting in this regard was held in Denver, May 30—June 2, 1955. United States Department of Agriculture representatives, the governors of the ten Great Plains states, and representatives of the USDA co-operative extension service attended. A program of conservation work within the various states, in co-operation with the government, was developed—of which you will be hearing more. We hope it is an effective one.

1956

THE BIRTH OF DAILY WEATHER REPORTING

When ancient man first began to till the land, centuries before the dawn of history, he was constantly surveying the heavens and talking with the older people in an endeavor to learn what the weather would be. His knowledge was limited to the small area in which he lived. The ancient proverbs and sayings of the oldsters were passed down by word of mouth. Perhaps one of the better known of these ancient proverbs is the one found in the Gospel of

St. Matthew, Chapter 16, Verses 2 and 3, "When it is evening, ye say, it will be fair weather for the sky is red, and in the morning it will be foul weather today, for the sky is red and lowering."

Here and there, prior to 1850, spasmodic attempts were made by individuals to work out some system of weather reporting. But such efforts were abortive. Space will not permit a detailed history. Notable, however, were the meteorological stations established by Frederick II, Grand Duke of Tuscany, in 1653...and the availability of thermometer and barometer at that time.

Among the danger spots of the world in 1854 was the Crimea, or as it was called in ancient times, Crim Tartary. Here the Allies, composed of the French, English, and Turks, were engaged in forcing Russia, who had attempted to overrun Turkey, back behind her own boundaries.

The war between the Allies and Russia developed into a series of battles around the Black Sea, finally ending in the tragic Battle of Balaklava. This resulted in the Russians being forced into a state of siege. But for the intervention of Fate, the Battle of Balaklava would have been merely another battle. The tragic aftermath of this battle, however, leading to the establishment of daily weather forecasting, made this battle immortal.

Early in the evening of November 13, 1854, after a series of days comparable to our Indian summer, a rain started. Soon it developed (on the fourteenth) into a tempest with gale-force winds. Tents were torn down and wooden tent flooring blown away together with the men's spare clothing and accouterments. The cold wind caused the greatest misery. Shipping in the harbor was destroyed, including France's largest battleship, the *Henri IV*. The huge steamboat owned by the British navy, the *Prince*, containing winter clothing and supplies, was sunk.

When the news reached England and France, the public clamor was high, but as in so many cases, it was soon hushed by their parliaments. There was one man in France who could not be silenced. This was Marshal Jean Baptiste Philibert Vaillant. He felt very keenly his responsibility to his Emperor Napoleon for the loss of the *Henri IV* and was determined that, if possible, some way would be found to warn the armed forces of these sudden and often tragic storms.

He secured the permission of the emperor to employ the services of the most brilliant scientist in all Europe, Urbain Jean Joseph LeVerrier. LeVerrier was undoubtedly the best selection that could have been made. He was in charge of the meteorological work at the Imperial Observatory in Paris. He had succeeded, purely by mathematical deductions, in discovering a new planet. On receiving his assignment from the emperor, he immediately communicated with all the European observatories asking that they send their data relative to weather observations for the eleventh to sixteenth of November, 1854. When he received these, with his assistants, he correlated the information and on January 31, 1855, he reported to the Royal Academy that a storm warning could have been issued to the military forces in the Crimea a day in advance of the debacle. Later, he submitted to the emperor a memorandum outlining a project for weather advisories which Napoleon approved at once, and ordered that necessary steps be taken to put these plans to work at once. He authorized the director general of telegraphic lines to co-operate with the plans.

Thus was born the daily weather-reporting system . . . as was, incidentally, the eternal fame of Florence Nightingale, a volunteer nurse at the scene of the Balaklava disaster, and the Light Brigade which made its famous disastrous charge at Balaklava in September.

1956—*W. Emory Wardwell*

FOR FORTY DAYS AND NIGHTS . . .

Psychologists agree that in thoughts, as well as actions, we earth people of 1951 are motivated to a large degree (perhaps 70 per cent) by the past. The palsy, for example, is seen as the continuous exercise we once undertook as fishes to keep ourselves afloat. In thought, not the least tenacious and frequent outcropping of legend is seen in our arbitrary acceptance of "forty days" for Lent, the rainy or dry period after St. Swithin's Day, etc.

Upon occasion, the Aztecs—as well as most ancient and honorable civilizations—divided the year into forty-day cycles. Hesiod, in the eighth century B.C., proclaimed the disappearance of the Pleiades for forty days and nights as the law of all mankind. There are too many Biblical and other historical references to this forty-day period for us, just because we cannot explain these, to dismiss them as old wives' tales.

In our estimate, an observer at about 42° North or South Latitude might easily conclude the forty-day cycle as one which makes excellent weather-forecasting sense. It has, apparently, a definite relation to the obliquity of the sun's rays upon the earth and to the temperatures of the earth's atmosphere—the chief cause of weather.

At the Equator, stable temperatures produce even weather. The winds come steadily from given directions. The rainy season is predicted successfully almost to the minute.

We, at 42° North, could forecast our weather accurately, too, could we determine our normal atmospheric temperatures for any given obliquity of the sun's rays. The accumulated excess or deficiency heat and cold figures from the normal would go far to determine what might be expected in the way of a balancing weather operation by Mother Nature.

The principle is simple and well understood. Precipitation, storms, weather extremes are nature's way of maintaining temperature balances. As the sun leaves us in the fall, the cooling of our atmosphere brings on bad weather. As it returns to us in the spring, the warming process does likewise. The apparent "lag"—or period of adjustment which is allowed to our atmosphere for catching up with the sun—seems to be approximately forty days.

Our observer then, on the fortieth parallel, might arrive at certain definite weather conclusions:

1. That severe "surprise" weather extremes, such as hurricanes and blizzards, are to be looked for only in two of nine seasons.

2. That the forty-day legend at Groundhog Day (February 2), at St. Swithin's Day (July 15), at Christmas, and at St. Paul's Day (January 25) is based on the fact that seasons actually do begin very close to those particular days.

3. That the ancients—as well as ourselves—have some basis in fact for our belief in forty-day cycles.

4. That there is some reason to believe that weather can be foretold in the equation between atmospheric temperatures and the obliquity of the sun's rays.

5. That actual weather records along the fortieth parallel actually prove nine seasons a far more accurate measure of weather than do the present zodiacal four seasons which in most places are no measure at all.

A tabulation which an observer might make of the nine seasons along the fortieth parallel—and certain weather extremes which have occurred within these seasons—follows. North or south of the fortieth parallel, one would expect these seasons to be fewer in number and of different lengths.

THE NINE SEASONS

1. *Spring*. May 1 to June 10.
2. *Early Summer*. June 11 to July 15.
3. *Summer*. July 15 to September 1. (Heat and storm records occasional.)
4. *Early Fall*. September 2 to October 15. September 8 to 16, 1944: Great Atlantic Hurricane. September 17 to 21, 1938: New England Hurricane. 1815: New England Hurricane.
5. *Fall*. October 16 to November 20.
6. *Early Winter*. November 21 to December 25.
7. *Winter*. December 26 to February 1. (Cold and snow records occasional.)
8. *Late Winter*. February 2 to March 15. February 9, 1934: Boston low record—18° (Also February 15, 1817). 1933: U. S.

Record low at Yellowstone Park, Wyoming, of 66 below. February 16, 1933: Turners Falls, Massachusetts, record low of 30 below. February 24, 1723: Highest tide Boston ever had. March 3, 1907: Nantucket icebound. March 11, 1888: Famous blizzard began with 20.9 inches of snow.

9. *False Spring*. March 16 to April 30.

1951

CONNECTICUT

I ONCE REMARKED to a friend of mine that a certain person looked like a Yankee. My friend said, "He's no Yankee. He comes from Worcester, Massachusetts." From which it may be inferred that we in Connecticut consider ourselves sole legatees of this ancient name.

In the early seventeenth century, Connecticut was the frontier. Small bands of settlers left Massachusetts Bay and Plymouth to journey westward to the Connecticut River Valley, where the first towns were established by 1635 or a year or two earlier at Wethersfield, Windsor, and Hartford. Other settlements followed, along the coast and up the streams which penetrated the interior.

These early Connecticut settlers were prompted to migrate not only by a desire for economic freedom but also by the urge for religious and political independence. It is for this reason, perhaps, that there grew up here a race of hardy, ingenious, and rather shrewd men and women, since neither the country nor the climate was especially favorable to the primary means of making a living by tilling the soil. These people were quick to seize upon manufacturing as supplementary, in some measure, to farming. Early in the eighteenth century, small factories developed along rivers which supplied water power. Iron, tin, and copper were mined from local deposits and transformed into salable products. Clocks were also manufactured at an early date. Later in the century, the first silk mill was established at Mansfield, which afterward led to the

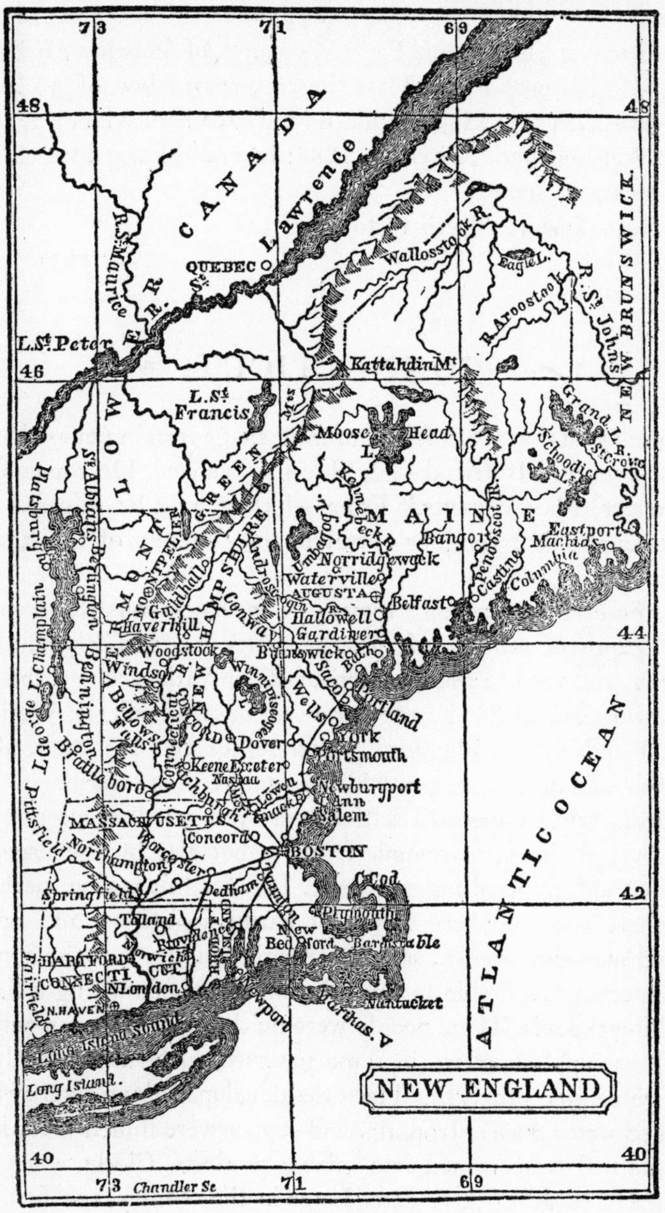

NEW ENGLAND
CANADA
NEW BRUNSWICK
MAINE
VERMONT
NEW HAMPSHIRE
MASSACHUSETTS
CONNECTICUT
ATLANTIC OCEAN
QUEBEC
L. St. Peter
L. St. Francis
Moose Head L.
Kattahdin Mt.
Wallosstook R.
Eagle L.
R. Aroostook
R. St. Johns
Grand L.
St. Croix R.
Schoodic Ls.
Eastport
Machias
Columbia
Castine
Penobscot R.
Bangor
Belfast
Norridgewock
Waterville
AUGUSTA
Hallowell
Gardiner
Brunswick
Bath
Portland
Saco
Wells
York
Portsmouth
Newburyport
Salem
BOSTON
C. Cod
Plymouth
Barnstable
Nantucket
New Bedford
Newport
Providence
Dedham
Concord
Lowell
Dover
Exeter
Keene
Nashua
CONCORD
Winnipiseogee
Conway
Haverhill
Woodstock
Windsor
Bellows Falls
Brattleboro
Bennington
Burlington
Plattsburg
L. Champlain
L. George
Pittsfield
Northampton
Worcester
Springfield
Tolland
HARTFORD
Norwich
N. London
N. HAVEN
Fairfield
Long Island Sound
Long Island
MONTPELIER
Guildhall
Androscoggin
Umbagog L.
Kennebeck R.
Connecticut R.
St. Maurice R.
St. Lawrence R.
48
46
44
42
40
73
71
69
Chandler Sc

1844

ROADS

To some of the principal towns, with their distances from Boston

☞ NOTICE, that the distances inserted are from one established tavern to another.

Fr. Boston to Newport over Seekonk, thro' Rehoboth.

	Miles.
Roxbury, Taft's	6
Dedham	4
——	3
Walpole	7
Wrentham	6
Attleborough	5
——	4
Rehoboth	7
Warren	8
Bristol	4
Ferry-House,	2
Portsmouth	7
Newport	5
	68

To Plymouth and Cape Cod.

Dorchester	4
Neponset Bridge } Quincy }	2
Weymouth	5
Scituate	6
Hanover	6
Pembroke	5
Duxbury	2
Kingston	3
Plymouth	4
	37
Plymouth	5
ditto	5
Sandwich	7
——	4
Barnstable	4
——	4
——	2
Yarmouth	2
Harwich	9
ditto	1
'rleans	5
Eastham	1
ditto	3
Wellfleet	8
——	2
Truro	8
Provincetown	9
	115

N. B. By the turnpike, eight miles short.

To Martha's Vineyard.

Sandwich	60
Falmouth	10
Falmouthtown	8
Wood's Hole	4
Over the Ferry to the Vineyard	9
	91

Road to Taunton, Somerset, Warren, Bristol, & Newport.

Dorchester	3
Milton	7
Canton	4
Sharon	4
Taunton	17
Dighton	7
Somerset	4
Swansey	3
Warren	2
——	4
Bristol	4
Over the Bridge to Newport	13
Corrected for 1825.	72

Road to N. Bedford.

Dorchester	4
Quincy	4
Weymouth	3
——	4
Abington	3
East Bridgewater	5
Bridgewater	3
Middleboro'	10
——	2
New Bedford	14
	52

To Walpole, Keene, Windsor, Vt., and Hanover.

Cambridgeport	2
——	2
Cambridge	2
West Cambridge	3
Lexington	3
——	3
Lincoln	2
Concord	2
Acton	7
Littleton	2
Groton	4
——	3
Pepperell	3
Townsend	5
New Ipswich	7
Village	3
Jeffrey	7
——	5
Marlborough	12
Keene	2
Walpole	9
do. village	5
Bellows Falls	4
Charlestown	4
——	4
Claremont	12
Cornish	4
Windsor	2
Hartland	5
ditto	5
Lebanon	8
Dartmouth Coll.	6
	140

To Montreal and Quebec.

Walpole Village	94
Rockingham	4
ditto	5
ditto	4
Chester	4
Cavendish	8
Ludlow	4
Mount Holly	4
Shrewsbury	8
Clarendon	8
Rutland	2
Pittsford	9
Brandon	8
Leicester	6
Salisbury	3
Middlebury	7
Vergennes	12
Ferrisburg	5
Charlotte	6
Sherburne	6
Burlington	5
Across the s'nd b'r	15
The gut between N. and S. Hero	12
Ferry to N. Hero	1
Harvey's Ferry	7
Alburg	1
Savage's Point	4
Latitude 45th deg.	3
——	8
——	13
St. John's	5
Half-way house	9
Laprairie	9
Ferry to Montreal	9
Trois Rivieres	9
Quebec	80
	492

To Montreal and Quebec.

Medford	5
Woburn	5
Burlington	3
Billerica	6
Chelmsford	4
Tyngsborough	5
Dunstable	5
Nashua	4
Merrimac	5
Amherst	6
Mount Vernon	2
Francistown	9
——	3
Hillsborough	9
Washington	7
Lempster	7
Claremont	10
Windsor, Vt.	9
Woodstock	4
Barnard	8
Royalton	8
Randolph	10
Brookfield	5
——	4
Williamstown	4
Barre	4
Montpelier	6
Moretown	7
Waterbury	7
Bolton	8
Richmond	5
Williston	5
Burlington	10
	210

To Dartmouth College, thro' Amherst, and Windsor.

Windsor (*for the route, see route to Montreal, &c.*)	107
Hartland	5
Lebanon	7
Hanover	6
	125

To Norwich and New London.

Attleborough	36
Providence	9
Johnson	3
——	5
Scituate	4
ditto	6
Coventry	4
Volentown	4
Plainfield	8
Newent	7
Norwich	7
Mohegan	4
New London	7
	104

Upper road to Exeter, Portland, and Bangor.

Medford	5
Reading	7
Andover	8
Haverhill	9
Plaistow	7
Kingston	6

1844

establishment of the world-famous Cheney Mills at South Manchester. As the technique of factory production developed, Connecticut industries grew, and by 1880, we were rather more an industrial than an agricultural state.

The products of our infant industries were distributed throughout neighboring states by Yankee peddlers. A prosperous shipping trade developed from the exchange of Connecticut goods for West Indian rum and molasses and Chinese silk.

Apparently this combination of producing ingenious wares and exchanging them for other goods or cash proved profitable. Many large fortunes were created and a relatively high standard of living for the state as a whole was established. The Connecticut Yankee rose from humble beginnings to wealth and influence.

Because of the opportunities in our large industrial centers, and because Connecticut lies midway between the two great ports of Boston and New York, many immigrants from Europe have sought homes here during the past hundred years. Some 65 per cent of our population is now either foreign born or but one generation removed from foreign-born parents.

In spite of later immigration, Connecticut is still Yankeeland. There are perhaps two main reasons why this is so. First, we have preserved our beautiful countryside. Farming still occupies a large part of our population. Here in the open season is a green and pleasant land, with rolling hills and fields, with old elm-shaded villages, with forests where the dogwood and mountain laurel bloom; with rivers and lakes and rushing streams that still keep in their names echoes of the long Indian past; with miles of fine beaches and friendly harbors along beautiful shores. It is not surprising that the Connecticut Yankee has survived in these surroundings and still dominates the lower house of our General Assembly which is made up of representatives from the 169 towns in the state.

The second reason why Connecticut is still Yankeeland lies, not in our countryside but, strangely enough, in the cities, where the traditional Yankees are far outnumbered by men and women of foreign birth or parents, where each national group has its societies named for the town or the saints of Europe. There can be no doubt of the love and sentiment of these people for their homeland. But they love Connecticut more. At no time recently has this sentiment been more apparent than during the observance of the three hundredth anniversary of the settlement of Connecticut, which occurred in 1935. The eager participation of groups of the so-called foreign-born was an inspiration. One of the features of the final state exercises was a parade, held in Hartford on a beautiful October day. A distinguished committee passed judgment on the many floats and awarded prizes for the most effective historical ones. The first prize went to a group of Italians for their float representing "The First Thanksgiving of Plymouth." The second prize went to a Swedish society.

All this shows that the traditions of the world-famous Yankee still prevail in Connecticut, where many others besides myself read *The Old Farmer's Almanac.*

1939—*Wilbur L. Cross, Governor*

CAPE COD

I SUPPOSE that, of all questions asked a writer of Cape Cod stories, the following is asked more frequently than any other:

"Is the Cape like the Cape you used to know as a boy? Or is it and are its people changed beyond recognition?"

I have answered the question a good many times, and in a recent book of mine, *Cape Cod Yesterdays,* I answered it more or less as follows:

This country of ours is, as we all must realize, rapidly becoming standardized. Good roads, motors, increasing and improving railway facilities, long-distance telephones, radios, airplanes—all of these are annihilating distance, and sections which were more or less isolated are now in close touch with other sections.

Consequently, the people of a locality are losing the local habits of life and customs of speech which made them distinctive. Prophesying is a risky profession but, nevertheless, it would seem fairly safe to prophesy that, and before very long, all Americans are going to be pretty much alike.

When the author was a boy in a Cape Cod village, there was a firm belief that there was something distinctive to a Cape Codder, something which made him different and recognizable wherever he might be—to another Cape Codder, that is. A friend of mine, born and brought up on the Cape, and who, having made a substantial fortune in a Midwestern city, had returned to his native village to spend the years left to him, told this story:

He said that he and his family were taking a trip up the Nile in one of the Cook steamers. Leaning over the rail near the bow of that steamer, he noticed a man whose appearance interested him. He watched this man for some time. Then he walked over and accosted him. "Pardon me," he said, "but I am going to ask you a personal question. What part of the Cape did you come from?"

The man turned and inspected him carefully. "I hail from Wellfleet," he said. "What part of the Cape did you come from?"

Now I can't vouch for the truth of this story, but knowing the man who told it, I believe it. Being a Cape Codder, I would want to believe it anyhow. "Capers" are proud of the Cape, its low rolling hills, its pine groves, its little lakes, its surf-boarded beaches, its white-painted or gray-shingled houses, its sturdy, law-abiding, dryly witty people. We brag of them whenever we have an opportunity.

Again, when the author was a youngster, there was a saying that the Cape Codder born and bred—or, excuse me, brought up—was perfectly certain of three things. First, that Cape Cod was the finest place in the world. Second, that Cape Codders were the finest people in the world. Third, that he himself was finer than any other Cape Codder.

The Cape was left so much more to itself then. There were summer boarders and visitors from the city, but not nearly so many of them. The winter populations of the towns were then almost as large as the summer populations. We welcomed our city friends, but we did not change our mode of life to suit their convenience. If we chose to "cal'late" or "presume likely" when expressing our opinions, we did so. We took our guests driving over the sandy roads, and if they ventured to wonder why our buggies and carryalls were several inches wider from wheel to wheel than those to which they were accustomed in urban districts, we let them wonder. The broad-gauged vehicles were made for us, made for Cape Cod customers, by the builders. They had been made that way for generations. They suited us, and that was sufficient.

We do not use them any more, but that is because our roads, the vast majority of them, are no longer rutted. We have our automobiles now and our roads are like city roads. Our towns are, in summer, crowded with city sojourners, and we are delighted to have them so. Our streets and our beaches are bordered with handsome cottages or homes where people come with their families in the late spring and remain until the fall. They have learned to love the Cape and its people. And, in learning to understand the locality and its habitants, they readily recognize the fact that the Cape Codder is still, in spite of his sophistication, just as sturdily independent and self-respecting as he always was.

1937—*Joseph C. Lincoln*

THE PERIODICAL CICADA

Seventeen-Year Locust

THERE ARE two groups, tribes, or races of this cicada, one appearing at intervals of seventeen, the other at intervals of thirteen years. The seventeen-year race usually appears in the more northerly, the thirteen-year race in the more southerly portions of the United States east of the Rocky Mountains. All the individuals of either race do not appear in any one year. In the case of each race, those appearing in a certain year are designated for convenience as a brood, and are identified with that year.

Unless unforeseen conditions prevail, the 1919 brood of cicadas —one of the largest—will appear during the latter part of May in Rutland County, Vermont, and possibly in Bristol County, Massachusetts. In 1920 members of the brood of that year will appear in Bristol, Franklin, and Hampshire Counties, Massachusetts; and in Hartford County, Connecticut.

The periodical cicada, often erroneously called the "seventeen-year locust," is, in the curious features of its life history, one of the most interesting of all the insects peculiar to the American continent. During thirteen or seventeen years its existence is unsuspected and unindicated by any superficial sign. At the end of these periods every generation, though numbering millions of individuals, with perfect regularity attains maturity at almost the same moment.

The cicada suddenly emerges over greater or smaller areas, filling the ground from which it issues with innumerable exit holes, swarming over trees and shrubs, and making the air vibrate with its shrill, discordant notes. Within two weeks the female begins to puncture the twigs in order to deposit her eggs, which vary in number from four hundred to six hundred. The part of the plant selected for a receptable for the eggs is almost invariably the twigs of the previous year's growth.

The young antlike larva, hatching from the egg a few weeks after the latter has been laid, escapes from the wounded limb, falls lightly to the ground, and quickly burrows out of sight, where it remains in solitude during the thirteen or seventeen years of its hypogeal existence. During the few weeks of its aerial life the cicada attends actively to the needs of continuing its species, rarely taking wing, and seldom taking food. For four or five weeks the male sings his song of love and courtship, and the female busies herself with the placing of the eggs which are to produce the subsequent generation thirteen or seventeen years later.

At the close of its short adult existence the cicada falls to the ground again, perhaps within a few feet of the point from which it issued, there to be dismembered and scattered about, carpeting the surface of the ground with its wings and fragments of its body.

The cicada is most abundant in old and undisturbed forest tracks, and confines its work for the most part to forest trees. In some instances fruit trees have been injured, although the damage is very slight in proportion to the fears aroused. One of the best means of destroying the cicada in the orchard is to gather them by hand in the early morning, when they are somewhat torpid and sluggish. Very satisfactory results have been obtained by using a strong kerosene emulsion. Spraying with Bordeaux mixture before their arrival has often been a means of driving the cicadas to other places.

No pruning or grafting should be done during the winter and spring prior to the expected appearance of the cicada in order to offer a larger twig growth, and distribute by this means the damage over a greater surface. Also defer the planting of orchards, especially in the vicinity of old orchards or forest land, until the danger is past. With young trees, the worst affected branches should be removed, and the less injured ones protected by covering the wounded parts with grafting wax or a moderately hard soap. These protective coverings should be renewed at least once a year, until the wounds are entirely healed over. In the case of a badly injured tree that has been recently budded or grafted, it may be well to cut it back nearly to the bud or graft, so that an entirely new top may be made.

1919

THE VITALITY OF BURIED SEEDS

MOTHER NATURE is a wise "old dame" and has made many interesting provisions in her plant kingdom for protecting seeds and perpetuating the species. Just how long seeds will retain their vitality has always been an interesting question, and extravagant statements have frequently been made and published regarding the germination of very old seeds.

The general impression has prevailed that seeds of certain plants, mostly weeds, are able to retain their vitality for a long time, although buried in the ground. Germination tests of many herbarium samples of seed of known age have been made, and in some instances seeds more than a hundred years old have germinated and produced plants.

In 1894, the *Gardener's Chronicle* cited a case of a charlock-infested field which had been seeded down to grass. After twenty-three years a loaded wagon drawn across the field in the spring when the ground was soft brought subsoil to the surface, and in the following summer ribbons of charlock grew in the wheel tracks.

Perhaps the first attempt to secure specific information on the length of time seeds are able to retain their vitality while buried in the soil was made by the late Dr. W. J. Beal of Michigan Agricultural College. In 1879, he buried at East Lansing, Michigan, twenty uncorked bottles of seed, each bottle containing fifty seeds of each of twenty different species of plant. One of these bottles has been taken up every five years, the last report being made after forty years, at which time ten of the twenty species germinated.

In 1902, the Seed Laboratory of the United States Department of Agriculture started a buried-seed experiment in which 112 samples of seed representing 107 species were used. A certain number of each kind of seed was mixed with sterilized soil and placed in common flowerpots. These pots, each covered with a porous saucer, were arranged in sets and buried in the soil at the Arlington Experiment Station near Washington. As a result of this method, the soil within the pots when taken up has resembled the soil outside in moisture and compactness.

The trench in which the pots were buried was about 9 feet wide at the top and 50 feet long. At one side the trench was made 8 inches deep; in the middle, 22 inches deep; and at other side,

42 inches deep. The trench thus had three distinct levels or shelves, each about three feet wide, of undisturbed soil. The sets of pots, 32 in all, were buried on each of these shelves, 8 sets on the shallow or A level, 12 sets on the middle or B level, and 12 sets on the deep or C level. This arrangement made it possible to take up a set from each of the different depths by digging across the trench without any unnecessary disturbance of the remaining sets.

The seeds upon being dug up have been tested at once for germination in the greenhouse. To date, six different removals have been made, the last one reported being in 1923, when the seeds had been buried for twenty years.

The following list shows the species which produced sprouts in 1923. Twelve of these marked with a * have produced sprouts from each depth each year tested. Tobacco is the only cultivated crop included in the twelve:

*Foxtail
Yellow foxtail
Green foxtail
Reed canary grass
Timothy
Kentucky bluegrass
Hair-grass dropseed
Sand dropseed
Yellow nut grass
Ramie
Smartweed
False buckwheat
Willow-leaved dock
Curled dock
*Broad-leaved dock
Sugar beet
Lamb's quarters
Goosefoot
Poke berry
Purslane
Black mustard
Field penny cress
Rough cinquefoil
Wild senna
Bush clover
Alsike clover
Red clover
White clover
Black locust
Velvet leaf
Rose mallow
Evening primrose
Celery
*Hedge bindweed
*White morning-glory
Dodder
Blue vervain
White vervain

*Jimson weed	Great ragweed
*Tobacco	Burdock
Black nightshade	*Canada thistle
*Great mullen	*Oxeye daisy
*Common plantain	Cotton thistle
Broad plantain	*Black-eyed Susan
*Ragweed	

Of the 107 species buried in 1902, 71 grew in 1903 after one year; 61 grew in 1905 after 3 years; 68 grew in 1908 after 6 years; 69 grew in 1912 after 10 years; 50 grew in 1918 after 16 years; and 51 grew in 1923 after 20 years.

The following findings of these experiments are of interest:

1. The depth at which seeds are buried has little effect upon the preservation of their vitality.

2. None of the cereals or legumes whose seeds are used as food germinated on being dug up.

3. The seeds of weeds and wild plants survived better than those of cultivated plants.

4. The weeds showing the highest germination and the fewest failures are those common and persistent in the locality where the tests were made.

From these findings it is quite evident that plowing under weeds which have gone to seed will not exterminate them. Each plowing of a field infested with weed seeds brings some of them near enough to the surface to germinate and at the same time buries others deeply enough to preserve their vitality. No normal crop-rotation system is long enough to effect the eradication of persistent weeds. This conclusion, however, does not lessen the importance of plowing weeds under before they go to seed.

1932

BUD FISHER

Creator of A. Mutt and J. Jeff

The first New England railroads went into operation in 1834. As late as 1842, the inhabitants of Dorchester, Massachusetts, voted in town meeting that these lines would be an "incalculable evil." In 1841, Robert B. Thomas included the railroads for the first time on his Old Farmer's Almanac *map of New England—thus admitting them to some sort of parity with the stagecoaches.*

Bud Fisher published the first American comic strip in 1907. Though some readers still refuse parity for the comic strip with the rest of the paper, it cannot be denied it has gained a major place in American publishing. The American News Company sale alone amounted to 69 million copies of comic books in 1942, 144 million in 1944, and 169 million in 1946, or over a copy for every living American man, woman, and child.

The Old Farmer's Almanac *thus comes somewhat late in the day to recognition of this truly American phenomena in publishing. Herewith this story of Bud Fisher, first American comic-strip artist.*

Back in 1907, horse players were just as avid for a winner as they are today. Bud Fisher, ever observant of the behaviorism of his fellow humans, saw in this field an opportunity for a comic artist that was a surer thing than the best bet of the day. Fisher lived in San Francisco at the time when the gee-gees were running at Emeryville, across the bay.

Born in Chicago, Harry Conway "Bud" Fisher had attended Hyde Park High School where he starred on the relay team. He had illustrious company, for such athletes as Walter Eckersall and Tom Hammond were also there at the time. He attended the University of Chicago for three months and, when his family moved to Reno, went along but made San Francisco his destination.

When the comic-strip idea first came to Fisher, he was only twenty-one, but he was two years older than that before he finally convinced John P. Young, then managing editor of the San Francisco *Chronicle*, that his idea was worth a gamble. Fisher's enthusiasm and perseverance won. He caught Mr. Young in a genial mood one night and approached him with some sample drawings.

"What's that?" Mr. Young asked Fisher, as he peered at the cartoons and pointed to the thin, weak-chinned character that was soon to make comic-strip history.

"That's me," Bud replied. "A. Mutt."

"He looks funny. We'll publish it."

This was the start of Augustus Mutt and the first comic strip ever published. Fisher had purposely given Mutt a long nose in sympathy to the horse players who were always adding body English to the pony they played, in the hope said horse would get his nose in front at the finish. Mutt was supposed to pick a horse a day and Fisher made him a composite of all the betters he observed. He portrayed their varied methods of trying to dope out a winner and A. Mutt soon had a big audience. There was a familiar note here that all horse players responded to. His cartoons gained greater popularity when the horses picked began to win, much to the bookies' chagrin.

Fisher's selections were strictly for gags, not speed. That is, the name of the horse would fit in with the humorous situation he intended to portray, so that the effect would be double-barreled. To anyone but a horse player, such a hit-and-miss proposition seems like a quick way to the poorhouse. But A. Mutt had luck. His horses won and soon yelling newsboys were selling the paper on the strength of Mutt's selections.

On one occasion, Mutt was in a hospital, recovering from an injury, looking over the day's entries. He glanced at the sky, the sun was shining. He looked back at the list of horses. There it was, a hunch bet—Bright Skies. Mutt threw away his crutches, leaped into the bay, and swam to the track just in time to plank down five dollars on the horse to win. He came in at odds of 300 to 1. Mutt was made and his body and balloons were by Fisher.

During one stretch, Fisher picked so many winners he tried to taper off. But his long shots persisted in bounding down the stretch in front.

Before long, the San Francisco *Examiner* offered Fisher a job at more money and he accepted. He copyrighted the title and character in his own name and added little Jeff to the comic. This was at the time when the sport pages were filled with news of the coming Johnson-Jeffries fight. Mutt had been sent to an asylum and there met the diminutive and bewhiskered Jeff, who claimed he was James J. Jeffries, heavyweight champion of the world. Jeff's claims were a challenge to Mutt to make the little fellow come off a bad second in any engagements the two had. Because it is human nature to side with the weak, Jeff soon had the sympathy of the public.

Mr. Hearst transferred Fisher to New York and Mutt and Jeff began to appear in all the Hearst newspapers. By this time the strip was nationally popular and Fisher was anxious to obtain more money. His contract called for two hundred dollars a week the first year; two hundred and fifty dollars a week for the second, third, and fourth years; and three hundred dollars for the fifth year.

Once, when visiting the New York *American* offices, Fisher was puffing away at a cigarette. There was a sign in the building prohibiting smoking, and when some executive called Mr. Fisher's attention to this, Bud's indifference nettled the man.

"Do you work here?" he inquired.

"Yes," Fisher replied.

"Then you're fired," spouted the executive.

"Mister," said Fisher calmly, "I don't know who you are, but if you can make that discharge stick, I'll give you a thousand dollars."

When his contract with Hearst expired in 1913, Fisher signed a contract with John N. Wheeler, enterprising New York newspaperman, to syndicate the strip at one thousand dollars a week and share in the profits. Hearst did not give up without a fight and a long lawsuit followed. Various artists were employed by the *American* to draw the strip while the court fight was going on. The court finally granted Fisher exclusive right to produce Mutt and Jeff, and protection from unfair competition of others reproducing them.

The fact that Fisher had copyrighted the strip a few years before was a stone wall which Hearst's experienced lawyers could not dent. By this victory, Fisher gained not only wealth for himself but made it possible for many comic artists who came after him to gain greater returns than they ever thought possible. Still, in fairness to Hearst, Fisher admitted later that he had done more to raise the pay of newspapermen and artists than any other publisher.

Syndicated on a wide scale by Mr. Wheeler, Mutt and Jeff was soon appearing in more than 250 newspapers, favorite comic of millions of readers. Fisher made the biggest fortune ever amassed by a comic artist from his drawing. There were years when his earnings from syndication exceeded four thousand dollars a week.

When Mr. Wheeler went to Mexico in quest of a story by Villa himself, Fisher accompanied him. Villa was fighting Carranza at the time, and Bud brought back a revolver the Mexican had given him. During World War I, he was commissioned a lieutenant in the American National Army but later resigned to join the Canadian forces in the hope of getting into action more quickly.

Although Mutt was no longer following the races and picking winners, Fisher's love for racing did not diminish. He gradually built up a stable of fifty horses, many of them stakes winners. He paid close to $60,000 for Sporting Blood, Latonia Handicap winner. Nellie Morse, named after Mr. Fisher's mother, won the Preakness. Mr. Mutt won the Saratoga Cup; and another horse, Cartoonist, showed great promise as a two-year-old which never materialized later. One day, Bud invited Mr. Wheeler and Ring Lardner to Saratoga where his Hyperion was running with Sande up. It looked like a sure thing until the horse bolted and threw Sande and all three for a loss.

Forty years have gone by since Mutt and Jeff was first published, but the strip is still popular. Bud Fisher continues to take an enthusiastic interest in his work. During this time, it has appeared in many countries and in many languages. From his wide experience, Fisher analyzes the successful ingredients of a real comic as a combination of funny drawing, funny situations, and funny lines, with funny situations as the most important.

1948—*Released by The Bell Syndicate, Inc.*

THEY CONSULT A MUSHROOM!

When our troubles prove too much for some of us, we consult a psychiatrist for help. But unsophisticated people have evolved other methods for solving their problems, none more fantastic and fascinating than that followed for centuries by certain Mexican Indians. They consult a mushroom!

Early Spanish friars were much distressed by this custom, but were unable to turn their converts from their ancient practice, and in parts of Mexico these rites are secretly followed to this day. The mushroom used, known as the "divine mushroom," is found on this continent and in Europe. Eaten in carefully prescribed quantities, it produces a trance state in the partaker, who experiences a sense of ecstasy and enlightenment, and is ravished by beautiful visions and colors. While the congregation are eating the mushroom, devout leaders, mostly women, conduct the solemn rites and chanting which are customary, and, after a lapse of some time, give answers and advice to those present. These leaders receive a high fee for their services. They give advice on health, locate missing articles, solve mysteries, and report on the welfare of absent relatives. Numbers of these people, of late years, have spent much time in the United States as migrant workers; many of them cannot write, nor can those left at home read, so this is their substitute for letters. An American investigator was deeply impressed by the serious and religious attitude of these gatherings, and convinced that extraordinary results were actually attained.

Chemical analysis has revealed that the "divine mushroom" contains lysergic acid: an interesting discovery, as this chemical has been used recently in this country in exploring the nature of mental disease. Volunteers who have taken it for medical enlightenment are plunged into a state resembling that of schizophrenia. When they return to normal, they can recall their sensations and give valuable descriptions of the state of mind and body they have experienced.

It is a fact that certain races have learned to identify many mushrooms, which they seek eagerly and for which they have charming folknames, often of an affectionate nature. No Russian, for instance, would ever speak harshly of a mushroom! They have simple, but accurate, rhymed descriptions which they learn as children. In Tolstoi's *Anna Karenina*, there is a charming account of a Russian family making merry gathering mushrooms in the forest. Other races do not recognize any good in mushrooms, cannot distinguish one from another, call them toadstools or harsher names, and never speak well of them. These attitudes of affection or loathing have persisted for ages. There is a new theory that a science of ethnomycology may be established upon this basis, by which racial groups may be traced far back into very ancient times by their attitudes to mushrooms.

On this continent grow more than 3,000 varieties of mushrooms, of which at least 700 are edible. Not all are interesting as food, but many have flavors far superior to those of the sole cultivated variety. We waste, yearly, tons of valuable, free, and delicious food, replete with vitamins and minerals. In Europe, the picture is reversed: during their seasons, wild mushrooms form an important part of the daily diet and great quantities are dried for winter use. During both World Wars they were gleaned so thoroughly, to supplement scanty food supplies, that fears were expressed that the prospects for future crops were being endangered. Many people gain part of their livelihood by gathering them for sale. Tons of them are sold in the great picturesque mushroom markets. So important are they as a common food that mushroom inspectors, who are required to pass strict government examinations, are present at all markets, to insure that no poisonous varieties are unwittingly offered for sale. Their universal use as a food has stimulated European scientists to seek for antidotes for the deadly ones. A French doctor has produced a serum which has had notable success in many cases. It is, unfortunately, unstable, and must be procured fresh from Paris in case of need. Nothing of this kind is available in the United States.

Commercial canning and drying are carried out in Europe in a large way. The truffle, an underground mushroom which grows near the roots of certain oaks, is considered the chief delicacy of the tribe. Truffles are no trifles, for the Italian peasants do a million-dollar business in them yearly, and at least $150,000 worth of them are imported each year into the United States. So costly are they that chefs in hotels, where they are largely used in gourmet cooking, keep their precious stock under lock and key. Pigs, goats, and dogs, whose delicate sense of smell can detect the presence of the underground truffles, are employed to aid the searchers.

Some of the "miracle" drugs are, of course, varieties of molds, which are merely microscopic brethren of the larger mushrooms. It is a relative of penicillin which forms the blue-green spots in Roquefort cheese, and various strains of this and other molds are responsible for its tangy flavor as well as that of luscious Camembert. Researchers are eagerly seeking further medical discoveries from some of the mushrooms common to our fields and forests. Investigations of their possibilities in the cure of glaucoma, arthritis, and cancer are in progress. In certain parts of Europe, cancer is strikingly absent; freedom from the scourge is attributed by the natives to their large consumption of *Boletus Edulis*, a delicacy growing wild in such profusion, and so esteemed, that trainloads of it are shipped into Vienna and other cities. Research at Michigan State and the Sloan-Kettering Institute has revealed that this and several other mushrooms (all found here) do possess tumor-inhibiting substances. So far, these reports are based on animal experiments only.

Like men, mushrooms use enzymes and acids in the process of digestion. Some people, whose digestions are faulty, are helped by a fungus enzyme, called taka-diastase.

Mushrooms come in an endless variety of colors, shapes, and flavors; can and do grow in strange situations: on the ground, on trees, on railroad ties, on telephone poles, in cellars, in walls, mines, and elevator shafts. They are possessed of surprising strength, frequently breaking up through cement floors and streets. One tiny fellow grows only on the hoofs of dead animals; another only on one special joint of the left hind leg of a certain beetle. A number of varieties are skillfully cultivated by ants and beetles in flourishing underground gardens. The ambrosia beetle eats nothing but the mushroom his family raises. It is believed that some of these insect-cultivated mushrooms contain vitamins not found elsewhere. The ants lick each leaf before carrying it underground to make compost beds. Since they maintain a pure culture of mushrooms in their garden, it is conjectured that the ant saliva is germicidal, and that its investigation may be of value to man.

Some mushrooms are phosphorescent in the dark; some have a power of movement, puzzling the learned, who cannot decide whether they should be classed as plants or animals. Their odd shapes, colors, and textures account for some of their common names, which include such picturesque ones as Witches' Butter, Judas' Ear, Devil's Snuff-box, Brownie Cap, and Plum Top. Their range of color is immense: they can match or surpass the colors of the most brilliant plumage or the softest, most exquisite hues of blossoms. Some possess delightful odors: that of sweet clover, anise, newly ground meal, orange flower blossoms, and cucumber, to name but a few. Others broadcast a rank smell of carrion or worse, utterly alluring to certain flies and beetles. Some have flavors so reminiscent of common foods that, when properly cooked and served, they have fooled the unwary into thinking they were eating chicken, oysters, beefsteak, or liver. A tiny fellow, its cap no larger than a shirt button, is an excellent substitute for a clove of garlic. Some may be dried for winter use, and are more delicious thus than when used fresh. One of the best for this purpose may be gathered in New England, where it grows in moss beds, far into December, even after light snows have fallen, for freezing does not harm it. Some dry themselves on their stems when the weather is sunny and hot, only to revive when rain falls again. Some grow so high up on elm trees that they are secured only by those skillful enough to toss an accurate lasso. One grows even in February, should winter be interrupted by a short mild spell.

The poisonous members of the tribe have given mushrooms a bad name. Although there are many poisonous wild plants, some deadly, people do not seem to fear plants as they do "toadstools." Only about thirty-six in this country are poisonous. Many of these are only mildly indigestible. The true killers belong almost entirely to one family. This has striking characteristics, easily learned. Some of the most delicious could not possibly be mistaken for anything harmful. One delicacy, growing in abundant troops on the forest floor, looks exactly like a small crocus or morning-glory daintily made of dark gray or blackish fine kidskin. Any intelligent person, under a good teacher, can soon learn to identify the bad fellows, and with ease acquire knowledge of many edible varieties. It is regrettable that more people do not do so, perhaps by joining one of the many mycological clubs, for they would thus embark on a hobby that offers a delicious food free for the picking, healthy walks—endless and growing fascination.

One large species, yellowish-red in color, is known as the Fly mushroom, for it is poisonous to those insects, a fact that is being investigated for its commercial possibilities. Cows dote on this mushroom and will race each other across a pasture to secure it; their predilection gives some concern to farmers in Nova Scotia, where the mushroom is especially abundant, for though it causes the cows no harm it does dry up their milk or render it bitter and unwholesome for humans. Although the Fly mushroom is poisonous to humans, certain Siberian tribes once were notorious for using an infusion made of dried specimens as an intoxicant, staging glorious binges that lasted for thirty-six hours or more. Even in this country, back in the last century when certain gay souls used to gather to sniff "laughing gas," there were "Panaeolus parties." These mushrooms, used in cautious quantities, induced hilarity and odd visions that were deemed vastly entertaining.

The reproduction of mushrooms is exceptionally odd, possessed as they are of four sexes; roughly speaking, A must be introduced to C, and B must meet up with D, and all this underground and in the dark! But the system works out well enough for some of the tribe have been around millions of years, longer far than man, and are possessed of such cunning modes of survival that some biologists believe that, like the meek, they may someday inherit the earth. When one considers that a medium-sized "Giant Puffball" (specimens have been found with a six-foot girth) has been computed to contain some 7,000,000,000,000 spores (seeds), it becomes apparent that they are taking no chances of race suicide. Should all the spores germinate our troubles would be solved, for this globe we share would be completely upholstered in puffballs.

1957—*Sybil Curtis*

INTEMPERANCE

Illustrated and Exemplified

TEMPERANCE SOCIETIES meant business in the 1830's. Doctors, lawyers, businessmen—everyone in fact—were being called on for a public show of colors in the matter, and they'd better be dry or else. Robert B. Thomas, founder of the *Almanac*, had been on both sides of this fence—some years scolding the drinkers, other years making merry with them in his book. But there can be little doubt his habits were abstemious and temperate and, when his turn came, we doubt if he was at all rebellious about going along with the American Temperance Society and the Boston Society for the Promotion of Temperance. His contribution was the printing of a twelve-page Temperance Supplement to his *Almanac* of 1834, the last page of which carried the endorsement of no fewer than seventy-five prominent Boston physicians. An abridgment of the text of this supplement follows along with nine of the twelve woodcuts it contained.

CHILD: Mother, what is this picture?

MOTHER: This is a picture of a nurse feeding a baby with gin and water made sweet with sugar.

CHILD: I thought only men and women used spirit.

MOTHER: Many mothers and nurses think spirit is good for babies and often give it to them to keep them quiet. But it is a hurtful practice and in consequence many persons have become drunkards.

CHILD: What is the little boy asking for?

MOTHER: His mother is preparing to give him some sweetened rum because the boy has seen his father drinking it, so he thinks he should have it, too.

CHILD: Why is that woman still up? The clock says after midnight.

MOTHER: She has to work hard at sewing to support her four children. You can see three of them in the bed and one in the cradle. Her husband is a drinking man and does not support her or his family.

MOTHER: Here you see that woman's husband drinking in a grogshop. The man asleep in the chair is called a moderate drinker.

CHILD: But who is the man behind the chair? He can hardly stand up.

MOTHER: We call him a tippler because he has been a drinker for many years and cannot resist going into every grogshop he passes.

CHILD: And the other one?

MOTHER: From riches to rags, that one. Used to be a fine man, but just look what drinking has done to him.

CHILD: And what is this place?

MOTHER: This is a tavern that sells rum on Election Day. That is where politicians take men to persuade them through treats to vote the way they want them to.

CHILD: But must all taverns sell rum?

MOTHER: No. The one kept by Mr. Henry Hoyt in Rochester doesn't, nor that kept by Mr. Jones on Genesee Street in Utica. Neither does the one run by N. Safford in Albany, and there are several in Boston and other places that don't.

MOTHER: Here you see two men who have left their work to go to the tavern you see near. As a result of their visit both have become drunk and one is fallen on the ground.

CHILD: What is his name?

MOTHER: You remember the picture of the woman sewing?

Well, he is that woman's husband. He will probably lie on that ground until morning and his children cannot go to school but must grow up in ignorance, and rags, because their father is a drunkard. My son, you *must never drink spirit at all*, for there is no such thing as a temperate drinker.

CHILD: Is this woman ill?

MOTHER: Yes, this is the woman you saw sewing and she is broken down now from overwork and may die. Her son, you can see, is defending her against her drunken husband.

CHILD: Do drunkards beat their children and wives?

MOTHER: Perhaps they don't mean to, but when they are intoxicated they may even commit murder. It looks here as if he intended only to drive her out of doors and into the dark and stormy night.

CHILD: Isn't this the same woman we saw sewing and so very ill later on from overwork?

MOTHER: Yes. The husband, while drunk, has committed an infamous crime and has been taken to prison. The little family have lost their home and are being taken to the poorhouse. All their property was sold by the sheriff to pay for the husband's liquor bills. My son, you must never drink ardent spirit.

A LETTER TO THE EDITOR

Dear Mr. Thomas:

The Old Farmer's Almanac is and has been used as a diary by seven different generations in our family in Hollis, Maine.

On the margins are written births, deaths, bird arrivals, marriages, when the frogs first peeped, when the ice went out of the Saco River—freshet dates and bridges carried away by floods, heavy showers, deep snowfalls, the arrival of new bossies and colts, baptisms, new ministers, beloved teachers—"dere techer" and some not so "dere."

In fact many history writers of towns around here find their accurate dates in these dog-eared yellowed piles of *Almanacs* carefully laid away up attic under the eaves in one of the old and odorous herring boxes, carefully papered on the outside—with scraps of bordering left over from the home papering.

Historic! Here's a sample—on the April, 1793, page—*"Sarah*

Phinney, my wife, died, aged 59." In the following October (scant time for the mill owner, Sam Leavitt, to wait)—*"Married Hannah Deering."*

Capt. Stephen Bean (1812 War) records on the 1833 *Almanac* that he *"left home while the stars were still falling like snow with his two-horse wain loaded with lamp black, which he sold to a line of tanneries going Westard as far as the State of New York."* His writing is still clear as script.

Jonathan Bean ("Grandpa Jattie") wrote on the May, 1838, page—*"brought home my 2d wife Sophia Hamblen from Gorham. We set out an elm tree in front of her house that day to remember it by."* (Note: that tree is still there.)

Tappan Sawyer Bean (named for his grandfather, the celebrated cabinetmaker), himself a master-mason, writes on the margin of June, 1877—*"went to St. John, N. B. where I helped build mills destroyed in the great fire."*

Mother wrote on March 13, 1877—*"Finished my rose-garland rug—white ground, today."* (I have it still.)

I wrote in April, 1896—*"Crossed swaying footbridge at midnight over Saco, on way home from acting in Class play."*

My son Clarence (aged 12) wrote on February 22, 1916—*"I won silver cup, 1st prize, for snowshoeing races at the Carnival."*

And so it goes—the handy diary for all ages and conditions. Hanging beside the kitchen window where we pick over the beans and file the saw—it's a real cozy companion. Dick, the canary, sings a little louder as it reflects his color, and the red geranium is brighter—by contrast.

Sincerely yours,
Lucina H. Lombard
Gorham, Maine
1942